HOLLYWOOD WOLF WHISTLE

CAR HORN

CHEVROLET

JAY CARNINE

Lobo

CALIFORNIA HOT RODDER

Published in 2000 by
Graffiti Publications Pty. Ltd.,
69 Forest Street, Castlemaine, Victoria, Australia
Phone International 61 3 5472 3653
Fax International 61 3 5472 3805
Email: graffiti@netcon.net.au
Website: www.graffitipub.com.au

Copyright 2000 by Jay Carnine
Publisher: Larry O'Toole
Design: Michael deWolfe
Illustrations: Alan Schofield
Old advertising illustrations from early Automotive magazines.

Cover photo features CK and his coupe.

Colour Separations: Sharpscan, West Melbourne
Printing: Centre State Printing, Maryborough

Graffiti Publications books are also available at discounts in bulk quantity for industrial or sales promotional use.
For details contact Graffiti Publications Ph: (613) 5472 3653

Printed and bound in Australia.

ISBN 0 949398 10 1

JAY CARNINE
DEDICATION
TO MY LOVELY AND MOST INTERESTING WIFE, GAY.

She is the oldest child in her family as I am in mine. Sometimes we have strong opinions and differing ones. I still prefer to spend time with her over all others. I like having a wife who is smart and has opinions and interests of her own. I am truly blessed, with a wife that is confident enough of herself not to be jealous of her husband's hobbies. Too many times in the past I've seen wives taking offense at the husband's interests and it usually leads to an embittered and bored husband or a divorce. If they stick together, in later years, she wonders why he's not interested in anything.

One of the things I really like about Gay is that she is a reader, a thinker a doer, and has opinions of her own. Sometimes I think a docile and boring wife would be nice, but when I think about it, I couldn't handle it. I like being married to a girl who is her own person, has her own opinions and interests and is willing to try most any new activity.

I feel fortunate that she allows me to come along with her on her journey through life.

CONTENTS

CHAPTER ONE
VERY FIRST HOT ROD 11

CHAPTER TWO
NO SLEEPERS HERE 17

CHAPTER THREE
FIRST CAR 21

CHAPTER FOUR
SAUGUS DRAG STRIP 31

CHAPTER FIVE
BRODIE KNOBS AND MODEL A 37

CHAPTER SIX
SLEEPERS 41

CHAPTER SEVEN
SAUGUS SPEEDWAY 47

CHAPTER EIGHT
DRAG RACE CARS AT SAN FERNANDO AND LONG BEACH 55

CHAPTER NINE
GOOD SOUNDS SLEEPER 61

CHAPTER TEN
AIR ATTACK AT THE DRAG STRIP 67

CHAPTER ELEVEN
THE STARTER'S WIFE 68

CHAPTER TWELVE
LEAVING MISS LILLY 71

CHAPTER THIRTEEN
NOSTALGIA ENGINE SWAP 77

CHAPTER FOURTEEN
ONE DAY AT SANTA MARIA 83

CHAPTER FIFTEEN
THE LAST DRAG RACE 89

CHAPTER SIXTEEN
THE BIG PACKARD 97

CHAPTER SEVENTEEN
SPOTS AND BOLT ONS 103

CHAPTER EIGHTEEN
SHOEBOX SERENADE 109

CHAPTER NINETEEN
IN BETWEEN RODS AND CUSTOMS 117

CHAPTER TWENTY
OLDS VS FORD 125

CHAPTER TWENTY-ONE
ADVENTURES WITH CK AND ME 129

CHAPTER TWENTY-TWO
SUNDAY DRIVE 141

CHAPTER TWENTY-THREE
ME AND CK HIT THE RACES 145

CHAPTER TWENTY-FOUR
THE BLACK HAT 155

CHAPTER TWENTY-FIVE
AUTO SHOP DAZE 161

CHAPTER TWENTY-SIX
SPOTS AND BOLT ONS 167

CHAPTER TWENTY-SEVEN
TERMINAL ISLAND TO INYOKERN 173

AFTER WORD
A FORTUNATE LIFE 191

FOREWORD

A SMALL PIECE ABOUT ME

I've been very fortunate in how my life has turned out so far. Married to an interesting and outgoing girl who is also my best friend. I'd rather spend time with her than anyone.

We have two daughters. Cheri, the oldest is married to Pat Scoles, an Air Force Sergeant and has turned into a bright and lovely young woman with a great family and has turned into quite the teacher. Both in the home schooling she's doing as well as Sunday school at her church. Pat and Cheri have two children, Cory and Kristin.

Debbie, the youngest. She always liked doing the boy stuff and to a great extent still does. Smart and observant, teaching her to drive was a snap. She just got in the stick shift Pinto and drove it off, not a problem. Her background as a dirt bike rider for many years probably made it very easy for her. She started riding dirt bikes at the age of three and has always had a love for things mechanical. She's a single mom and has one child, Melissa.

The three grandchildren; eighteen year old Cory Scoles who's ready to fly in from North Las Vegas, move in and help build the '31. He definitely got converted a couple of Christmases ago when they were here and I let him drive the '32. Big engine, little car, a watershed experience in anybody's life.

Fifteen year old Kristin Scoles, she lives in North Las Vegas also and is turning into quite the artist, recently having had several of her pastels in a show. A quiet and shy girl, but she does stand up for herself and is a most interesting person to those that take the time to listen.

Nine year old, going on 21, Melissa Carnine lives in Visalia as we do. She's kind of a toughie, stands up for herself pretty well and absolutely consumes information. She likes helping in the garage, riding in the roadster and especially likes riding in the '50 Plymouth coupe. I think it had something to do with her long blonde hair getting mussed in the roadster. She's over that though. I pick her up after school now and then and usually take the roadster. As she quickly discovered, the roadster is a bit of a points maker with the boys.

Aside from my immediate family, there's my seriously involved in drag racing little brother and my trap shooting sister. Both pretty skilled in their chosen hobbies and sister ends up on the mens squad shooting against them now and then. For most guys, not a problem, for a few, Olympic Class Backpedaling......

My grandfather worked in farming, on farms, and eventually owned a big Nebraska wheat farm which he gave back when the depression came along, as did most of America. Grandad came to California in the early '30s. His experiences on the farm and his experiences with big engines, really big ones, allowed him to work right through the depression pouring and fitting babbitt bearings in these things. It was a skill that was required, even though the economy had slowed down, steam engines, generators and the like were still required. He went to work in the Southern California oil fields in the mid '30s or thereabouts. He was a good machinist and an excellent mechanic.

Kinda the same story with my dad. He did the same things right along with his dad and when his turn came he went to work in the Southern California oil fields at the end of the '30s. Same company, but at a coastal location. Grandad was inland a ways. Dad too, was a good machinist and a really excellent mechanic. It was always a source of pride for me when I found out that other companies, now and then, would try to hire him away from the oil fields. He was loyal, and the job was a pretty good one, eventually leading into a supervisory position. He went the whole way to retirement working for the same company.

A long story so far, but I have the time to write things down and time, as I'm sure most would agree is the most important thing of all. A real scarcity for the working guy, a boon for the retired, but a boon only if you have an interest to fill it. Bluntly put, if you don't have an interest or hobby fairly well established prior to retirement, you're not gonna make it. Life's a lot more interesting when you are doing something and working towards a goal. I used to have friends that bought a color TV in their early 20s, curled up in a corner with it and I think they're still there. I'm 59 and retired three years ago during a company downsizing which turned out to be a real blessing. For most of us, we heard freedom calling and we answered. Over 80% of the crew left and it was worth your life to stand in the doorway.

I was an operator of a Southern California Edison high voltage bulk power switching/dispatch center. The company called us operators, but the majority of other companies called us dispatchers and that's a slightly better description of what we did. It was a really interesting job, somewhat technically oriented, but more like a constantly evolving dynamic chess game.

A bulk power system is a life entity unto itself. Every day was different, from the routine ones of just monitoring the system and heading off potential problems, to the windstorms, brush fires, lightning storms, heavy duty rainstorms, snow and ice, earthquakes and even the heat storms. Heck, we even had salt storms on the coast. Some of the guys didn't care for the storms as it interfered with what they hoped would be a calm shift. I liked 'em, at least during the storms, the paperwork afterward was a bit of a pain, but a necessary one. Since it was a 24 hour a day, 365 days a year endeavor, the next crew needed to know where they were at. Best part about the power biz was working with very bright and talented people.

Once I attained driving age, it pretty much was hot rods for me. My involvement waxed and waned several times over the years, but when I think back on those times, I really was still doing it. Having a hot rod '63 Chevy pickup to haul the dirt bikes was a definite necessity. In fact, most of my family transportation had been hot rodded to a degree. Typical would have been our '62 Ford wagon with stick shift, 3.89 diff, Shelby 390 FE engine that was the wife's car. I kinda figure, that if you're going to rebuild them, you may as well get a little extra out of the deal.

I've been a tool junkie all my life and now have a few that make life really easy. A small lathe and mill really gets you away from the file/hacksaw syndrome. There's nothing wrong with working with what you have, but I found them to be great time savers as well as saving a lot of money while building hot rods. With tools like this you are not limited, what was a tough job to start with, turns out to be interesting and easy. With a welder and a few machine tools, if you can dream a part, you can make it.

I've been interested in, and involved in other hobbies aside from the hot rod bit. Funny part about some of them is, I'd be thinking about the hot rods while doing the other thing. When I'm doing the hot rod bit, I never find myself thinking about the other hobbies, most of which have been relegated to the back burner and probably won't see the light of day again. There's always something new to try.

I'm a voracious reader and fairly consume the printed page, mostly about the hobby and things that relate to it. I read some history as well as a few novels, perhaps two or three every year unless someone recommends a really good one. Being blessed with, or perhaps it's a curse, a really good memory, a lot of these little hot rod adventures are very fresh in my mind and I find them easy to write about.

I find one thing about retirement is, that we live pretty much as man has always lived including the caveman. Now that I'm not involved with the artificiality of time, and the constraints thereof, I find that my life follows the daily cycles of the sun. Now that I don't have to get up early I do, 0500-0700 and most days right at 0600. I like to spend the quiet times in the morning writing and perusing the e-mail and devote a couple of hours writing to one or the other. Coffee's not bad either.

In the end, hot rodders are not too far removed from the caveman. We have our little adventures and retreat back to the cave and discuss them with the others. Seems to me, sitting around the campfire and reviewing the recent Mastodon hunt is pretty much like bench racing. 'Course, the very best bench racing is perhaps done when camped out at the end of the salt flats, dry lakes or the drag strip. Sitting around a small fire on a dark and star laden night, beverage of choice at hand and some interesting friends taking part makes it all worthwhile. At least for a, not too far removed from the caveman, hot rod type guy like me.......

Jay Carnine
Visalia, California
May, 2000

"...This set up a lock to lock slide, and once I realized it wouldn't crash, I started to enjoy it and get a little crazy in front of the crowd on succeeding races. All stops after that were big sweeping brake slides, going both left and right, and with a final stop switching ends. It was just too cool and I had a great time..."

CHAPTER ONE
VERY FIRST HOT ROD
KINDA FUNNY HOW WE GET STARTED IN THIS HOBBY.
OR ANY OTHER, FOR THAT MATTER.

Dad was always interested in cars and had owned several hot rods in the past. I believe he had one of the very first chopped cars in Southern California in 1942, a '36 Ford five window coupe.

For me, it may have started in grade school when I noticed the older guys paid a lot of attention to one of the teachers' cars that was a bit modified. I don't remember much about it, although it did have skirts and was lower than the other cars in the parking lot and it was black.

I do remember going to L.A. in the late forties as a little guy and seeing quite a few cars inside a very large building with some of them being roadsters. Dad and my uncle were really fascinated by them and talked about them all the way home to the small coastal town where we lived.

What impressed me the most was a large table, around 4'x10', perhaps Micarta covered or maybe well finished Masonite that had little cars of many different types following a painted road. These little cars had no rotating wheels, but had magnets on the bottom with felt pads glued on. Apparently a chain drive of some type, with magnets installed under the table surface and running in guides dragged the little cars along the winding roadway on the tabletop. There were no slots or guides on the tabletop, simply a painted-on roadway and areas painted to look like grass and dirt. It was pretty fascinating and dad let me stay and watch for quite a while. (I think he was a bit fascinated too.)

The above photo was taken at Kenney Grove Park, Fillmore, California, the old home town. That's my dad sitting on the tire of my topless roadster, talking to an old hot rod/oil patch friend.

Dad owned a '42 Ford sedan at the time. It had pipes, shaved heads and a beautiful black paint job. He was pretty particular when he washed and waxed it, and it seemed to me to always look good.

These sedans were really roomy, and when men got in the back seat change tended to roll out of their pockets. That also happened to me. When we got home after a trip to town I asked dad if I could pull the back seat and get my two dimes back. (Big money at the time). Dad knew I could put it back okay so he let me do it. My sister didn't want to help, so I pulled it by myself. I struck a gold mine. I found over $6.00 in change in there.

When I ran in the house to show dad, I could tell he kinda wished he'd pulled it himself. He was always more than fair and let me keep it all. At that time $6.00 was a fair chunk of pocket money for an adult, let alone a nine year old kid. My sister was a bit put out. I carried this money around in a bag for over a week until it was all spent. Such a deal!

Dad was one heck of a good mechanic and worked in the oil patch. In fact, he was so darned good that every once in a while some other oil company or oil patch related outfit would offer him a job. He was pretty loyal and stayed where he was, eventually getting into supervision which was a whole other world for him. He did well at it. He was patient and fair, but I don't think it was one of his favorite jobs. I still call him for advice on things mechanical to this day.

What's been amazing is his capability to disassemble things without some of the special tooling required, with no damage to either tool or component, to get things running again by re-using equipment other mechanics would remove and discard. There were lots of clever fixes and shimming of things and since I got to go to work with him on quite a few of the emergency call-outs on weekends and nights, it was a valuable experience for me. None of this was "Mickey Mouse". It was just good, old-fashioned skill and common sense. He was good friends with the company welder, a very talented guy and considered by many to be one of the better welders in the oil industry.

Dad recovers on the front wheel of the roadster right after sticking a couple of cups of coffee in him. He nearly froze riding the 30 miles from Ventura to Fillmore with only a sweatshirt and a vest in 37 degree weather, which he felt would be warm enough. I told him, but he wouldn't listen. (Waited many years to say that!)

Our small town was mainly known for the oil patch and the citrus crops. The Junior Chamber of Commerce (JC) let it be known that this year, on the 4th of July there would be a soap box race as part of the festivities. Due to the town being heavily involved in the citrus industry the race was called the "Citrus Crate Derby" If the oil patch had a few more guys in the JC it could have been called the "Oil Patch Races" or similar.

The JC guys set out some great rules. Unlike the genuine soap box derby, where the kid had to use the genuine soap box derby wheels and build the car all by himself. The "Citrus Crate Derby" rules were simple; one car, four wheels of any kind, a brake system, no body required, 200lb. maximum including driver and best of all, dads were allowed to help in the building.

Dad was a really good wood worker and quite skilled in metal fabrication and had already made some neat toys for us as we grew up. He was a bit of an artist also. One favorite that sister and I talk about occasionally were two rocking horses. They had wooden frames, a long car leaf spring anchored at the front end, a seat and the requisite horses head, properly painted on the other end. Mine was slightly larger than sisters. These things were great and no one else had anything even close.

Dad sketched out some plans for the "racer" and showed them to the welder. Over about a three month period they had built a car out of metal scraps lying around the welding shop. The frame was a simple ladder frame, made of, I believe, fairly high quality tubing, about one inch diameter. It also had; a hoop for a cowl and steering column mount that went just in front of the driver, a similar hoop, smaller, that went in front over the drivers, lighter weight hoop that went behind the driver and was braced to accept a seat back. Tires were valve pump covers off a "Big Bertha" mud pump. (A piece of oil field equipment) These were about 10 inches in diameter, fairly narrow and were mounted to home made wheels about eight inches in diameter.

Wheels were simple 1/8 inch plates cut out by the welder and ground to the round shape and with a bearing receptacle in one side. Eight of these plates were required for the four wheels. The wheels were held together by four home made bolts that had a stepped pattern cut into them and were tacked on the inside of the outer plate. They also had a lathe turned decorative center piece with a stepped pattern to match the bolts. In a small way, they looked a bit like the first Center Line wheels that came along later.

The inner plates with double race ball bearings were installed on the axles and bolted up with the large center nut, the tire (solid rubber) was held in place, the outer plate installed and the tacked in place bolts pushed through the inner plate and bolted together with an all metal locking nut. Spinning the wheels showed them to run very true and they would spin for a long time. There was no suspension.

Brakes were the outside contracting type, with only a forward shoe that clamped onto a piece of large tubing that was welded to the inside of both rear wheels. Shoes with appropriate linings riveted on were applied via a mechanism by a hand brake on the right side of the large cowl hoop. The brake handle was pivoted on a bushing on the right side of the cowl hoop and had a large single ball bearing brazed on for a handle. The brake mechanism was hung under the driver's seat area of the frame. They were strong enough to lock the wheels at any speed and were a great source of fun.

Front wheel axle stubs were welded to a small piece of channel that pivoted on a bolt mounted through a vertical piece of tubing (with a bit of caster plugged in) that was welded to the front outside of the frame on each side and were retained by one of the all metal lock nuts. Steering linkage was very car-like and was used to adjust and align the front end.

The tie rod was a piece of 3/8 inch rod, threaded to accept "Hall-Scott" carburetor linkage ends. (Hall-Scott was an industrial engine used at the oil wells to drive pumps and the like). The carburetor linkage ends looked just like a scaled up version of some of the good quality, right angle links seen on some of today's aftermarket throttle linkages. They screwed on to the tie rod ends, took jam nuts and had a 3/8 inch NF male threaded end that exited the body at a 90 degree angle to the female end and bolted to the steering arms that were flame cut from 3/16 inch plate. Same deal with the drag link. It came off a tab welded to the bottom of the center mounted steering column that rode in bushings attached to the hoops front and rear. The drag link went from the tab to the left steering arm that had two holes to accept the carburetor linkage ends and was similar to the Vega cross steering arms we use today. Turning the steering wheel, lock to lock took only 1/3 of a turn total. To say it was quick steering would be an understatement. Since I really wasn't used to anything else, I adapted quickly.

The steering wheel was a piece of about 3/4 inch OD copper tubing bent into a perfect circle, the ends brazed together, with a lathe turned brass center adapted to the steering column and having four polished stainless steel spokes arranged in a shallow "X" pattern. Tabs were welded to the frame to accept a 3/4 inch plywood floor front and rear.

After making several trial runs down one of the hills near the oil company welding shop we decided all was well and started making the body. I say "we", but I was pretty much the gopher and got to do some of the menial jobs. That was fine with me, I really enjoyed being in on the building of this little car.

Dad and the welder were really getting into this, and so far, had created a thing of mechanical beauty. The body was simple, with no compound curves. Flat aluminum with a curve rolled in using a large piece of pipe, and made of one piece was used to cover the nose going from hoop to hoop and leaving the front end open. The tail section was formed similarly, although two pieces were used and joined on a vertical 3/4 inch plywood former running from the top of the seat back to the tail section floor. A piece to cover the open nose section was formed from two pieces of aluminum that looked a bit like expanded metal, but was flat and had no sharp edges.

Both the grille to nose joint and the two tail section joints were covered by a piece of thin aluminum tubing, flattened and held on by small bolts for the front piece and wood screws for the rear two pieces. No sharp edges were exposed. The car was spray painted fire engine red.

As dad was pretty good with a sign painters brush he painted the number nine on both sides of the nose piece and the tail section using a bright, oil field silver enamel. The numbers looked like dull chrome when dry.

The steering wheel was polished so the copper wheel, stainless rods and brass center pieces shined brightly. Even the brake knob was polished. The wheels were painted red and the bolts and center pieces were black. The seat floor and back were upholstered with lightly padded black naugahyde like material. When it was done, it was eerily similar to the Indianapolis race cars of the thirties.

Race day came and we took it to the staging area in front of the library. The JC's had blocked off two blocks of a fairly steep section of Main Street for the races. The little car really wowed the troops. We gathered quite a crowd. It was pretty evident that a lot of work and craftsmanship had gone into this little car. I was proud of the car, and really proud of dad. He was smiling a bit himself.

The cars were broken into two classes depending mainly on wheel diameter. There were several genuine soap box cars there, that had the official soap box wheels and they may have been faster. All of those cars were in "A" class. We were in "B" class. There was a pretty good turnout of cars with about 12-15 in total. As this race had been well advertised, there was quite a crowd lined up along the two block downhill area.

I watched the first round of "A" class cars run and noted they were really sailing down the fairly steep hill. I think too, that the JC guys didn't realize these little cars would get rolling so fast.

Our turn on the ramp came, we launched and it was all very slow motion for a bit. As we picked up speed, I decided this was really cool, especially since I was pulling away from the other car. About quarter way down the second block, we had really picked up speed and were really hurtling down the hill. We were probably not far from touching on 50 mph.

As my car had exceptionally good and powerful brakes for a soap box racer I could get it stopped about 1/4 way down the next block. Some of the other cars took most of the block to get stopped.

The drums had fresh paint on them and since the brakes had a high co-efficient of friction they would easily lock the wheels. This set up a lock to lock slide, and once I realized it wouldn't crash, I started to enjoy it and get a little crazy in front of the crowd on succeeding races. All stops after that were big sweeping brake slides, going both left and right, and with a final stop switching ends. It was just too cool and I had a great time.

We won class "B" with the car and the JCs gave the winners and runners-up nice little trophies. I've won a few other trophies over the years, but this is the only one I've kept and displayed. It still sits on my bookcase and I enjoy seeing it there. I've seen dad looking at it from time to time when he's been up to visit.

After the races, the local radio station guy dragged us off to the judge's stand and interviewed us. He got a lot of yes, no and maybes out of me. The paper took several pictures of the car and printed one. After the radio interview, a kid from the Junior High School I attended came over and talked about the car for a bit. He was known as a bit of a tough guy and ran with an older group that had cars. He always treated me well and I liked him. The newspaper at that time was delivered in the afternoon.

Next day, when it came, I ran out and grabbed it hoping to see if our picture was in the paper. I was stunned to see that the kid I talked to at the races had been killed in a car wreck a couple of hours later. My favorite uncle had been killed on Iwo Jima in WW2 when I was a little guy, but I was too young to understand at the time. This was my first inkling that death really could be around the corner if you weren't careful. I was a pretty good kid, but I started paying a lot more attention to what dad and mom said after that.

For several years after the races, my friends and I used to take the little soap box racer to one of the little used beach access roads and take turns running it down the hill. Once in the tight confines of the cockpit, it was a bit difficult to get out. In fact it was a little hard to get in, but being kids and being flexible it was no problem. We used to run to the bottom of the hill, and without touching the brakes crank a hard left and make a sliding almost 180 degree turn to the flat road below. The car handled well and never turned over, a good thing, as a couple of rollovers could have been really damaging.

The last ride I took in it, we pushed it across town with a couple of other guys that also had a soap box racer and spent about an hour pushing them both to the top of a steep winding hill. We set off in both cars, not worried in the least about any traffic coming up the hill and raced down. The soap box racer, although slightly faster got left behind pretty fast because he wasn't as crazy as I was and I had much the better brakes. Just about every turn was a sliding turn under total control, and the car had never gone faster. I hesitate to estimate how fast we were going. Suffice to say, the trip down the hill took virtually no time at all.

The JC guys not being dummies moved the races to a less steep hill next to the hospital across town. The move was done for several reasons. The hill was not so steep. Shutting down traffic here was not as big a problem as shutting it off downtown. Best of all, it was right next to the hospital.

The car got parked for a while and little brother sorta inherited it. Shortly after I left home and unbeknownst to dad and myself he sold it to the kid down the street for $10.00. I found out and went over there a couple of days later to see about getting it back and found that the kid had torn the hand-made aluminum body off and tried to adapt an old Briggs & Stratton lawn mower engine to it. His dad, being a non-mechanical type didn't want it cluttering up the garage and promptly took it to the dump. I always thought the dad and the kid were competitors for the "Village Idiot" title and felt this one kinda put 'em right up there with the front runners.

Dad and I were a bit miffed at little brother, but he was such a good kid we soon forgave him. What the heck, I only have one brother ....

"...In fact it was in the opening shots of one of the hot rod movies made in the mid to late fifties, (I believe it was filmed at San Fernando Drag Strip). If you see the movie, you'll see the Deuce frying the tires, the rear swinging back and forth and not accelerating very hard..."

CHAPTER TWO
NO SLEEPERS HERE
TIMES CHANGE.

Life really changed when the '55 Chevy came to town. Probably the fastest car in my hometown was a '32 five-window. The kid that owned it ran a couple of different DeSoto Hemi engines in it. His dad owned the DeSoto agency. For the record he was a very nice guy, two years older and one grade ahead of me. He would take the time to talk to anyone. He was one of a few kids from wealthy families I knew (and I wasn't one – had to do the whole nine yards to earn hot rod money) that did appreciate what they had. He worked in his dad's dealership to earn his money.

The car originally had (I'm guessing here on the size) a 291 inch DeSoto Hemi with Herbert roller cam, four two barrels in one row. It was one of the best looking intakes and engine combo's I ever saw. He had to cut the front lower part of the hood side louvers away to make room for the wide DeSoto. It was a well-built car with Bell dropped axle, probably '40 Ford brakes, later Ford pickup steering box, '39 trans., stock Ford rear end (probably '40-'48), dash load of Stewart Warner instruments and a cherry primered body.

He started drag racing it and was quite successful. Later on he made the requisite trip to Tijuana for tuck and roll. (Which I'm tempted to do if I build another one. I think I will.)

After collecting a lot of broken '39 transmission parts and after a couple of years, a 341

Hemi engine became available. (Guessing again on the CID) A '38 Buick transmission went behind it and a Halibrand quickchange rear was installed. Another Herbert roller was installed along with 6x2 barrels. We're talking major eyewash here.

I don't remember if this was an aluminum cast intake or one of the Crower "U-Fab" intakes. It was probably a Crower. Crower sold a kit with flanges cut for your engine, two approximately 2-1/2 – 3 inch diameter tubes for the intake plenums and eight short tubes to connect the plenums to the intake flanges. Four short bibs about 1-1/2 – 2 inch in diameter accepted two straight radiator hoses that were the balance tubes, there were four end caps for the plenum and six (or eight if desired) plates cut to match the venerable Stromberg 97s. With some welding and a little paint you ended up with a really neat intake manifold.

The car was then painted and had one of the first sets of "Moon" discs in town installed. (I had the second set). He also ran blackwalls at a time when everyone else was running whites. I liked the look and copied it for my '50 coupe. (I tried to buy his old engine with cam and intake for my '50 Coupe, but by the time payday rolled around someone else had taken it – for $100.00. Big money at the time). Anyway, this was the fastest car in town. (At the time of this story the 291 inch DeSoto was in the Deuce).

My friend's dad owned a barber shop and one of the barbers was a skinny guy about 25 years old. We liked him as he would always talk cars with us. He bought a new '55 Chevy two door V-8 with stick shift. He installed pipes (a requisite at the time) and did a little fine tuning on the engine. Word went around, he wanted to race the '32.

We went straight to the shop on our bikes and asked him if it was true. We figured he didn't have a chance and really gave him a bad time. He was a good sport, took it all in and just smiled. We were beginning to wonder if he knew something that we didn't. Being 15 and somewhat opinionated (both of us) as only 15 years olds can be, we decided there was no way he could win.

He told us he was ready, but the kid with the Deuce didn't seem to want to race. This was over a several week period. We found it hard to believe, as the Deuce (to us) was the fastest and greatest car around.

Well they finally raced, the Chevy beating the Deuce, but not by a whole lot. We were stunned that a factory car could be that fast. Thinking back on it, I realized that a new age had dawned.

A little after that the kid with the Deuce installed the larger engine, Buick trans etc. and began drag racing pretty steady. He was very successful. In fact it was in the opening shots of one of the hot rod movies made in the mid to late fifties, (I believe it was filmed at San Fernando Drag Strip). If you see the movie, you'll see the Deuce frying the tires, the rear swinging back and forth and not accelerating very hard.

When asked he told us he had the rear tires spinning with the brakes applied. This was a common trick that some did to leave a really long stretch of rubber on the street. (Pretty hard on brakes though). Being very unsophisticated about such things, we figured that long rubber marks were a sign of really high horsepower. (Since we didn't know the brake trick.)

We were quite overwhelmed on some of our first trips to a drag strip that ran top fuelers. These guys laid down some serious rubber. We loved it.

Driving techniques at the time seemed to be – nail it and hang on! We were to learn later that fuel drivers were really quite skilled and did a lot of pedaling down the track.

As a small aside we witnessed the first "over 200 mph" runs at San Fernando drag strip. At the time just a few cars around the country had broken the 200 mph barrier. This may have been specifically a record attempt as it was a single run during time trials. We could tell this was a really good run as the dragster slicks lit up a little bit out of the hole and lightly hazed the tires most of the way down with the front wheels gently raising about 6-10 inches and gently setting down several times during the run. The tires quit hazing in front of the traps and looked to be locked into the strip surface.

The crowd knew they had witnessed something special and were dead quiet. The strip announcer came up on the PA system, asked for the starter and I believe the strip owner to come to the timing stand. We saw several other guys go in. Nothing more came out of the PA for a while and no more cars were run. Finally the announcer came on and told us the dragster had run 205 mph. The clocks were witnessed by several people including a couple of fuel competitors. The crowd went wild and it was a few minutes before racing resumed. We felt we had witnessed history in the making.

And the Deuce coupe?

I had gained a job at the gas station that was part of the DeSoto agency. The Deuce used to come in all the time for gas and I got to see the car fairly often. It was steadily pulling away from street duty and going toward strictly drag racing. It still had all the upholstery and street trim though, and still looked great. In fact this car would compare favorably with most of the trailer queens we see in the hobby today. It was that nice. He drove it a lot even though he had a newer car.

The last time I saw it on the street was a summer evening about dusk. The gas station fronted the four-lane through town. I was out at the pumps and heard what sounded like a motorcycle gang coming down the road. If you've ever heard a group of noisy bikes, you'll know what I mean. You can feel the sound before you can hear it. I looked down the street for the motorcycles and saw his car coming, but darned if I could see the bikes. He pulled into the gas station. The Deuce was making one heck of a lot of noise and was the source of what I thought was the bike group. A friend of his that worked at a muffler shop was in the right seat. They were both grinning widely. They had spent the day building an exhaust system that was eight straight pipes. It ran from exhaust port all the way to the back and under the rear bumper. It was the greatest exhaust system that I ever saw.

I still haven't heard or seen anything that compares, and I have attended a whole lotta drag races and rod runs since then.

The kid got real serious about drag racing, bought a roadster that was built strictly for the drag strip and built a blown DeSoto engine. He raced this a lot and eventually drifted away from cars. Although, the last time I saw him, he had restored a very early car and was having a good time with that.

I had by now joined a group of guys in a car club. The club rented a building in the country that was probably an old independent garage. It had a large office that we held the meetings in, a pit, a big workbench, room to park several project cars and best of all an oxy/acetylene welder that we could use. I went out there one day to use the welder and lo and behold, the Deuce, now with the engine, transmission and Halibrand quickchange gone, but rolling around on a stock rear end, was sitting in a corner.

One of our club members had purchased it and with the help of one of the older members that could actually weld quite well and do bodywork, were busy altering the firewall for an Olds engine with Cad-LaSalle trans. He paid $400.00 for an engine-less but well done, finished car. I never even heard it was for sale, but it didn't make any difference as $400.00 was about two months pay for me at my part time job. A little after that I quit the club and heard no more about the Deuce. I just hope it didn't end up pursuing a career as a trailer queen.

"...Lazy guys would simply place blocks under the front bumper and heat the coils until they collapsed and the car stopped on the blocks. I'm sure you can see the flaw here, many times the car was a lot lower than desired and a bit crooked..."

CHAPTER THREE

FIRST CAR

MY FIRST CAR WAS ALSO MY DAD'S FIRST NEW CAR

A black, '50 Ford two door Sedan, custom model with the 100 hp V-8, OD trans, push-button radio, heater, turn signals and electric clock. (I believe it also came with a tinted windshield.) This was the fully optioned car at the time.

The only other option, later in the model year was the Crestliner model with special side chrome strips dividing a nice factory two-tone paint job. Two color choices were available, black and maroon, which to me looked really good, and the chartreuse and black, which about blew out your eyeballs. These cars had slightly different interior trim and a good looking X-pattern steering wheel that a lot of guys installed in the standard car. The Crestliners were available in the two door sedan and the convertible.

Black cars seem to be a family custom. Granddad owned a black '49 Ford two door sedan. My favorite cousin, sort of a big brother to me, owned a black '40 Coupe and later a black '49 Ford two door sedan. Little brother today owns a black '74 Ford shortbed 1/2 ton, black Suburban and the black Henry J race car. My only contribution today is my black roadster, although I did own a black '51 Plymouth and dad had owned several black Fords, namely a chopped '36 coupe, '42 and '48 sedan prior to the '50. Dad drove the '50 for about five years until a '54 Chevy driver rear-ended us in the fog and rain in Fullerton, California. The

Black cars seem to be a family custom. My only contribution today is my black roadster, although I did own a black '51 Plymouth and dad had owned several black Fords.

Chevy driver had a bit of internal fog also, and I believe was hauled off to jail.

The impact drove us into the back of a '51 or so Pontiac. The collision bent up the front and rear of the little sedan pretty good. The insurance company totaled the car out and dad bought it back. It had excellent running gear and a well cared for engine. With the insurance money he purchased a metallic blue six cylinder '50 Ford sedan. I remember he and mom discussing the new V-8 '50 prior to purchase and he was talking about getting a six cylinder model. Mom cautioned against it as he had always had V-8s. It was probably one of those conversations married folks have, that are designed to make the other think they were in on an already made decision. Not that I've ever done any of those you understand.

I was really surprised to find he had bought a six. It was a really clean car and ran well. It was still a six. Sixes were okay if you owned Chevy, lots of kids did. A six in a Ford was something you sorta wanted to hide. Fords at the time were considered the performance vehicle to own. Some of the well tuned Chevy sixes would hold their own pretty well. Not to mention the '49-'50 Oldsmobiles that really ripped up the highways.

Some of the early pioneers of engine swapping got hold of a '49-'50 Cadillac engine somewhere and swapped it into the '49 and '50 Fords. These were known as "Fordillacs" and got to be somewhat common with most large towns having one or two. There was also a company in LA that specialized in this. Putting a brand new crate Caddy engine in a virtually new Ford.

All of the Fordillacs I ever saw were the Coupe, custom model. Fords of the '49-'51 era came in two levels. The Deluxe, which was the cheaper model and the Custom which had side trim and a little better interior although you could get side trim as an option on the Deluxe.

Funny thing about the Deluxe was the Coupes had no rear seat, simply a floor level flat sheet metal platform where the rear seat went and was covered in molded rubber. Sort of an enclosed "Ute" if you will. Salesmen loved these seatless Coupes and bought many of them. The other main difference was the rear quarter windows on the Deluxe Coupes were sealed shut and the Custom Coupes had swing open rear quarter windows that worked similar to the wind-wings.

For the younger set, wind-wings were small front side windows that opened, by pushing out as far as 160 degrees or so in Fords, and other makes had winder cranks that opened them a bit past the 90 degree mark. These were really nice on the days you drove with the windows down, with the wind-wings cranked out a bit, the bees and wasps tended not to get in the car when at speed. Occasionally it happened, but not like a modern car. I've had more than one bee or wasp in my Pinto and later on the '88 Mustang.

There's just nothing like getting a wasp in your shirt, coming to a sliding sideways halt from a 55 mph highway and ripping off your shirt while passerby wonder what happened. Of course when it happened to your female passenger, it was downright distracting.

Anyway, dad knew a lot of automotive people in town and he cut a deal with an older guy that ran one of the better body shops, along with his son who was a very good painter. Deal was, they would work on it when they had time and dad would be allowed to help and repair what he could of the body. Not knowing any better, I didn't hold out much hope for the little sedan.

Since dad, at least to me, always went cool places, I would usually go to the body shop with him and learned quite a bit from both dad and the two shop owners. After about a year, the car emerged from the shop with new paint and new chrome. It looked really good. It felt to me a lot stronger than the six cylinder sedan we were driving now. Probably just me dreaming out loud, horsepower figures for both cars were similar. The V-8 was 100 hp and I believe the six was 95 hp. I had been driving for a little over a year by now and had just turned 15. Dad always took me for driving lessons on the Brea, California oil patch roads when we visited the grandparents. He and granddad worked for the same oil company although in different locations.

A few months later I got the much desired learners permit. 'Course prior to this time I had decided that I should wash both cars and got pretty regular about doing them. Having permission to drive them around the large front yard was a definite plus and I fairly wore out the lawn and I only tore one chrome strip off Mom's car (the six) going through the gate.

Finally I got my license. In California (as I'm sure it is in every other state and country) this is a day of liberation for the young. Freedom. Being my own man. Being able to go anywhere. ('Course I had to get permission first.) I'm sure you've been there. Never did I dream there were so many good reasons to have the car for the day, or evening. Being an average student, my folks were glad to see me go to the library so much. Guess they figured we were really studying some heavy duty stuff as we were always at the library.

Three friends and myself were driving now, so someone could always weasel a car somehow. We didn't lie about going to the library, we always went. Course as soon as we looked up one or two items to finish a school paper and not finding any girls we knew (or girls that would actually leave the library with us) we soon beat it to more interesting places. Later on I learned the girls had done a bit of car-weaseling themselves and weren't about to join a bunch of hot rodders (at least that's what we thought) and abandon a chance to cruise around a bit themselves.

This was the era of the drive-in. Never was a better device invented for young people to meet and mix in. There was always something going on and it was a great place to hang out. Admission was simply the price of a soda. Our local drive in, with the exception of the roller skating car-hops was just about the same as the one in American Graffiti. It was located on a point of land where the two main streets through town split. There was always a good car show for the passer-by. Lots of hot rods, usually coupes and sedans, Fords and Chevies, and an occasional roadster. Customs were popular too, although seeing a finished one was rare. They were usually just finishing a body mod or about to start one. Primer spots on either hot rods, customs or stockers were a badge of honor.

Our drive-in car-hops walked and didn't take any back talk. Most of them were mature women in their twenties, so we gave them a wide berth. If they got mad at you, you would get a tongue lashing that would make a crusty old Sea Captain proud. No cussing was done and about all you could do was slide down in your seat until it was over. Even that didn't help as the girls just leaned in the window and hollered louder. After that, we just sorta slunk out of the place.

When Summer came, dad steered me toward a job at a local parts house/machine shop. I was glad to get a job and had been looking hard for one. My hearts desire was to get a hot rod and I knew the only way to attain this goal was to work for it. I really liked working there. I didn't even ask how much I was making until the third day. When I asked, I was hoping it would be at least $50.00 monthly. I was totally stunned when the boss matter of factly told me my starting wage would be $200.00 per month. I don't think he saw my jaw hit the floor and hopefully didn't see me walking in circles for the next couple of hours.

Thoughts of roadsters and coupes soon entered my mind. I soon learned about taxes and such on the first payday. What a rip. The machinist had known dad for years and taught me a lot of things. Driving the delivery truck was a blast too. One of them (and my favorite one) was a '40 Ford pickup with twin pipes, floor box and a really crisp running flathead. It was the personal truck of one of the owners and he was a bit of a hot rodder. The twin pipes had "Smitty" mufflers, the hot set-up muffler of the era. It sounded great.

Usually I drove the other truck, a '48 Ford that had an engine hoist installed to pick up and deliver engines etc. I learned about tying down the load the hard way in the '48 by putting an 85A engine in the back near the tail gate. The floor was overlaid with diamond plate. (I know – you see this one coming.) Had to slam on the brakes on the two lane out of town, when the engine hit the front of the bed I thought I'd been rear-ended by at least a diesel truck. Always tied em down after that. (I may be dumb, but I learn fast.)

With this new found income, many plans and schemes were hatched that would hopefully end in the ownership of a car. Dad had always been very generous in letting me drive the V-8 '50, and it was my favorite. Heck, the six was an old folks car. He sold it to me for $300.00 This car was six years old, in immaculate shape and really good looking. It really was worth considerably more than the $300.00 Looking back, I think the price was carefully calculated to allow me to buy the car, pay for insurance for one year, buy gas to go to work and have a chunk left over to carry me through the school year. Fat chance.

There's no such thing as a young hot rodder with spare money. First thing on the agenda was a set of pipes. Pipes were an absolute necessity. It showed you were really serious about having a fast car. Course the great sounds out of some of the V8s and sixes as well was reward enough for most of us.

I ordered the accessory left side exhaust pipe, left and right tail pipes and the requisite straight through mufflers. Mine weren't Smittys as they were only available through muffler shops. They were a nice pair of steel packs.

I got the new left side exhaust pipe, muffler and tail pipe installed ok, even though the tail pipe front was hanging under the rear crossmember as there was no punched out hole for the pipe to fit through. It hung a bit low, but wasn't too bad. After driving that around for a day or so, and cruising by the handball courts in the high school alley to hear the great sounds, I took it home and started on the right side.

Being utterly brilliant at the time, I didn't know and had not thought that perhaps the tail pipe should be removed first. By the time dad got home from work I had the original stock muffler just about beat to death with his biggest hammer. (A four pounder) He kinda laughed at me and went in the house. (I'm sure this was a great story at the oil patch garage where he worked, as every time I went out there the mechanics would always tell me how great the pipes sounded. They were pretty nice guys and never gave me bad time about it. They were pretty subtle.)

Dad came out with his coveralls on, unbolted the tailpipe, unbolted the front of the muffler and a few light taps slid the whole thing off. I was amazed. Once it was out of there, bolting on the new tailpipe and muffler was a cinch. The following Saturday morning dad took the car to his friends muffler shop, cut out the crossmember and properly mounted the tailpipe, had the tailpipe ends straightened, aligned and installed chrome tips.

The little '50 not only sounded great, it looked great too. As all hot rodders have done, it was on to the next modification, lowering the car. Surprisingly, dad gave me permission to lower it. He'd been fairly adamant about keeping it stock except for the pipes. I think I caught him in a really good mood. He was always a pretty happy guy and easy to get along with, but this one was a surprise to me. I think his hot rodding tendencies were coming back a bit.

This was also the era of the "rake" or "dago". Hot rods generally ran nose down, and customs ran tail down with the best customs running both ends equally low. Some of the guys with '40s through '48s (Fords) got the front ends really low with four and five inch dropped axles and six inch long spring shackles. The six inch long shackles were used by those of us that couldn't afford the dropped axles. The shackles spoiled the handling a bit, but who cared, it looked cool. (Only dropped the car a couple of inches though.)

The '40-'48 Ford guys would also install the taller Model A rear spring (all As and '40-'48s were equipped with transverse springs.) and get the back up pretty high. They always looked better with the rear stock, big tires and the front low with little tires.

The earlier Chevy guys, '40 to '54 or so and us '49-'53 Ford guys generally cut the front coils to lower the front end. 1-1/2coils cut and sawing the rubber bumper in half worked about right and rode fair. I cut two coils first time out, it laid on the rubber bumper. Then I had to fit new springs that were cut one coil. That worked out well. The first time around I used end wrenches, took a bit of doing. Dad later brought home a set of 1/2 inch drive sockets that used to belong to granddad. That was a whole new world of efficiency for me. I've still got the socket set and still use 'em.

Lazy guys would simply place blocks under the front bumper and heat the coils until they collapsed and the car stopped on the blocks. (I'm sure you can see the flaw here, many times the car was a lot lower than desired and a bit crooked. After some of the guys that did this got some experience they were able to get down about where they wanted). These were always bad riding cars unless a minimal amount of lowering was done. Smarter guys, with access to a torch would use a spring clamp to lock in the coil height, get the front end in the air and cut out one coil or so a 1/4 or 1/3 at a time and drag out the pieces with pliers. With no torch, we would remove our coils and take them to an oil field welding shop or send them to work with dad where the welders would cut them. Generally it was free at the welding shop, if they had the torch running. Most times they did, and they were a pretty generous lot.

One really sad story about lowering methods was concerning four kids in a neighboring town that placed several chunks of broken cement sidewalk in the trunk of their car to lower the rear. The car went off the road, hit a tree and the cement pieces swept through the car and occupants. All were dead at the scene.

The '50 Fords we ran usually had the stock 15 inch wheels which were probably six inches wide. Tires of choice were 5:50x15 front. (Standard Volkswagen size) and 8:20x15 rear (standard Cadillac size). Later on we found the big T-Birds (four seaters) had 7x14 wheels and we would run those. And even later still we found a small shop that widened stock wheels to eight inches and beyond. We ran those in the back and sometimes the front for the Can-Am look. (But not on the Fifties cars, only on other later models.)

Front tires were about 24-25 inches diameter and the rears about 28 inches diameter. Wide whitewalls were just about all that was available in the early fifties. (As far as whitewalls go.) They generally came on the Caddies and Chryslers etc. Tire companies started making smaller ones in response to demand from the Ford and Chevy owners. Later on, (about mid-fifties), they went to a slightly narrower whitewall that didn't wrap around the tire sidewall so far. Some of the radical customs still ran the really wide whites though. Most of us ran the medium width whitewall. Later on, Uniroyal came out with a thin band whitewall that became popular and still later they brought out an even thinner band, red-wall that was considered a performance tire.

A red-wall sounds weird, but it was really a good looking, sorta competition flavored tire. We all wanted them, but they were expensive. The Deuce five window with the DeSoto engine was the first guy in town to run blackwalls on a hot rod. He was also the first to run the bolt-on Moon discs. I liked the look and copied it for my '50 Ford sedan and was the second car in town to do this. A few weeks later, several cars were sporting the blackwall/Moon disc look.

During this time and a bit before, a tire blackening product was available that you painted on to your tires to make them look really black. When the whitewalls came out, they were immediately followed by a paint product that you painted on your tires to obtain the whitewall look. The trouble with this stuff was you had to re-paint it once a month or so as it yellowed.

A later product was the "Port-a-Wall". A molded white rubber disc you mounted between rim and tire and they shaped themselves against the tire giving the appearance of whitewalls. These were actually a pretty good product and looked good.

The little Ford sedan was a really good car and never really let me down. I tore a few transmissions and a couple of axles out of it during overzealous driving, but soon learned to quickly fix them. One of the greater mysteries was how did they get the needle bearings to stay in the cluster gear until you could get the counter shaft in. Dad always had a good answer and showed me how to pack them in grease to sorta glue em in place. He let me work at my own pace, and always had an answer that would do the job. When I worked on the car, he usually stayed inside and let me try to figure it out for myself. He was really strict about using the floor stands and other safety measures. (Little brother walked to school for a week when dad caught him using grey concrete blocks for jackstands. Especially since we had four really nice stands dad had built sitting right inside the garage.)

Dad worked with a really talented guy named Ed. He had gone so far as to grind his own camshaft for his '50 Studebaker on the company lathe. Ed was also an excellent painter. A deal was struck, where I would buy all the materials, lead, paint, sandpaper and sand the car down, Ed and dad would paint it for me. Such a deal. I dragged about four of my friends over on a Saturday and had a sanding party and got the paint so far down that a new primer coat was required. Some of them had sanded down to bare metal. What did we know? We were young, strong and energetic. (What is it that W.C.Fields said? Youth is wasted on the young.)

When the car was ready, we took it to the oil patch garage on a Saturday afternoon. Dad's boss was cool and stopped by and helped for a bit. In one long day and evening, we nosed and partially decked it, filled a few trim holes, taped and painted it. Next morning we brought it the 15 miles home and re-installed the bumpers and hub caps.

One of my '50 Ford coupes was this version with green body, primed front clip, stainless hood scoop and no front bumper. This photo was taken just before the rear wheels were radiused for drag slicks and it went racing only.

The hub caps were '56 Chevy small caps the Chevy parts guy had given me off a large stack of take offs. (Chevies were shipped with small caps and the optional large caps were installed at the dealers.) The little sedan had black wheels, the Chevy hub caps with Ford beauty rings and Titian Red paint. Nosed and partially decked, lowered and white wall tires and twin pipes it was really a knockout of a car.

Ed, the painter, had obtained some finely ground gold metal flake, (more like gold dust) and mixed it into the paint giving it a bit more of the metallic look. It wasn't a metal-flake, more of a gold highlight. It was different, good looking and I never saw any other cars that did it.

The Titian Red was a '54 and maybe '55 Buick color. There was a second color also known as Titian Red that Buick brought out in 1956. This superseded the original Titian Red and was very maroon in color and didn't look nearly as good as the original. (The second color may have also been called Tahitian Red.) The original was very red, metallic, and close to a Candy Apple Red. Buick changed it as it faded pretty fast unless kept well waxed. (Never a problem for a hot rodder – what is it someone recently said: "Rub em till they shine, drive 'em till they smoke". Good words and ones that we lived by.)

I was working in another automotive parts/machine shop at the time and one of my duties was mixing paint for the local body shops. Dupont sent out the new formula cards with instructions to destroy the old formula. Yeah, right. Every paint mixing outfit in town had a separate file box for deleted colors and all the old color chip books stored away.

I drove the little sedan for about two years and developed a lust for a '50 Ford Coupe. I found a cherry one in Santa Barbara with a bad engine and picked it up for $100.00 By that time the sedan had been painted once again, a '56 Chevy color "Dusk Plum", one of the colors used on the sorta purple looking and white two tone paint jobs on these. It also had, as a result of a trip to Tijuana, Mexico, a tuck and roll package shelf and a tarp over the back seat. Back seat tarps were popular for quite a while and were really great to toss jackets and the like under so that the car still looked clean.

I do remember more than one couple getting in the car and crawling under the tarp for the trip to the drive in movies. The ticket girls never looked and I don't think they cared. I do remember a lot of giggling and laughing coming from under there though.

The sedan was stripped of all the best parts and a nice little '50 coupe was built. The poor little sedan was taken to the junk yard and we received $25.00 from the owner. We were pleased, but it pains me a bit today, to know we threw away a really cherry sedan.

As you will read later, the sedan was the car we took to Saugus drag strip and San Fernando drag strips first time out. We even went so far as to get a triple intake manifold on the sedan and run it at San Fernando. It cranked off a ferocious 70 mph. The sedan had a fairly fresh factory rebuilt flathead engine, with the aforementioned triples and this was pulled and put in the coupe. This coupe was the first of four that I owned, all '50s except for one '49 which I bought from my best friend CK, when he went in the Army. (I'm pleased to report that CK and I are still friends. He even introduced me to my wife and we're still friends after that. He told me I would like her, and he wasn't wrong.)

The '49 was a neat little car with a stock flathead and took me a lot of places and never let me down. It was eventually sold to an ex-friend of CK's and another '50 coupe was obtained. This coupe was the one that was considerably built up and had an Olds engine stuck in it.

To end this part of the story, I'll simply list the cars I've owned.
'50 Ford sedan, stock for the most part, bought from dad.
'50 Ford coupe, slightly built flathead, bought from Santa Barbara.
'51 Plymouth four door, bought from dad who bought it from my uncle when dad's Buick was wrecked in Arkansas.
'49 Ford coupe, bought from CK.
'31 Ford Model A coupe, bought from an old girl friend, drove it for the summer, sold it for

what I paid for it. Thought about making a hot rod out of it, since it wasn't a Deuce, I passed. Now look at all the great Model A hot rods kickin' around.
'50 Ford coupe, built flathead, later a built Olds.
'50 Ford coupe, the built Olds de-tuned a bit and run on the street.
'53 Ford four door, six, automatic, given to us by the wife's grandparents when we married, had 11,000miles on it. It was a great little car after I figured out brother in  *law had severely retarded the ignition during a tune-up without a timing light and not a whole lot of knowledge.*
'54 Ford coupe, V-8, automatic. Bought from a co-workers daughter for $125.00 It had a bad idler arm and they were afraid to drive it. Replaced the arm for $9.00 and drove it for a while. Sold it to wife's brother, a really good guy, he had it for three days and put it sideways into a brick wall. It went to the junkyard after that. (Didn't hurt brother in law a bit, except for his feelings.)
'57 Buick Roadmaster hardtop, white, bought from WB's dad, great car, crummy brakes.
'59 Ford Ranchero, stick shift, auto rear, serious highway flyer with a 292. Bought from

brother in law with the '57 Buick swapped into the deal. (Wife's brother).

'59 Ford Ranchero, automatic, 352, this one later got a Shelby 390 FE series engine with three speed stick and headers. Bought from other brother in law. (Sisters husband).

'61 Ford four door hard top. Given to us by wife's mother. Gave the '53 four door to brother in law. Big mistake as the '53 had a freshly overhauled engine. My decision though, brother in law was happy to get the '53.

'62 Ford four door wagon. This one had the Shelby 390 engine and trans installed that was in the '59 Ranchero. The Ranchero was given up due to rust starting after driving down many miles of Mexico's beaches. This was a neat car and pretty fast. It came to be known as the "Red Rocket" or as my older daughter called it "The Pink Pig". She was embarrassed to be seen in it. In fact she put off getting her license for a year as she didn't want to drive it. Probably because it was a stick. This poor car died an undignified death when my house was flooded in 1978. I had time to get one vehicle out and chose my '63 Chevy pickup.

'63 Chevy 1/2 ton shortbed, big window, fleetside pickup. Ended up with a good running stock four barrel 327, Corvette four speed manual transmission, mags and Indian red Porsche paint. Neat truck, put many miles on it.

'67 Barracuda coupe, automatic, power pack 273 engine, folks bought it new. Should have kept it.

'72 Ford Pinto. Bought it from a co-worker who bought it new to commute to a new job 40 miles away. A month later he got a job close to home and a company car. This Pinto had 32,000 miles on it when I got it in '84, had the

original tires with lots of tread left. They washed it once a week, waxed it every three months and put it in the garage every time they were through with it. Generally it was used by the wife for trips to the grocery store. Otherwise they used the company car. The cherriest used car I ever owned.

'77 Ford 3/4 ton 4x4, built 400M engine, automatic, white, mags, camper shell. Another good truck. Bought from brother in law who bought it new.

The '32 Roadster. Purchased in 1985 and got it running in 1992.

'88 Ford Mustang GT, purchased new, first new car, still got it, trouble free car.

'89 Ford Ranger longbed 4x4, stick, 2.9 liter V6, camper shell, first new truck, trouble free so far.

Cars owned, but didn't get running:

'29 A highboy roadster.

'34 Ford Vicky, lightly wrecked, cut up and disposed of during a bit of ignorance. (Don't whine – you did it too.)

'23 T roadster pickup, a clone of the 77 Sunset strip car with Olds engine. Got very close to running, ended up selling it for some good reason.

'50 Ford coupe, Buick Nailhead powered, a nicely done swap was completed when I got it in a swap for a couple of transmissions, engine needed a rebuild, swapped many parts with the Olds powered coupe and sold it.

'54 Ford sedan, granddad's old car, destroyed beyond repair by little brother's friend.

'59 Ranchero, was going to swap in the Shelby 390 from the other '59 Ranchero and then the very straight '62 Ford wagon came along. Took it to the junkyard.

'39 Ford four door sedan, had a complete car, with all the parts except the steering box, ready to start building. 350 small block Chevy, Turbo 350 etc. Sold due to lack of time with all the work days and no days off I was getting stuck with. Sold it really cheap, as I didn't have much invested. Phone rang off the hook for days.

So far it's been interesting ....

"...The flagman brought us to a stop and we backed up. I was getting a little bent about now as I had been making fair starts and stopped right on the start line. I didn't notice the car was still in reverse. The flagman flagged us off. My car started burning rubber in reverse, people were running, scrambling, falling down. It was Panic City for a bit..."

CHAPTER FOUR
SAUGUS DRAG STRIP
THE FIRST TIME. 1956.

The first drag strip we ever went to was Saugus. We left home, a small Southern California coastal town, on a Sunday morning in my first car, the '50 Ford two door sedan. It was black, totally stock with the exception of pipes, seat belts and '56 Chevy small hub caps. There were four of us in the car including little brother. At nine years old, he was as car crazy as the rest of us. He was pretty cool for a little guy and we took him most places with us.

We were really going someplace now. Of course, the furthest we had been from home to date was about 25 miles out of town. Dad was pretty cool about it and told us how to get to the area, located about 60 miles from home. We didn't have a clue as to where the strip actually was located. Mom – well you know how moms are, she worried a lot. It was really something, going to a place we had only heard about. We had hopes we might see some of the cars we had only read about in magazines.

We got to the Saugus area and a local gave us directions to the strip. Turns out it was an old airport, (Airport 6 I believe) and not a hot rod in sight. We drove down the taxi-way to a hangar/office building. An old guy came out and told us that they only ran on Saturday nights due to the airport being still in operation and planes operated out of there in the daylight hours. He was pretty cool and told us that the San Fernando drag strip operated on Sundays.

We went back to town and got directions to San Fernando (who would have thought to bring a map!)

Once in San Fernando we were able to find the strip easily. Just follow the noise. The fuelers could be heard all over town and the noise was the eventual cause of the curfew. Open headers were only allowed between 12:00 noon and 3:00 PM. It made for a great show as far as spectating went.

The strip opened about 9:00 am and time trials were run through the mufflers until noon. After that, open header time trials were run until 1.30 pm at which time eliminations started. It made for a great show that was run out in short order and it was all over at 3:00 pm. San Fernando was always one of our favorite strips, mainly due to the short, quick program. There was always time to stop at the lake and go swimming on the way home. We were usually ready after spending the day in 100°+ temperatures and being either on the hot asphalt surface or in the no-shade grandstands built right on the asphalt.

Once we arrived at the strip we found we didn't have enough money to get everybody in. The bane of youth – no money. In fact it still seems to be a bit of a bane. We turned around and drove around to the north end where you could park the car and see fairly well from the Foothill Boulevard bridge.

After watching a bit, I got the idea to take all our money, get myself in and enter the car. Totally brilliant – I still can't believe the guys went for it. After entering and finding my way to the staging lanes I made a time trial run. Boy, was I disappointed when I got my time slip. Here was the truth in black and white, 65 mph at about 19.90 et. I was so sure my car would turn at least 90 mph. The little sedan was just as fast as any other '49-'51 Ford kicking around town. Just goes to show that these cars were not as fast as we thought they were. An interesting lesson about wishful thinking.

Spending a little time in the grandstands while waiting for eliminations, I watched a couple of '56 Plymouth Furys run. I had been reading about these in Motor Trend and elsewhere. These were one of the first factory hot rods. They had distinctive gold trim and a special factory paint job, factory installed twin pipes and two small four barrels. They used wedge motors. I do know they were bored and stroked (303 cubic inch vs. 277 cubic inch, 9.25 compression ratio vs. 8.0 compression ratio and 240 horsepower). Just from what we had read, we thought these Plymouths had to be the fastest cars around. I don't remember what times they turned.

The thing that shocked me, were the '55-'56 Chevies that were kicking tail on these two cars. I had no idea the Chevies were that fast, It was obvious I had a lot to learn. And one of the things I was learning was to look out for the Chevies. It was the proverbial handwriting on the wall.

Eliminations came and I was promptly eliminated by a smooth running '49 Ford coupe from the Valley. With the racing over, I returned to pick up the guys on Foothill Boulevard. It was a hot day and they were dying of thirst. We went straight to the local drive in, got sodas and headed for the lake. Hitting the cool lake waters after spending the day in 100 degree temps was something we always looked forward to after a day at the drags. We usually got there late enough that the rangers had gone for the day and access was free. Lucky for us as it seemed we were always low on funds.

After swimming a while, we headed home. It was getting pretty close to being dark. Quite a day. We learned a lot. We had never seen a drag strip before. Now we had seen two in one day and raced on one. The bug had bitten us, and for a couple of us it bit really hard.

After wandering around town for a couple of weeks, we decided to make the trek to Saugus drag strip again. This time we would be really smart and go on Saturday night. That's kinda the way it was. We had no idea who to contact to see if they might actually be racing. (And we weren't the only ones.) We just got in the car and went. So what if it was a wasted trip. We got to drive our car somewhere and that was enough for most of us.

The week before we went, we decided to get serious about the racing biz. We took the sedan to dad's friend's muffler shop and had a pair of cutouts installed. Now these things were illegal, the police would bust you for them now and then. We were too dumb to tuck them away, out of sight under the car. Not us – we had 'em behind the front tires under the rocker panel with the Official Chrome Plated Caps, right out where everybody could see them. Why spend money on serious speed equipment if no one knew you had it?

That was part of the hot rod mystique. Right along with no hood if you had multiple carburetion. Part of the game was just looking fast. If you looked fast enough and could pull the choke out just right when idling through the drive-in you probably wouldn't have to race anyone. Except for a few locals who knew how fast your car really wasn't.

The cutouts the muffler shop guy put on for us were really a work of art as compared to ones installed at other shops. He got a couple of pieces of curved pipe and took a long cut out of one of the curves, tapered it to fit the exhaust pipe and did a lot of work to make a cutout that looked like it would flow well. Not anything like the other shops that would torch a hole in the exhaust pipe and stick a straight pipe in at almost a 90 degree angle.

This guy was a bit of an artist with a torch and a pretty good tuner/engine builder. He raced jalopies. (His ride at that time was a GMC six powered '32 Ford five window coupe which sorta explains where a lot of the five windows went). It had pretty outstanding workmanship as compared to other jalopies of the time. He explained what he was doing as he went along. He didn't seem to mind the four of us wandering around in the pit and the shop. I think he kinda got a kick out of us since we knew so much about cars. (At least we thought so.)

We took the car out to a straight road in a fairly desolate area, pulled the caps and just plain got high on the noise. We made a couple of runs with the cutouts open and decided it really made a lot of difference. Ignorance is bliss!

The cutout block-off plates were diamond shaped, had rounded corners and two bolt holes to match a typical exhaust flange. When running open, the hot set-up was to loosen the bolts, swing the plates 180 degrees and tighten the one bolt. The nifty Official Chrome Plated Cap remained attached and looked "too cool".

Great sport was to find your buddy's car in a parking lot at night, preferably when he was at the movies with a date (newer the girl the better) and open his cutouts for him and leave. It scared the heck out of them when the car was started. I had this one pulled on me several times. The fear factor is definitely there. I did this to a friend one night, he never carried tools in his car, a '54 Olds, and was forced to drive home on Saturday night right through town with cutouts open. He was lucky he didn't get a ticket.

Shortly afterward my Chrome Plated caps disappeared, never to be seen again. I thought I had seen them on a car, but they were somewhat common so there was no way to ID them. Dad helped me make a new set out of 1/2" aluminum and turned a round design in the ends to make them easily identifiable. Those disappeared too. Never saw 'em again.

The final solution for me was to buy another set of chrome plated caps and install them with Allen bolts. Hardly any of the hot rod group around town carried Allen wrenches so the caps stayed put. After installing our first piece of real speed equipment, we took off for Saugus with five in the car. We headed out to do some serious racing and show the Valley boys what it was all about.

Of course part way through the trip, once we were really out in the country, we had to pull over and open the caps. Our thoughts were; "Whose gonna catch us out here in the sticks?" Never gave a passing thought about the California Highway Patrol, L.A. County Sheriff or local police in the small towns we passed through and anybody else that didn't care for the noise our little group of desperadoes was making.

We got to the drag strip late in the afternoon, racing didn't start until a little before dark. We were in Nirvana while waiting in line. A McCullough blown, white '55 T-Bird was in front of us. (McCullough eventually became Paxton.) A Chrysler Hemi powered '53 Ford F 100 was in back of us. A couple of coupes and roadsters were there, but I didn't see them race.

With the line at a standstill, we were able to walk up and down and see some really great cars. It compared to walking through the pages of hot rod magazine. There was quite a turnout of hot rods and a few we would later see featured in the mags.

The T-Bird, as we were to see, would exceed 100 mph with ease. (100 mph was a pretty magic figure at that time – if your street driven car could exceed 100 it was really something.) MPH times were the most important to us as that was what we identified with. We did not realize how important ETs were. We were to learn.

The strip used large lights on tall stands to light the area. We found that headlights were required shortly after the finish line. There was less than a 1/4 mile of asphalt in the shutdown area, about 1/8 mile of gravel and then you were facing a sagebrush covered hill.

We made one time trial run. A big jump in times was expected due to the power adding cutouts. The car turned 66 mph at about 19.90 (There must be more to this hop-up stuff than we thought.) We were in a stock class and were eventually paired up with a green '53 Chevy coupe. Right behind us, and surrounded by spectators, was one of the fastest dragsters in the country at the time, the Yeakel Brothers Cadillac powered rail. (Yeakel Bros. owned a Caddy dealership in the Valley). This car consistently ran 144 mph on fuel.

The starting system in use at the time was a flagman. We were soon to learn about being the flagman's buddy. I had pretty good reactions and put a good hole shot on the Chevy. The flagman was supposed to make it a fair start, so he flagged us to a stop. We backed up, lined up again, he flagged us off, once again I put a hole shot on the Chevy. The flagman brought us to a stop and we backed up. I was getting a little bent about now as I had been making fair starts and stopped right on the start line. I didn't notice the car was still in reverse. The flagman flagged us off. My car started burning rubber in reverse, people were running, scrambling, falling down. It was Panic City for a bit. It really confused me for a second, here I am all braced for the massive G forces from the launch, and all of a sudden I'm traveling toward the ceiling and the steering wheel. The safety belt held me down as it should and I was able to stop the car before it went very far, maybe 5-10 feet at the most. I got some serious glares from the Yeakel Bros. pit crew, and who could blame them.

Well the race got flagged off okay, the Chevy got the hole shot, and of course we weren't called back for that one. First round eliminations were getting to be a way of life with me.

We parked the car and stayed around to watch the racing. It was too cool. The noise, the crowd, dust, rubber haze, all the great cars. It was a total and vivid experience. There were no grandstands, the crowd stood along the side of the race track and would lean and/or step in so they could see the race cars coming. This was on both sides of the track. When the cars approached they would lean back or step back, and when the cars had passed they would lean in again and look in the opposite direction and watch them race to the finish line. A guy at the finish line with a flag would indicate the winner. It worked well, but once in a while there would be some arguing about who won.

The beer stand was a popular place and there were several people wobbling around after a while. One of the worst wobblers was driving a '49 Ford ice cream truck. He had been selling ice cream to the crowd and eventually he got so drunk he was just leaning on the fender. A few in the crowd started passing out ice cream from the back while the driver was just about passed out in the front. The truck was emptied in no time at all. About an hour later the ice cream truck showed up in the staging lanes, drunk guy and all. The starter didn't know he was drunk and let him run. He made a good straight run, shifted pretty well and turned 50 mph. He got to the end of the strip, pulled way off to one side, parked and promptly fell asleep.

The best was at the very end. The Yeakel Bros. Dragster lined up for a single. They left hard, smoking the tires. It was quite a sight to a group of kids that had only read about this car. Here it was right in front of us, burning rubber for a long way. Rubber smoke hung over the strip as the dragster went through the traps a little over 140 mph. There were no chutes used at that time. The driver couldn't get the dragster stopped on the asphalt, went through the gravel section without slowing down at all and launched himself a couple of hundred yards up the hill. He didn't turn over, hit anything or even bend it up much from what we could see. A lot of the crowd, including us, drove to the end of the strip as racing was over for the night, (it was about midnight) and walked up the hill to see what we could see. The car didn't seem to be hurt at all. We watched for a while and eventually left. We heard later they had to get two pickups in there, tie on to the dragster and drag it down off the hill.

We drove home, bench racing all the way. It had been quite an evening. The cutouts were still open and stayed open all the way home. We still had our shoe polish class #9 on the window where it stayed for several days. Heck – we were real racers now ......

If you live or lived in, the Saugus-Newhall area you may be surprised to learn there was a drag strip in the area. I don't know when it opened, but I believe it closed about 1957 or '58. It was located East of the Santa Clara river and North of Soledad Canyon Road, right on top of what is known as the "North Oaks" tract of homes. It ran east and west. Originally they ran the cars to the west, but too many of the faster cars couldn't stop at the end and crossed the road (scaring heck out of the citizens using the road) and eventually launched themselves into the river bed which was usually dry. It was tough to drag 'em out of the riverbed.

After a while they ran cars to the east where the only barrier was the sagebrush covered hill. Fate takes some interesting twists. On our way out to the Saugus drag strip we passed a high voltage power station. We had no idea what it was. We had never seen anything like it. It looked like a yard full of things straight from a monster movie. About five years later I was working there.

A couple of years after that, one of the Yeakel Bros. died in a plane crash. He came out of the fog and low clouds, totally disoriented, and went straight into the golf course fairway behind the station.

Years later I went surf fishing with the '54 Olds owner. He had a couple of rusty, chrome plated cutout caps in his tackle box. He was using them as weights. He saw me looking and just smiled. I never did ask him where they came from ....

"...Two guys were in front and two in the rumble seat. One rumble seat occupant, (Skip) was ejected and landed running on the lawn of the house. Since he was running at 25-30 mph or so, he soon went down and slid into the rose bushes. He did get across the lawn pretty fast though..."

CHAPTER FIVE
BRODIE KNOBS AND MODEL A s
BRODIE KNOBS WENT OUT OF STYLE FOR GOOD REASON

Knocking your knuckles or fingers was one. Catching the shirt sleeve was another. One of the main reasons was, they tended to chew up the steering wheel where they were mounted. Sometimes a strip of inner tube rubber taped under the mount helped, but it eventually wore through and still ate the steering wheel. This wasn't too big of a problem for us as we usually ended up painting the steering wheel with enamel to match the exterior color, sometimes a nice contrasting color, usually done when the car was painted. I think the knobs were used because most started with bolt-on stuff and this was one of the cheapest and easiest ones. They had a bit of the outlaw image too. Especially if you had one with a photo of a scantily clad young lady, the scantier the better.

Other names that were common in my area were what I think was the "official" name – Steering Knob. They were sometimes called Spinners. Brodie or Brody knob was the common name for us. That came about from the fun activity called spinning brodies, at least until the car got upside down. Other areas called them spinning brodies, spinning doughnuts. It was always interesting to get an out of state car-guy into school or work and learn their local terms for some things.

The brodie/brody name came from, at least this is the way I heard the story, a guy named Steve Brody jumped off a high bridge intent on suicide, I think it may have been the Golden Gate Bridge, and lived through it. One of the very few to do so. Police of course, like any other working group have their own slang/language soon termed a rapid change of direction a "brody". The original use applied to just about anything including a changing of the mind. Eventually, at least in my area, it came to mean either switching ends in a short half turn or just spinning circles on a big parking lot.

Brodie knobs went out of style for good reason. Knocking your knuckles or fingers was one. Catching the shirt sleeve was another. One of the main reasons was, they tended to chew up the steering wheel where they were mounted.

We used to do these on a deserted gravel road at the beach. It came to an end for me when my '50 Ford sedan didn't switch ends, but simply slid along sideways coming to a stop and coming very close to turning over. My '31 Model A coupe owning friend who was in the back seat of the '50 at the time, and was a recent immigrant from Kansas. He thought it was cool.

Returning from the skating rink late on a dark night, Kansas, in his little rumble seat "A" caught up to us. "Us" being my girlfriend and the other girl my skating partner. We were on a two lane at the edge of town and they passed us doing about 45 in a 25 mph zone. Since we were actually doing 25 it was easy for us to crank a hard right at the intersection to get away from them. It was always a fun game, but not this time. Kansas turned hard left at about the same time, never slowing down from 45 and was thinking the little coupe would switch ends.

Not to be. Well, not exactly anyway. We watched the "A" roll onto its right side, then switch ends and slide into the curb with the tail end pretty hard. Two guys were in front and two in the rumble seat. One rumble seat occupant, (Skip) was ejected and landed running on the lawn of the house. Since he was running at 25-30 mph or so, he soon went down and slid into the rose bushes. He did get across the lawn pretty fast though. The other guy hunkered down, stayed in the seat and was okay. The driver was also okay as was the inside passenger, although he soon had his Levis in shreds, mainly due to the battery dumping the majority of it's acid all over his well worn Levis.

For us, we thought we'd seen the death of a couple of them and it was hard to go back. The girls wanted to leave as they were horrified at the pretty spectacular crash. I turned around right away and went back. It was a pretty grim scene for a bit, as here lay the Model "A" and there was not much movement. Skip was still lying in the rose bushes. Glass was all over the street and smoke was coming from the "A". When we pulled up, I got out; the girls were scared and stayed in the car. Pretty soon the guys in the "A" started coming around. They were shaken up and unhurt for the most part, although Skip had some interesting cuts and was pretty much covered in mud.

I always thought the brodie knob in the "A" was partially responsible for the crash as Kansas had simply cranked it hard and full left without slowing down at all. He never did remember exactly what happened. The hardest part was going home with him and facing the music. Although it wasn't too bad for us, his dad dismissed us pretty quickly and he had to stay and face the music.

Kansas was grounded for quite a while and walked for even longer. Skip healed up with no scars. The shredded Levis guy got new Levis and still hung around with us. The other rumble seat occupant would still talk to us, but not ride anywhere with us after that one. He thought we were the wild bunch or something along those lines. Fancy that!

An interesting side note to all this was that the curb and lawn the "A" ended up lying on, belonged to the folks of another girl who was the girlfriend of a good friend of mine and she was also a competition skater that we skated against from time to time. You just never know where life is going to land you.

Witnessing the crash was good for the two girls. My girlfriend was a pretty calm and safe driver. The crash showed her what could happen and things could get real serious real quick. My skating partner thought she could handle a car pretty well and was forever bombing around the countryside, many times sideways. A free spirit for sure. She slowed down a bit after that one. But only a little .....

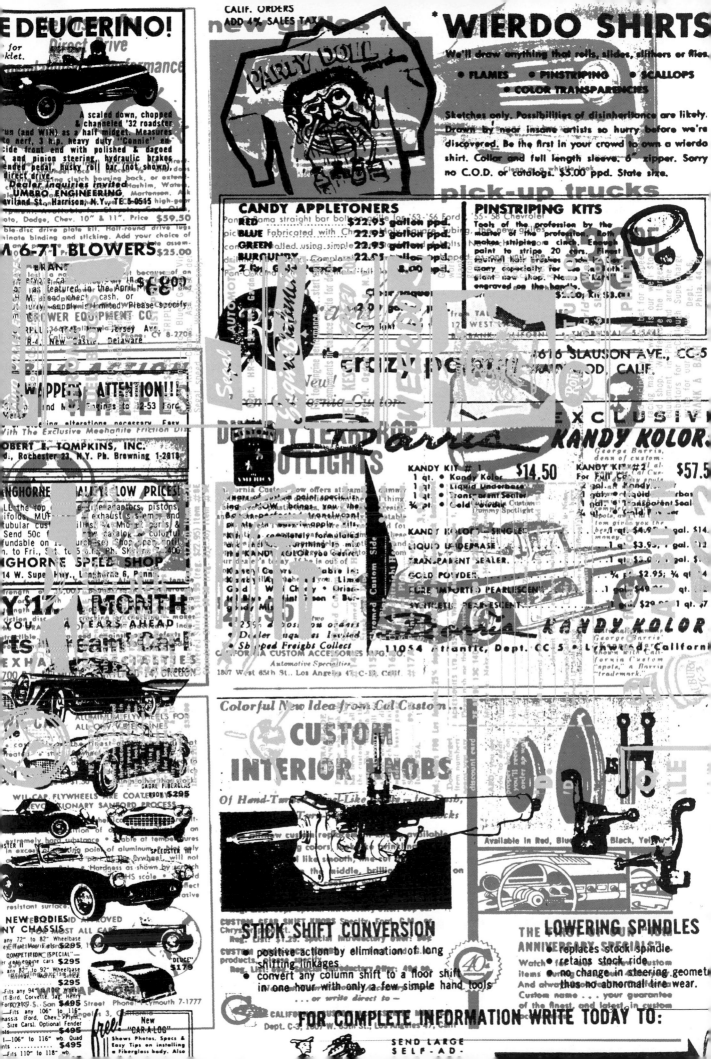

"...He slowed down with us. Both cars went into second gear and we nailed the throttle. It was pretty even until we ran out of revs at 6200, I shifted and he kept right on revving in second gear, shifted and pulled away. What a shock. He had done to us what we had done to so many others..."

CHAPTER SIX
SLEEPERS

ONE OF MY FAVOURITE CARS FROM THE PAST WAS A '50 FORD COUPE THAT I RAN IN THE MID-SIXTIES.

When initially on the road it had 335 inch '56 Olds engine (324 inch bored .060" over). There were some serious overbores in some of these engines. Some guys would bore the '49 Olds (303 inches) .250" over and not be in too much danger of striking water. They ended up with a 345 cid engine.

The '49 Olds had the desirable rifle drilled rods which all the drag race guys liked. A '37 Cad-LaSalle three speed transmission was installed which had a stock floor shift. This was just about the time Hurst started making their shifter. That was a real boon as genuine floor shifts were hard to come by. (In fact we made our own floor shifts by getting a junkyard '40 to '53 or so Ford column shift, shortened it to about four to six inches long, mounted it to a bracket mounted on the tail shaft bolts and put Chevy column shift arms on the transmission shifter shafts. Sometimes these would slip. I came home from Santa Monica one night with a vise-grip clamping the two-three shift arm

on. Later we got smart and filed a notch in the shifter shaft and installed larger bolts – no more slips.

The other popular transmission was the '38 Buick which originally came with a torque tube and was more difficult to adapt to engine swaps. The Cad-LaSalle trans. was very popular and got somewhat scarce. In fact most of the Cadillac dealerships would not sell transmission parts to someone they perceived as a hot rodder. They wanted to save 'em for the Caddy owners. All that did was teach us to wear slacks and a button shirt and lie when at the Caddy dealers.

My '50 Ford coupe from the mid-sixties had a 335 cubic inch '56 Olds engine for street use. The car was later converted to more serious race car use.

The "hot" setup with these floor shift transmissions was to run the stock length or extended shift lever, chrome plated, with an eight ball or aluminum skull on top. It was the epitome of cool.

Some guys ran the '39 Ford trans (which was somewhat weak) in the '40-'48 series of Fords. It was a floor-shift with torque tube or closed drive-line type transmission. Some of the '49 and later guys would adapt the '39 transmission using the Mercury bellhousing and pickup open driveline pieces. This was mainly done because floor shifts were fun to drive and looked really cool. The '39 transmission used to get puked out on the street regularly. The most spectacularly broken one I ever saw was behind a hot flathead. It broke so badly the sides and bottom of the trans. were gone and gears, oil and other pieces littered the street.

As the stock Ford rear end (this was an open drive line) was fairly weak and would break axles at the slightest provocation, even with stock motors, we discovered the Spicer rear end out of the '52-'54 Ford station wagons would bolt right in and was fairly strong. With the fairly hard slicks and/or street tires we ran we never broke one, although I did toss a couple of driveshafts out on the street. Standard non-overdrive ratios in the original rear end were about 3.73 or 3.89. Overdrive ratios were 4.11. Station wagons generally had lower gearing.

These spicer rear ends, (no carrier – integral rear end with cover plate) came with 4.11 gears. Overdrive versions had 4.27 ratios. Just the thing for an aspiring drag racer. Standard brake drum diameter was 11 inch.

In fact, we discovered (after an emergency stop on the freeway) that brakes really should be balanced. With 10 inch drums in the front and 11 inch in the back it would switch ends under hard braking. A little thinking and some junkyard wanderings pointed us to the '52-'53 Ford station wagons. Their front brakes were 11 inch and were a bolt in swap. We used the '53 spindles, kingpins and all. A brake parts warehouse in North Hollywood, right around the corner from CT Automotive which was really handy, (we loved to go to CT, it was one of America's premier speed shops) would install Velvetouch brake linings on your cores. These were a "Sintered" metallic lining that was popular with the circle racing guys and went a long way toward curing brake fade on drum brake cars – especially heavier ones. (Sintered means powdered – the finely powdered metal, including ceramic material and whatever else they used in the mix was baked in what I was told was a 1900°F oven with a ceramic binder to glue them to the shoes.) These linings worked well, didn't fade, took a while to break in, were hard on drums and were not real great when cold. (When did anything like that ever stop a hot rodder?)

Traction systems were home made copies of the "Traction Masters". A simple piece of one inch tubing maybe 32 inches long overall with cut-off shock absorber rings and rubber bushings welded on the ends. A pair of brackets were welded underneath the leaf spring bolt plate and a bracket welded in front of the rear spring front hanger. One inch bolts were used with aircraft lock nuts. They worked fairly well.

In order to stay within the sleeper image we didn't always use the "Traction Master" setup. We would get an extra rear spring second leaf, (the second leaf just under the main leaf) cut it just behind the spring mounting pad, mount it on top of the main leaf under the housing with the long end facing forward. It was retained by the original spring u-bolts etc. and was clamped by three clamps, two in front and one in back. The car still rode well and I believe this setup gave better bite out of the hole than the "Traction Master" setup. (It was copied from the Chrysler Super Stockers – we weren't dumb – we stole every good idea we could get our hands on.)

Flywheel was a Schiefer aluminum that weighed about 10lb as compared to a stock one that weighed about 36lb. If you had a good crisp running motor it would really wrap up in a hurry when the motor was winged. (Thereby impressing the drive-in contingent)

The clutch was a heavy-duty Police/Taxi model. Diameter 11 inches (if you ran a 10 inch clutch you were a nobody – even guys with flatheads either stuck in an 11 inch clutch or lied about it!)

Cam was an Engle #153 if I remember correctly, it had .500" lift and about 288 degrees duration (advertised – the .050" ratings came in later). It also ran the Engle kit, pushrods, springs, retainers, 1.8 ratio rockers (stock was 1.5) etc. This was fairly radical for the street.

Street driving in the rain was real interesting with this cam. Vacuum levels were about 9-10 inches at idle. The vacuum wipers would usually stop at the stop lights and start again when the revs came up. Passing was something you had to plan ahead for. Once you pulled out to pass, the wipers would quit and you couldn't see a thing. Really fun passing big trucks.

Heads were stock. Some of the sharper guys realizing air flow was what it was all about learned to do porting. It was very scientific – many W.A.G. were made - the porting tool was taken out when "looks pretty good" was attained. Of course the amateur porters soon learned what worked and what didn't and had a leg up on the rest of us.

Ignition was a "Ducoil". A dual coil system that was popular for a while and really worked well on the high-winding Chevy small block. (The small block Chevy gets picked on a lot, but a lot of things we take for granted today came directly from this engine – it revved so high when hopped up, it ran into all sorts of ignition and valve train problems on the top end). In fact Junior Fuelers of the era (almost always Chevy powered) ran such high rpms they would get so much oil up in the higher areas of the motor that the oil pump could and would suck air before it drained back. The fix generally was a 1-1/2 inch radiator hose clamped to bibs welded on the front of each rocker cover and the pan making for rapid oil return) It had two of everything (points, condensers etc.) and a double ended rotor. Four of the cylinders were fired from the rotor center post that ran to one end of the rotor as on the stock distributor, the other four were fired by a graphite rotor rubbing block that ran on a flat brass ring on the underside of the cap to the other end of the rotor. (Hope that's somewhat clear.) We did end up with a different firing order. In fact we had two different ones dymo-taped to the firewall. One to run the valves and the other for the plug wires. Some of the spectators that came by in the pits got really confused over that one.

If you wanted headers you had to make them "your own self". We bought a flange kit from CT Automotive in North Hollywood. These came with short stubs formed to fit the square exhaust port. You arc-welded these to the 1/4 inch flange and four two inch pipes were welded to these. Exits were under the fender-well. The two inch pipes went directly to a "Dragfast" collector that was oval shaped, about 12 inches wide and 2-1/4 inches in depth. It had four holes in the top and about eight inches down had a cast aluminum cap with "Dragfast" cast into it that was retained with three 1/4 inch bolts. A hole was cut into the side for two inch exhaust pipes and tubing ran to stock Thunderbird mufflers selected for their silencing capabilities. These were connected to two inch tailpipes.

Since this was a "sleeper" in it's original form, quietness and stock appearance were important. In fact only the right tailpipe showed under the bumper, the left one was tucked under and out of sight and exhaust gasses exited downward. The only thing that gave away the sleeper image was the sounds from the hot motor dumping into the collector cans. This car sounded much "badder" than it really was. It scared away a lot of would-be competition. We used to really get some double takes from the Police when they pulled up next to us at an intersection.

The car was a stock Ford color, had all the original chrome trim and was not dropped in front as was popular at the time. It ran stock size whitewall tires, small hubcaps and beauty rings. The tachometer was tucked under the dash and later went on the column.

The first intake was a factory four barrel manifold. It worked okay but we really needed a multi-carb. setup. (Mainly for the eyewash effect.) Eventually went to a 3x2 barrel setup running #7013008 Rochesters (I don't know why that number has stuck with me, but it has.) These were about one size down from the popular Pontiac Rochester two barrels that most guys liked to run. The ones I ran were off Chevies and were easier to find at the junkyard. (The Pontiac's were about the biggest two barrel available.)

In those days carburetors/carburetion systems were rated in "venturi square inches" and not in CFM. (Factories no doubt used CFM figures – we had no idea what a flow-bench was.) The rest of the engine was stock, had about a 10:1 compression ratio.

Later on we went to 6x2 barrel Stromberg 48s. These were similar to the well known 97s but had larger venturis. (And they had really serious eyewash capabilities.) I used to run Olympia beer cans with the top and bottom cut out for intake stacks, 11 ouncers for top end and 16 ouncers for bottom end. The 16 ouncers poking through the hood under a stainless scoop were pretty impressive looking. They sounded great too – with the headers capped it sounded like the hood was going right down the carbs. At wide open throttle the efficiency of these 6x2 barrel and 8x2 barrel setups approached the efficiency of fuel injectors. Obviously they had to be correctly jetted to accomplish this. Generally we copied one another in the jetting department and tried to learn to read plugs. We probably got away with overly lean conditions due to the short wide-open throttle times at the strip.

Gasolines at the time were rated at 102 octane. East coasters could get I believe "Sunoco Blue", rated at 105 octane. Some of the guys running serious compression ratios of 11.5:1 or better would go into airports and get the aviation gas. (Usually you took a five gallon can to the airport, parked behind the hangar and walked around the corner and bought gas for your "airplane". If you drove up to the pumps in your car they usually wouldn't sell to you – offroad taxes and all that.)

We did well with this car on the street, but met our match in the form of another sleeper, '51 Chevy coupe running a small block Chevy disguised similarly to ours. He pulled up next to us on an empty freeway, looked us over and smiled. We slowed down to about 35 mph. (Figured that would make it our race and this poor guy with the six would eat dust) He slowed down with us. Both cars went into second gear and we nailed the throttle. It was pretty even until we ran out of revs at 6200, I shifted and he kept right on revving in second gear, shifted and pulled away. What a shock. He had done to us what we had done to so many others. We met up later and he was kind enough to show us his engine and setup. He wouldn't admit it, but I've always thought he was running one of the 364 inch small block Chevy strokers.

After having a grand time in the sleeper mode we converted to the race car thing. Slicks, cutout wheel wells, no rear seat, no front bumper, open headers etc. We usually ran at the San Fernando Drag Strip. It was a great place to race. Wandering through the parking lot was usually as good a car show as any car show around. Some of the early birds were allowed to park their cars and spectate from the side of the strip across from the fire up/return road. This was at about the 1000 foot mark and made for some good viewing. San Fernando ran a good, quick program as they had a noise curfew. Open headers were only allowed between 12 noon and 3:00 pm. 12 noon to 1:30 pm was for time trials and 1:30 to 3:00 pm was for all of the races. When they called your class you better be ready.

We won a lot of trophies here even though we were 1-1/2 to two seconds slower than the national record. This was due mainly to attending a lot of the races. Many of the cars we raced against were slightly hopped up, a bit slower and were stuck in the C/Gas class.

Being familiar with the starting system was probably the main reason for our success. San Fernando ran one of the starting systems that eventually led to the Xmas Tree. It was called a "Leaver-Loser" system. They ran it quite a while after other strips went to the Xmas Tree. It had (in each lane) a stage light (1), an amber light, green light and the familiar red light. When staged, the stage light was on, when the starter pushed the button the amber light lit starting a random selection timed relay that ran 1/2 to 1-1/2 seconds and then the green light came on. We soon learned to leave when the amber started to dim. The red light you all know about. Many of the out of town faster cars red-lighted because they were used to the 1/2 second timing between lights on the Xmas Tree that other strips ran.

C/Gas and other classes were determined by dividing the car weight by the CID of the engine. We were fortunate in not having to run in D/Gas. Theoretically it was a slower class, but was loaded with '55-'57 Chevies with 283 motors. They were generally faster than most of us, especially when outfitted with somewhat serious motors.

Some of the guys in D/Gas started Cherry-Picking in C/Gas by overestimating their engine size. Kinda doing it backwards, but it worked for them. Of course, sometimes we would do things like having little brother stand on the scales with the car in the hope we could get into D/Gas, which, at the beginning we thought would be a bit of "Cherry-Picking" we could do on our own.

First time in, we got destroyed in the first round. So much for that idea. Occasionally a car in one of the gas classes next to us would start up and everone's eyes would start watering. This guy didn't need a fuel test, he was worse than the fuelers that fired up on the fireup/return road and u-turned in front of us.

We did see considerable disparity in amounts of gas used (shall we call it gas mileage?) at the track with either system. Usually we started with 3/8 tank of gas. The 3x2s would allow us to run time trials (two -four runs) and the eliminations. With the 6x2s we found we could run time trials, but had to get gas to have enough to finish eliminations.

We used to drive to the north end of the strip, enter Foothill and go about 1/4 mile to the gas station. We had slicks and open headers. Occasionally the police would see us, but if we were behaving they would leave us alone. Sometimes some really radical cars would come in for gas. I saw a Fiat altered in there once. No brake front spokers, little radiator, huge slicks, four pipe exhaust on each side. I was a bit stunned, but the gas station guys didn't bat an eye.

Another strip we raced at was Long Beach. They had staging lanes with doors similar to what the horse race tracks use. Nobody snuck by these. Later on they had electrically driven rollers to start the fuel dragsters. They used to run a really quick Top Fuel show, especially since this was in the days before burnouts. Sometimes coastal fog would wet the track down and end racing for the night. Usually they had really good air.

They had a really good bracket system in that if you broke out at either end (ie: 13.0 to 13.99 ET class) you were disqualified. They ought to use this today. (At the recent March Meet at Bakersfield we watched a guy in a 10 second car run with a dial-in of 13.2 or so. He dominated the class as all he had to do was catch up. That's not racing and does a dis-service to the rest of the bracket racers. I don't think he proved a damn thing.)

We also went to Santa Maria. They had a great strip. The pits were across a country road that was parallel to the race track. You initially staged in the pits and the stage guy would wave you across the road to the line-up area. The return road was the country road. At times people would actually be driving down the country road and would be surprised at having to stop and wait while a dragster fired up in the long pit area and idled across the intersection. Some serious jaw-dropping was going on here.

The best part was when the when a car load of folks were was driving down the road, paralleling the strip. (There was a big line of Eucalyptus trees planted between the strip and the road – tall trees – a native of Australia and planted in California for windbreaks). Two dragsters would leave and the tremendous noises would scare heck out of the folks in the car. Generally they didn't know what was happening or where the noise was coming from. The strip ran slightly uphill halfway and downhill the rest, including the shut-down area. (Times compared favorably with other California strips.) After eliminations the track allowed racers to choose anyone in any class they wanted to race against. This made for some great match-ups. I used to let the little brother drive in these as a small reward for helping with the car. Being a really great little brother didn't hurt either. We got along well. He drag races to this day and now I do the pit crew thing.

At the very end of the shut-off area was an old farm house with porch etc. Every race day the family would have friends over, barbecue, drink beer and lemonade on the front porch and watch the race cars come down the not very steep hill. Turnoff was to the left, right in front of them. It was a great free show.

Tiring of drag racing and finding another really Cherry '50 coupe we pulled most of the goodies out of the by now mostly for drag racing coupe, sold it to the guy down the street who stuck a Caddy in it and built the second coupe for the street.

The engine in my little coupe finally spun a rod bearing and ruined the crank. (Didn't realize at the time that bearings ought to be inspected now and then after considerable high rpm use.) Between moving to a new job in San Bernardino and other things it never did get fixed.

Finally I moved back to Fillmore and sold the car to an ex-Barris bodyman that was branching out on his own. I saw it two other times after that, once driving around San Fernando, (with a small block Chevy under the hood – oh well!) and another time in the Saugus area, parked by the side of the road. I called the police after the second day and it had been reported stolen.

Even today I would like to have it back. (California license plate # IVB 520.)

"...I agreed to do the job. Friday afternoon I started sanding the car and B came out and said to only knock down the roughest spots. I was learning, but old habits die hard. I made a point to get a piece of chain and made a static ground. Saturday morning was clear and warm. I made a w.a.g. on the thinning required with gas, mixed it with the paint and in a vacant lot next to the shop started shooting..."

CHAPTER SEVEN
SAUGUS SPEEDWAY
SIDEWAYS IN SECOND GEAR

During the time the first version of the Olds powered '50 Ford coupe was being built I took it into the muffler shop in the new town I had just moved to – for welding of course. In this case it was the clutch transfer tab mount.

The owner, (we'll call him B – his track name bore the initials of WB, but we've already got one of those) was a guy in his late twenties, and he was a steady competitor at the Saugus Speedway. (For those of you with Tex Smith's book "Roaring Roadsters!" it was also known as Bonelli Stadium and was a track with a long and rich history.) He was one of the top ranking stock car drivers as well as being an excellent builder and of course the owner. I always felt (and I wasn't alone in my thinking) that he should have gone a long way in the ranks of racing, but he had a family and wasn't wild about all the travel involved. Probably a common story for many very skilled drivers. He welded the tab mount in for me, did a nice job and charged a reasonable and fair price.

So far the little town I had moved to had turned out to be pretty nice. B was a source for welding that didn't charge an arm and a leg, spoke "car" fluently, raced and built cars and engines and best of all a small group of local hot rodders hung out there. I got to know him, fairly well and pit crewed for him for a couple of years. It was quite an education.

This stock car racing was a whole new ball game. One in

which a lot of different and new knowledge soon became available. Some of the guys in the hot rod gang from home went for appearance a little more than performance. Those of us in the black primered '49-'50 Ford coupe gang spent the majority of our money on performance items. In fact, near the end, when we started going our separate ways, only WB had painted his nice little '49, a knockout fire engine red. It sure looked good now, sitting in the middle of all our primered coupes. We consoled ourselves with the fact that it was the slowest car of the bunch.

The biggest difference between the hot rod crowd I had come from and the stock car racing crowd was that hot rods were considered rolling treasures and much care was lavished on them.

Stock cars were rougher appearing, and even though just as well built, were considered expendable items in the quest for the checkered flag. That's probably the reason there are not too many small track stock cars at the museums. When retired they were usually severely wrecked and always well stripped of any potentially useful parts.

Up to this time, in building hot rods, we strived to make everything as functional and perfect as we could with our limited skills and tools. The stock cars were constructed in a different, but safe and sturdy manner. Items that the hot rod gang would cut to size, thread and make threaded receptacles for were simply welded in place on the stock cars. Removal? No problem – out with the cutting torch!

Things the hot rodders would spend two evenings fabricating and installing got cut down to size with torch and grinder and welded in place in an hour or two by the stock car guys. Speed and ease of construction was their goal. It was an eye opening experience for me and a good one. These guys could put together some really nice cars in a short period of time, paint 'em and go racing.

Ever wonder where all the great '49-'50 Olds coupes and fastbacks went? Right here. The speedway ate these things up like candy. The '49-'50 Olds coupes and sedans, but especially the coupes, were always a popular car with the younger set, but were getting hard to find, even in the early sixties. I saw some real beauties get cut down and set up for stock car racing. A lot of Olds small hardware, windows, trim chrome, radios seats, you name it got simply tossed to the side in the quest for speed. (Appropriate whining right here is okay. It's all right, I was there and helped, and did a bit of whining myself.) The Olds coupes were always one of my favorite cars and I never got to own one.

We, (the hot rod gang) loved cars. If they turned out to be good looking, we loved 'em even more. And if they were fast, we were totally in love. These stock car guys, they were a different breed. They had no other interest than speed; that and turning left. It was an all consuming interest. Nothing else counted. I got quite an education just being around them when the cars were built and also when they were raced.

Rules? The stock car guys were masters at interpreting the rule book. The cars, while safe, and let's face it, only an idiot would short change himself in the safety area, ran right up to the edge of the rule. There was no cheating on roll bar construction and other safety items, (at least none I heard). Other areas were fair game, builders took every advantage they could. Cheating wasn't blatant, but rather sophisticated and took many forms. Some information was shared, most was not. Sort of a "passing it on to the next generation" kind of thing. The cars were well built, generally handled fairly well and were safe to drive.

A lot of imaginative things were done in the engine department. One rule was, if you drove an Olds it better have an Olds engine. The same applied to the rest, Ford in a Ford, etc. At the time I came in, only a very few flathead Fords were running and only one fairly successfully. It was a '49 coupe, (a lot of these were consumed by the stock car tracks too, although nothing like the Olds) that ran a pretty strong engine. It sounded meaner than heck going down the straightaway in second gear. The engine only had a single two barrel carb and looked totally stock. I worked for the same company as the flathead driver and found out many years later that he ran a hidden nitro system. A hidden pump would put small amounts of nitromethane, cut with alcohol, (don't know the percentages) into a drip line in the air filter where it was aimed straight down the carb throat. It was only turned on in times of need as it was a bit hard on parts. Like many things, the perceived improvement in power may have been only in the mind.

One of the rulings, made in the usual attempt to even things out for everyone, was only a single two barrel carb could be run. Racers soon found that the Pontiac Rochester two barrel had larger venturis than any other two barrel so it was the carb of choice. Things got kinda funny after a while, you'd wander the junkyard, see all the cars hoodless or with the hood up. Almost every Chevy there had an intact two barrel. I don't believe I ever saw a Pontiac in the wrecking yard with a two barrel still installed. (Sorta like the last Vega steering box hunt we went on. We found one box out of about 20 cars!)

There was also competition from the hot rod crowd for the Pontiac two barrel, many were used on triple intakes and a lot were used on the Manafre 4 x 2 barrel intake made for small block Chevies. The Manafre was an interesting intake in that it was generally jetted fairly lean for a good low end and mid-range. The top end was richened up by a separate line that ran to each carburetor and was pointed straight down the carb. When the rpms got over a certain level a button was pushed energizing an electric fuel pump. The button was usually mounted on the steering wheel. Dyno tests were printed in a couple of the enthusiast mags of the era and it was a good intake setup that did produce power exceeding many of the more common racing intakes of the time. It was a neat looking rig, as the carburetors were arranged in a square pattern.

With the stock car crowd, the choice in intake manifolds was equally interesting. Almost always, and always with the experienced guys, it was a four barrel manifold with a two barrel to four barrel carb adapter mounted upside down. These adapters were originally made for would-be hot rodders to bolt a four barrel carb onto their two barrel intake, but you were pretty much fooling yourself, not much was gained. The makers must have wondered what happened when the stock car guys started buying these things left and right. B had done a bit of experimenting and comparing the two barrel intake manifold against the four barrel intake manifold with two barrel adapter and found the latter to be a bit stronger and worth the trouble.

B had done a lot of interesting and slightly different things on his car.
One was the rear axle ratio that he ran. Ratios were a jealously guarded secret with the racers and they didn't say much about them. They didn't say much about their engines either. In fact, they just plain didn't say much. (One of our younger pit crew guys let some information slip to another car owner. He came close to losing his unpaid volunteer job over that. He was bottom dog for a while. I was learning that stock car racing was a serious business in a lot of areas.)

The ratio of choice seemed to be the 4.11 which worked well with second gear, which was the gear these cars always ran in. The track was supposed to be a 1/3 mile and in truth did look slightly bigger than the 1/4 mile tracks we had seen at the flat track races. I believe B ran either a 4.27 or more likely a 4.33 diff. Most of the guys could build some really strong engines, some had the money to spend, but B could either keep up on the straights or pull them a little bit and reel em in. He had a different technique on the comers, more on that shortly.

One of the things I really liked about circle track racing, unlike drag racing where the smallest of errors will put you out of contention, was that circle track allows a bit of time for recovery. Engine basics were similar to the hot rod engines, but special attention was paid to cam choice so the two barrel would pull good off the comers and down the straights. Extra attention was paid to the oiling systems. These engines had to live at elevated rpm levels for considerable lengths of time.

Hot rodders in our group, not knowing much in the way of header science simply slapped on the biggest primaries and collectors we could buy. Circle track guys learned early about proper sized headers and collectors, probably due to being forced to make the two barrel carb breathe as well as possible.

Transmissions of choice in the Olds were generally the Olds and the longer Cad-LaSalle side shift transmissions. In fact B had so many spare Cad-LaSalle parts, he supplied the parts I had broken allowing me to get back on the road with the coupe. I only broke one Cad-La Salle trans in the coupe and that was due to the rear u-joint coming unglued on the second-high shift. The resulting driveshaft flailing broke the trans rear housing and bent the tailshaft, not to mention putting a pretty good kink in the driveshaft itself.

That sorta answers the question of; "Where'd all the Cad-LaSalle transmissions go?" The answer was, we were in competition with the stock car crowd. Between the hot rodders and the circle track guys, a Caddy owner didn't stand a chance. Now that I think about it, all the Cad-LaSalle transmissions my friends and I got were always obtained a long ways from any circle racing track. In the LA area and the San Fernando Valley area these transmissions were just about impossible to find.

Wheels were simple on the circle track cars. A rotary welding fixture was built that allowed the spider to be accurately cut out of a standard Olds wheel. This was then trimmed to size and used to mount a complete and totally stock wheel. This cut down spider was then welded to the new wheel rim and the spider effectively made a double spidered wheel. The 1/2 inch 20 lug studs were removed and tossed. 9/16 inch studs, (and they may have been 5/8 inch) considerably longer than stock, were then used with the proper lug nut, probably a common light truck item and the wheels bolted on. It made a pretty good wheel. I never saw one break under normal racing conditions. Wrecks don't count, every thing bends or breaks in one of these.

B altered his steering arms for quicker steering. He had also learned (from the proverbial old hand) how to set up a car for circle track racing. His car did handle well and he ended up with a small adjunct to his business doing front ends for other racers. But he always held back a bit for himself. After all, he was in racing to win and the track paid out real money as vs. the drag strips which only gave out trophies in most of the classes.

I used to think that owning a drag strip, aside from all the hard work had to be the perfect business. The racers (the show) paid to get in and race. The spectators paid to get in and watch. The payout for first place only was usually a cheap trophy that couldn't have cost more than $3.00. Such a deal! We really didn't care; we simply wanted to race.

B found out that I had painted a few cars, including the Olds powered coupe that had been very close to startup when in his shop for welding. He asked me to paint his backup race car he was building up. The realities of stock car racing were, you better have another one ready to go in case the primary car gets bent or totaled, which was fairly often. It was a pretty complete car, lacking only engine, trans and wiring. I asked him if he wanted me to pick up the paint supplies, he said he knew what to get and he had to run some errands anyway. His shop was a one man deal. He had found he could trust us with his cash, tools and sodas and felt no qualms about leaving us in charge. We didn't do any customer oriented work, simply worked on the race cars and told the customers B would be right back. Most customers knew B well, liked his work and didn't mind waiting.

When B came back with the paint supplies I was pretty surprised. I expected several gallons of thinners, primer, color, sandpaper, bondo and glazing putty. What he walked up with was a couple of sheets of 180 grit wet and dry and a gallon of Dupont's standard black car enamel. At least he'd bought some good paint. I asked him where the primer was and he told me that stock cars get banged up so fast that primer was not worth the trouble or money. I asked him where the thinner was. He dragged out an old Dupont thinner can and said they had it at the Texaco next door. I took it next door and asked for some enamel reducer. They kinda got a strange look and asked what I was going to do with it. When I told them, their faces brightened up, one guy took the can and went straight to the regular gas pump and proceeded to fill it. When I asked them what was the deal, they said to ask B. B explained that thinner was also costly so gasoline was the thinner. I had more than a few second thoughts, as working for the power company had taught me a lot about static electricity. (In fact an adjacent power utility had an unusual fatality. A contract lineman was building a new 230,000 volt line, one that was not near any other lines or power facilities and was simply sitting in the desert not connected to anything. Induced voltages from adjacent high voltage equipment was always a concern and was taken care of by proper grounding procedures. Induced voltages were not a concern here, but static electricity should have been. This poor lineman had climbed the tower and contacted the conductor that was charged with static electricity due to the wind. He was promptly electrocuted when the static electricity charge bled off to ground through his body to the tower.)

I agreed to do the job. Friday afternoon I started sanding the car and B came out and said to only knock down the roughest spots. I was learning, but old habits die hard. I made a point to get a piece of chain and made a static ground. Saturday morning was clear and warm. I made a w.a.g. on the thinning required with gas, mixed it with the paint and in a vacant lot next to the shop started shooting. The car was in the sunshine and the body was hot. No problem, this stuff flowed out a bit and cured like right now. It actually got a fair gloss and looked pretty good. Later I was to find that it chipped off in large flakes when damaged a bit and wasn't durable. This wasn't a big deal, not too many two year old stock cars were around anyway. A new one, sometimes two were built almost every year. (I really debated about recounting this piece on the gasoline thinned paint. I believe all of us realize what a risky business it was and is. Shooting this concoction in a garage and once ignited would probably be similar to a low yield nuclear event. You couldn't pay me enough to do it again. 'Nuff said!)

Other interesting things were the addition of a fairly large rear axle housing breather, especially when compared to the stock one. A large fill plug was welded to the back of the diff housing to allow the quick addition of rear end oil. The lubes used in these circle track cars had a bit of voodoo about them. There were many secret mixtures, with red lead being one of the favorite additives and some slow flowing black stuff which I thought was perhaps pure molybdenum disulphide, if such a thing was even available. I watched, but didn't ask too many questions when the diff lubes were being mixed up.

As mentioned, the exhaust system was different. The main difference was the collector was sometimes four feet-six inches long, extended to the front of the rear wheel housing and exited the car to the side there. A baloney style cut was favored and the collector/tailpipe worked well in keeping exhaust fumes out of the driver's face.

B had a small air scoop mounted on the roof just behind the windshield and in front of the driver. The outlet was inside the car and pointed directly at the driver. No one else ran one of these. I thought it was kinda funny, but realized what could happen when the leading driver in a long race started slowing down. I thought initially that he was getting a bit nervous after being in the lead for a while and was trying to cool it a bit. The other drivers were rapidly catching up. After a bit we could see he was starting to slump at the wheel and then everyone started passing him. All this didn't take too long, the starter was aware of the situation too and tossed out the yellow flag when the slumping began. We did have a very good and fair starter. The cars slowed down and the slumper finally passed out and hit the wall with minimal damage to the car and none to him. The red flag came out then and everybody pretty much stopped where they were. The ambulance crew got to him and stuck oxygen in him for a while until he came around. It was simply carbon monoxide poisoning. B's periscope, as we called it didn't look so silly now. The only glass allowed in these cars was the windshield and with the remaining windows gone exhaust fumes would drift in the open back window. We heard that the guy complained about having the worst headache in his life.

First time out as a pit crewman I found that all the cars looked great under the lights. Close examination showed them to be no smoother than ours. Our crew consisted of myself, a California Highway Patrolman about 25, a 21 year old and a 15 year old that lived down the street from B. The 15 year old was so nutso for racing he rode his bike several miles across town to the shop each day after school.

Initially, pit crews were located in the center of the track. Tow vehicles and tools were placed pretty much in the center and away from the corners. The rule was, keep your eyes and ears open, as sometimes guys would lose it on the straights and come into the pit area. I always felt it was a recipe for disaster, but it was great being right there in the center of action.

Pit crews were a bit like spectators at a tennis match. They would watch their car run and were constantly turning in circles to keep up. The infield pits came to an end one night when the main race was flagged off. A couple of cars lost it badly on entering turn three on the back straight and about four cars stacked up against the wall totally blocking the track. The remaining cars were still accelerating down the straight and proceeded to smack into the now stopped foursome. The middle of the pack and end runners started coming into the pit area to avoid the wrecked cars. It was pretty amazing in the pits, just about every single crewman started running toward the wreck in the corner even though cars were still coming down the straightaway. That little stunt forced a lot of the cars into the wreck as they had nowhere else to go. It was like a sea of Lemmings, once one started, the rest followed, including me and the 21 and 15 year olds.

The C.H.P. guy was about the only cool head there, he hollered at us to stop and we did before we got more than a few steps away. Once the dust settled, we found several wrecks, most in the corner, a couple on the straightaway and some cars were seriously damaged. One poor little '55 Chevy ended up smashed up against the wall with an Olds against the front, one against the side and one sitting on the trunk lid. The other end of the up in the air Olds was sitting on the hood of another Olds. The Chevy was pretty badly bent. No drivers or crew members were hurt, but it could have been quite a disaster.

B's car was totally unscathed, he was near the front of the pack and had simply driven around the initial wreck in the infield dirt, He was always a pretty calm guy and it stood him well this time out. The track operators realized a major disaster had been missed, mainly by sheer luck. Next race the pits were no longer in the center of the track and I never saw another pit crew there again.

Not too long after the pit crews were moved to the South grandstands a really good one happened. About one lap after the start of the main event all the lights went off. It was pretty dark as it was a fairly moonless night. The line serving the track had tripped out leaving the entire canyon area in the dark. Working for the power company I knew the automatic equipment would close the circuit breaker after a 30 second delay. After the 30 seconds were up, the lights came back on. We expected to see several wrecks and who knows what else. Racing hadn't even slowed down, the guys were still going full tilt and from what we could tell no one had lost position.

After the main event had ended, many of the race cars would park in the infield and fans would be allowed on the track to look at the race cars. A lot of guys would bring their trailers and car haulers to the infield and load up there. The lights went out again and stayed out. Some drunk had decided to contest the right of way with a power pole and lost. Loading up the race car was a bit of a pain with the low battery flashlight we had.

As I alluded to earlier, B's style of driving was different from just about everybody else. He had a mentor, a retired guy that had a wealth of experience and advised B on a lot of things. This is where B learned chassis setup and how to drive the corners. The driving technique was simple. The track was a simple oval with a very short bit of straight connecting turns one and two and three and four, a bit like Indy. Most drivers simply set up a drift and treated these slightly separate turns like one long turn. B also did that at times when required, but generally he slid into turn one under power, squared it off and drove straight at turn two where he slid into that under power, squared it off a bit less than he did at turn one and got a good drive off turn two. Of course this was repeated at turns three and four.

The pit crews were now in the South stands and we had an excellent vantage point to watch. You could tell that B pulled away very slightly from other cars due to getting through the turns a bit quicker. I was always surprised that no one else seemed to notice, as it looked like a good way to do it. I always thought that driving this way and running slightly shorter gears accounted for his consistent success.

I built a couple of Olds short blocks for B's cars. I learned a lot about clearancing and blue-printing blocks and learned to do a few things that we didn't do on our drag racing engines. B usually double checked my work, and rightly so. I checked the heck out of it myself; I didn't want to be embarrassed by a failure due to something simple and preventable.

I also wired several of his cars because I had a source for rubber covered clamps, tie wraps and similar and he had been impressed by the wiring on my '50 Ford coupe. Probably the only novel thing about the '50s wiring was the use of terminal strips to break up the wiring and have a good way to trouble shoot. It was handy; the simple removal of a few of the terminal block screws on the firewall and the engine was ready to come out as far as wiring was concerned.

I was very conscious about protecting the wiring from engine hot areas and sharp metal edges. We used grommets everywhere we could and protected the wiring by running it inside rubber hose. Many clamps and tie wraps were used, many more than any hot rod I had ever been involved with. It made a lot of sense as a failure here could cost a lot of money if the car quit.

For a while B effectively ran two cars. He had last year's car, which was in pretty good shape. The 21 year old (G) in our pit crew decided to get into racing and B let him use the old car. G replaced the front fender clip and bought the parts for a fresh engine. I built the short block here as well as degreeing the cam and sticking the heads on, things that B usually reserved for himself. I did a pretty good job as the engine lasted out the season with only minor maintenance.

The standard shift stuff and trans were obtained from B's pile of drive line parts in the back of the shop. I painted this car too, using the same paint/thinner combo. (I just knew there was going to be a really good explosion one day, but it never happened, probably because the fumes were well dissipated by painting outside.)

G turned out to be a pretty fair driver and left the novice class behind pretty quickly. Of course when he started running with the big boys he ended up in the middle of the pack. He got in a bit of trouble with the track officials once, when black flagged for an oil leak, he didn't realize the flag was pointed at him. After quite a few laps and with the starter just about spitting nails he finally caught on and pulled off the track. After the race, B and G walked over to the flag stand, G apologized to the starter and with a bit of diplomatic help from B was able to avoid a suspension.

The circle track stuff came to an end for me when I transferred to a new job 100 miles away. I still visited friends in the old town now and then and we usually made it to the speedway on Saturday night where we could watch B race. G had gone into the service by that time and I never saw him again. During these weekend visits we would hit San Fernando drag strip on Sundays and sometimes Long Beach drag strip. It worked out well as I had four days off every five weeks and we had an easy trip home on Monday morning.

The new home was not too far from the Fontana drag strip and many times I would spectate over there. Riverside Race Track was not too far in the other direction and we went there almost every year for the Times Grand Prix. For a while there, California was awash in drag strips, circle tracks and off road racing. The population boom put an end to most of that. The only drag strips still operational in Southern California now are Carlsbad, near San Diego, Palmdale, North of L.A. and Bakersfield, way North of L.A. Terminal Island at the Port of Los Angeles opens up once in a while but I think it's going now. It's been a bit of an on again, off again thing. Hope they can keep it running. Fontana has a new Super Speedway that either just opened or is about to open. I hear that no provisions have been made for a drag strip. Too bad, as it's in a good location and a drag strip would probably do well there. 'Course now the big cities and a lot of the small ones are experiencing the same problems they had in the fifties that led to the creation of all the local drag strips in the first place!

Street racing is alive and well ....

"...The little '33 ran a B&M Hydro, a popular trans at the time. On the first time trial with all the new stuff the car launched straight and true. And when second gear was hit the whole rear end just peeled right out of the car and went its own way, complete with both slicks and a bent up driveshaft..."

CHAPTER EIGHT
DRAG RACE CARS
AT SAN FERNANDO AND LONG BEACH

One car I'd like to see found, but it probably ended it's days as a drag racer or may even be on the street as a street rod, was a yellow '34 three window that used to run at San Fernando in the late fifties. It was somewhat similar to the famed Mooneyham-Sharp coupe but with fenders. It had a large #25 painted on the door if I remember correctly and it ran an injected Hemi. What made it impressive, besides the low stance and bright yellow paint was the times it ran – 125 mph on gas!

ETs were clocked at the time, but for most of us novices the mph figures were what impressed us. 'Course the smart guys were going for a low ET and taking all the money.

A guy named Jazzy Nelson had a Fiat coupe with flathead and it ran in the 10s in the early-mid fifties. Awesome performance for a flathead, especially when you consider the time period. He ended up Top Eliminator at many of the early days drag races.

A few impressive cars that ran at San Fernando in the late '50s, early '60s: (in my opinion) included Tony Nancy's flathead 22 jr roadster. Tony, being one of the very best West Coast upholsterers built equally nice cars. The fit and finish was state of the art for the era. They ran good too. He was the winner in his class most times.

Another was President Lincoln, a rumored to be (although it was stated as being so by the track announcer) 555 inch Lincoln motored Top Fueler. He beat the Chryslers fairly often. We loved it because it was so different and was very well built.

My favourite fueler is still the Greer-Black-Prudhomme car, now fully restored as shown here. The John Winderski fueler runs a close second and was similar to the Greer-Black-Prudhomme car, but longer.

There was a '29 Model A highboy sedan that ran a flathead and I believe Jack Chrisman ran it. It turned good times for it's altered class.

A mid-fifties Austin Healy, a good looking British sports car, running small block Chevy, was well built, ran good times and really ran good times after installing a 6.71 blower. 160 mph times were common as was the occasional giant wheel stand. This was an exceptional mph for the time period for this type car.

The drag strip starter was a partner in a '55 Nomad that had a stroked (no surprise, his day job was counter guy at CT Automotive where strokers were knocked out by the dozens) small block Chevy and was injected. Seems like it ran 118-125 mph or so on gas and they went to fuel and ran about 151 mph.

One of the greatest cars that ever showed up at San Fernando was the John Winderski Top Fueler (hope I spelled his name right). The car was named Black Beauty. This was a car similar to the Greer-Black-Prudhomme fueler and had a considerably longer wheelbase. The body was flawless and well designed. It was painted with a knockout paint job and was black (surprise) in color. Most of the smaller items were chromed as well as some of the larger ones. It ran a blown Chrysler and ran very competitively with other Top Fuelers in the Southland and was right up front in the finals or winning most times out.

My favorite Top Fueler is still the Greer-Black-Prudhomme car, but the Black Beauty dragster runs a very close second, at least for me. If an award was given for "most beautiful car at the strip", this car would have won every time. Winderski was a tall, kinda quiet guy. He was friendly enough, and didn't mind if you were in the pits checking out the car as long as you weren't in the way. Sadly he was killed at Long Beach drag strip. I'm not sure what transpired, but I think the engine came unglued in the traps at around 200mph. Pieces of the car went everywhere and the majority of the Hemi engine went down the shut off area, through the sand trap, through the cyclone fence and rolled right out onto the street that was at 90 degrees to the drag strip direction. No one ever thought that would happen as the street was a long ways away.

Tragedy did happen at the drags now and then. Most times it was very safe and about the worst that happened was a spin out just past the start line or sometimes a wild ride through the sand traps.

One accident that took a life at San Fernando should never have happened. An older rail, home built and fairly well done, running a carbureted small block Chevy came to the line. This little car was obviously a budget operation, but it did pass tech. The problem was, the header on the right bank was tossing quite a bit of oil on the right slick, easily viewed from our vantage point at the front of the staging lanes. The car was in the right lane and the slick was probably out of the starters vision. The starter is the final check for race car safety and they don't miss much. The car left, spinning the tires a bit, (no small wonder) and made a run to about 140 mph. No chute came out and he kept right on going. At San Fernando about 2/3 of the way down the paved shut off area a very slight right turn was made, (never a problem) and then under the Foothill Boulevard bridge and into the sand traps and river bed. Most everybody got stopped before running out of the sand traps. This poor driver hit the left side bridge abutment, probably in a slide due to the oiled down tire and possibly lost the brakes. I don't know, that was never explained. He still had a lot of speed on when he hit according to witnesses. We waited in the staging lanes for about 90 minutes until the ambulance came back. (Only the biggest races had two ambulances.)

We went back to San Fernando the following week and on the first time trial ran down to the end of the shut off area and took a look at the bridge from the return road. There were rubber scuff marks about 6-8 feet up on the bridge abutment and evidence of where a lot of oil had been. Sometimes on a Sunday at work, if things took me into the valley I would park the company car on Foothill Boulevard, near the bridge over the river adjacent to the drag strip. Sitting on the bridge and eating lunch while watching the race cars was about as entertaining a lunch hour that a guy could have. It was kinda interesting to hear and see the top fuelers shut down as they came winding down the shut off area.

One guy ran way past the finish and then popped the chute. The car finally got stopped about 200 yards from where I was. It did a lot of sliding back and forth across both lanes once it had slowed to under 100 mph. The driver got out in a real hurry and started hopping around on one leg. The other rail, with chute still out, rolled down, stopped and the driver got out to lend a hand. Turns out the drive shaft coupler or similar had broken and the pieces had broken the drivers leg as they were exiting the car. Drive line shields were a requirement at this time and I'm sure the car had one. It probably came a bit unglued too.

We used to see a lot of drag bikes run at Long Beach. One of the very wildest sounding ones was a dual engined Kawasaki Triple. These were three cylinder two strokes and sounded wild enough with one engine running expansion chambers, let alone two on the same bike. (I think the engines were 500cc). This thing was unbelievable. I don't remember what times he ran, they were very competitive and ran up front most of the time. The very best and most interesting bike was a twin engined Harley. A guy named Bob George built it. It had a pair of stroked 74s. They were probably 80 inches plus and may have been 100 inches. Some of the Harley guys ran some big engines, 100 inches was about the max for a stroker at that time. What made this bike so interesting was that it had all the street trim, headlight, taillight etc. on it. I think it was originally built for the street. At the time it seemed most Harley guys went right along with the hot rod theme of more is better and twice as much is best of all. Little brother and I were discussing how they planned to start the thing. I figured it would get a tow-start from another Harley they had with them. Not so, Mr. George, being a big strong guy, simply climbed on and kick started the darned thing. It definitely took some effort and if you've ever kick started a Harley I'm sure you can imagine trying to start two at once. Timing between engines was probably set up so as to make life easy. With the engine cold and after 6-7 kicks it lit off. Heck that was good for any stock Harley at the time. (Little brother stuck an accelerator pump carb on his '62 Harley Sportster and it got to be a 1-2 kicker every time. That seems to be the secret with Harleys, a shot of prime makes life easy.)

Anyway, once the bike was started, Bob, sitting astride the bike, idled it over to the start line with the rider walking along, putting on the helmet, zipping up the full leathers etc. Once near the start line the rider got on. In keeping with the requirements for "light weight = good acceleration", the rider probably weighed about 130-140 lbs. The rider was fearless, the bike handled fairly well and promptly cranked off an ET in the mid 9s. Very good performance at the time. The bike was later taken to Bonneville and posted speeds either very close to or in excess of 200 mph. 200 mph on an open bike is a tough nut to crack. One picture I've seen of a bike at Bonneville running about 200 mph showed the rider laying flat out, legs and feet hanging out the back and flying along in the windstream with the only connection his grip on the handlebars. Sorta like a banner flying in the wind. From what I've read and heard, this is pretty much the norm for an open bike at these very high speeds.

A short bit about the infamous "welded spiders" and how they worked out on the street and at the drag strip. As far as the welded spiders went, and they were simply an early days attempt to make both wheels drive equally. At times they left a lot to be desired, sometimes, a whole lot. On a dirt track with its lack of traction, they worked quite well. Driveline breakage was fairly uncommon in this venue. Welded spiders on the street or strip though, was a whole other ball game. They worked, but only up to a point. Everybody I knew that tried this one broke an axle. Usually by simply going around a corner and not even accelerating very hard. Since there was no "differentiating" going on within the diff, the axles simply twisted back and forth until they broke. That is exactly what happens when you flex a piece of wire back and forth creating heat at the molecular level and changing the crystalline grain structure of the metal. Initially it work hardens, gets soft and then breaks. For the lucky majority, on a slow corner. For the unlucky few during hard acceleration.

Once these cars broke an axle they usually made a fairly hard and quick turn toward the broken side. this was usually not caught by the driver because the initial indications are; the car is just starting to drift under power. Once the driver realizes the car is not coming back, it's too late – Wreck City in more than a few cases I saw.

The most spectacular one I saw was at San Fernando Drag Strip in the early '60s. Aside from the Top Fuelers, or simply A/F – standing for A Fuel – the top dogs in the gas classes – meaning the doorslammers, a term not used at the time – were the A/GS cars. The letter A standing for the top of the class, G for gasoline and S for supercharged. Later the blown cars were designated AA/G and BB/G and so on. The unsupercharged cars being labeled A/G etc. The blown and unblown cars originally ran in the same classes. Installing a blower simply booted you into the next class up. It didn't take too long for some of the thinkers and doers to start making some serious boost and before long a few of the B/G class cars with blowers, now running in A/G, took over the A/G class entirely. As you could imagine, some serious whining went up, not unlike that seen in the recent nitrous/supercharger wars when Scotty Cannon starting cleaning up with a blown car.

In truth, moving the blown cars up one class was a bit unfair and was recognized as such by the NHRA. NHRA then broke the ranks of the gas class cars even further with separate classes for blown and unblown. The Stone-Woods-Cook '41 Willys, (my favorite) and the Mazmanian '41 Willys, (a close second) fell into the A/GS class and put on one heck of a show. S-W-C at the time ran a blown Olds, and Mazmanian started out with a Chrysler Hemi in the Willys as far as I know.

Shortly after the initial matchups, these two famous, and deservedly so, cars became the stellar attractions of the infamous "Cam Wars". The "Cam Wars" being the brainchild of Ed Iskenderian who placed a brash, little bit tongue in cheek, advertisement in National Dragster extolling the virtues of Iskenderian cams. Engle cams responded in kind and it wasn't long before the ads were in the magazines. They were a great series of ads and we couldn't wait to see what the latest match race had wrought and what the latest ad would be. The S-W-C car ran Engle cams and the Mazmanian car ran Iskenderian cams. The S-W-C car's Olds engine was soon replaced with the popular Chrysler Hemi and it was off to the races for sure. I was fortunate to have seen several of the S-W-C and Mazmanian match races. Being doorslammers, and looking like something you might see on the street, mainly in LA or the San Fernando Valley – launching and accelerating so hard that it was darned near unbelievable – had most of us dreaming dreams on a grand scale. If only.....!

Not all the successful cars ran the big Chrysler though. An interesting little car soon showed up in the A/GS ranks running a blown small block Chevy. It was soon turning very competitive times. This particular car a '33 Willys coupe, a body style that a few were starting to use. The '33 body being a bit smaller and lighter than the popular and good looking '41 Willys coupes. The '33 was a good choice as the drag racing class breakdowns were delineated by pounds per cubic inch. Even giving up some cubic inches, the advantages were obvious. The little '33 weighing less than the '41s were a prime candidate for more of a rearward weight bias. Combine that with the smaller cubic inch Chevy small block which allowed an even lighter overall weight than the Chrysler engined '41s and the advantage was obvious. Keep in mind that class delineations were determined by dividing the weight of the car by the cubic inches of the engine. Big car – more weight. Little car – less weight. Simple as that.

The HP differences between Chevy and Chrysler may not have been as much as some thought either. With a good solid short block, a change to an overdriven blower pulley was easy and most times successful. Occasionally though, one paid the price for overboosting and took his engine home in a bag.

The '33 was run by a small consortium of three guys. Namely, Altizer-Finders-Kibler. The car was a strong runner and usually in the hunt for A/GS top honors. During time trials at San Fernando, the little coupe lined up in the left lane to make a single pass. It launched, really hard like always. About 50feet out, it started a turn to the left that drove the car up onto the hay bales lining that side of the track. Somewhere in here, the left rear wheel, broken axle stub and all came out. The car completed about a 270° on top of the hay bales and when it came down, the right front wheel hit the pavement hard and was broken off as well. It was short and violent and all over in a matter of seconds. I relate this short story just to point out what can happen to a solidly locked rear. Not to mention that at the wheel was a driver generally perceived at being one of the very best. He didn't stand a chance, and neither would we. Granted, a lot of spools are run at the drags nowadays, but the saving point is the very strong aftermarket alloy axles. Said axles being pretty much what's saving us from ourselves.

'Course, what's getting a lot of cars now is simply failures in some of the four bar systems running Heim joints. This one got Jim Data – a long time friend of little brother's and mine – about 3-4 years ago when his fiberglass bodied, DRCE engine, tube framed, about two month old '57 Pontiac two door made a 157 mph hard right turn into the guard rail at Famoso when a Heim joint broke. The resulting crash, quite spectacular to say the least totaled the car. He has a new race car - another fiberglass bodied '57 Pontiac completed just last spring. The new car is a knockout and has a couple of races under its belt and has done well so far. Winning B/Gas at the recent Pomona Goodguys race. From what I hear it's got some serious big and strong rod ends on the four bars. Small wonder.

Jim Data's '57 Pontiac.

A short but interesting little bit on the '33 Willys is that one week later we were surprised to see them at Lions Drag Strip at Long Beach. They were a serious and hard working race crew, but we thought it pretty amazing that they got it back on the track so fast. As far as we could tell it had a brand new 'glass front end, 'glass driver's door, left rear fender, new front axle and of course a new rear axle to replace the broken one, along with the requisite gray primer spots on the bright red body. We mentioned that we had 8mm film of the spectacular wreck and offered to make them a copy. They weren't even interested and who could blame them?

'Course since Lions ran on Saturdays and far into the night sometimes, Murphy was still about. The little '33 ran a B&M Hydro, a popular trans at the time. On the first time trial with all the new stuff the car launched straight and true. And when second gear was hit the whole rear end just peeled right out of the car and went its own way, complete with both slicks and a bent up driveshaft. Seems like the rear suspension brackets or rod ends had given up the ghost, allowing the complete rear end to leave. The little '33 slid to an embarrassed stop dragging on its gasser-style rear bumper. A tough break for a hard working crew. More than a few weeks elapsed before we saw the car again....

"...Like most of the Mustang owners of the era, this was probably the most powerful car he'd ever driven and I imagine he felt pretty invincible. That was until he got swamped by the old Ford. He didn't like it though, he ended up sailing down the freeway giving us the single digit salute..."

CHAPTER NINE
GOOD SOUNDS SLEEPER
I WAS RECENTLY ASKED A QUESTION THAT TOUCHES ON A LOT OF CARS I REMEMBER, AND A FEW THAT I OWNED.

The ones that I remember, I remember very well. Each one being a small, but important life changing experience. At least to me.

Roadsters are my favorite and I saw quite a few at a very early age, but the one I remember best was a flathead powered black '32 highboy driven by a high school teacher. At the time it was a bit impractical and also a hard to find car, not that any of us wouldn't have taken it, rain and cold be damned. Real life intrudes into dreams and hopes in just about every case, sometimes you settle for what's available and what you can really afford.

That's how it was for me, and for my first car, a '50 Ford sedan I bought from dad. Stock for the most part, it served its purpose well and I pretty much learned about it inside and out.

Finding a '50 Ford coupe was always on my mind though. I liked the '50s, still do and wouldn't mind having another one. It would have to be a coupe though. The sedans are cool and I see a few nowadays that I like, but the coupes just have that intangible something.

The Australians call the '49 and '50 Fords, which is what our group owned, "Spinners" and it's such a great nickname I'm surprised it didn't get picked up and used over here. Even better is the Aussie nickname of "Twin Spinner" for the '51s. Shoebox works here in the US, and the '49-'51 Fords are the first ones I can remember being called shoeboxes, but you gotta admit, "Spinner" just rolls off the tongue quite well. A name, at least to me, on a parallel with the justifiably famous Deuce.

After running second, and way second a few times, we figured that a swap to an overhead valve, even with it remaining totally stock, would give you a car that didn't have to fear too many others.

I owned several of the '50 Fords, one sedan, mostly coupes and then there's my favorite one. This one was my first coupe, obtained right after the sedan and it had a very lightly built flathead in it. This was right after high school, where the main thing that counted was how fast your car was.

Some spent their money on appearance items, but most that I knew were looking for horsepower. For the most part we didn't care where it came from. Raw, brutal and just barely harnessed horsepower was what it was all about. In truth, for most of us, the horsepower was not too raw, nor brutal and it was easily harnessed. We had dreams though.

There were a few locals that had reached that goal. One, a guy from an adjacent town, ran a Wayne headed Jimmy in a '41 Chevy coupe. It was a tough one to beat. The similar and strongly built same era flathead Ford coupes had a tough time in keeping up with this car, let alone beating it. Our slightly heavier, later model coupes being way down on horsepower with our lightly built, not much money spent, is this thing timed right, flatheads, were easy pickins for the little Chevy coupe. After running second, and way second a few times, we figured that a swap to an overhead valve, even with it remaining totally stock, would give you a car that didn't have to fear too many others. It wasn't long before the killer Jimmy powered coupe succumbed to some of these even bigger engined coupes and sedans.

I went the overhead route as soon as I could and ended up with a fair running stock Olds engine with four speed Hydro in my coupe that did okay for a short while. I found a deal on a new #95 Engle cam, a big one, including lifters for cheap at the local speed shop. That got tossed in, in short order. It was cheap because the guy that originally ordered it left a big deposit and never went back to pick it up. The speed shop, wanting to get rid of it, made me more than a fair deal.

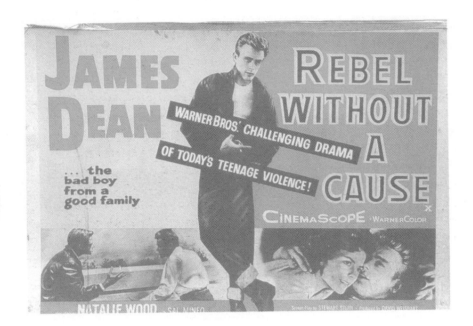

Tossing it in, that's pretty much what we did, not having a clue about degree wheels and the like. In fact, not too many of the era really knew about degree wheels, let alone how to use them. No money for minor things like correct length pushrods, adjustable rockers, and things like that, we just stuck the cam in straight up and set the solid lifter adjustment with adjustable pushrods that we bought from a friend. Sometimes the adjustable pushrods are all you can use, and many times are what a lot of the early Hemi guys have to use, but me, I hated 'em. It took three wrenches and a feeler gauge to adjust them, and I'm sure you can see right away you're about two hands short right off the bat. Since the adjustable pushrods were probably for a different engine they were slightly too long. Being a rather brilliant guy the fix was easy. I got a hand full of thin hardened washers at the parts house and stuck em under the rocker stands. I was busy adjusting away when dad came out and asked how that was going to work out.

"Okay", I assured him, just like I really knew what the heck I was talking about! He asked me if the rockers were oiled through the pushrods, I didn't really know, hated to admit it, so I just agreed that it did. Dad was a patient guy and I think a little pleased that I could do things my immediate peer group could not, simple stuff, like pulling a distributor and getting it back in, and in time, engine swaps and things like that. Easy for me and hard for my friends. I wasn't any smarter than they were, but I was not afraid to do it and I always learned something along the way. I think dad gave me way too much credit and probably would have been surprised at what I did not know. My biggest mechanical advantage was simply fearlessness, that and a stack of Hot Rod magazines, dog-eared and well studied, but apparently not studied close enough, enabled me to muddle through most things.

I'm sure that most of you see the big failing here. The rockers oiled through the rocker shaft and with the washers raising the rocker shaft up just enough to enable the use of the adjustable pushrods the rocker stand oil hole was now effectively open to the world. That created a couple of problems. No oil to the rocker shaft, ergo, no oil to the rockers, not to mention, with such a big internal oil leak, one on each bank, the engine oil pressure was way low. It must have pumped some though as it ran for several days like this. Just a minor problem compounded by my willingness to forgo the use of an oil pressure gauge. Since the six volt Ford sender didn't fit the 12 volt Olds pressure tap hole, I just plugged it off figuring I'd buy a new mechanical Stewart-Warner gauge on pay day.

Ignorance is bliss they say, and maybe it is. Too bad ignorance is not money, I'd sure have my share of it by now. After a couple of days the Olds started knocking a rod pretty good and was shut down – for quite a while as it turned out. I got married, Sweetie's grandparents gave us a clean low mileage '53 Ford four door, but still had the coupe and all the parts. 'Course the cam picked up a flat lobe. Who knew about cam lube, let alone a break in run just for the cam?

Somewhere in here I picked up a Model T roadster and had a good start toward an Olds short block with new pistons, etc. And I still had the coupe, although Sweetie's grandparents were getting a little tired of it in their garage. I came to the realization that building the T was going to take a lot more resources than I had at the time, being newly married and all that. So the T was sold and showed up on the streets a few months later with a good running junkyard Olds engine, Hydro, orange paint, white tuck and roll and looking a lot like the Sunset Strip Grabowski car. 'Course now it was owned by somebody else and he sold it a few months later for about five times what he'd paid for it as "nearly a runner". The biggest change was the orange paint and upholstery. The Olds short block got sold too and I still had the bad crank engine sitting in the coupe.

During a move with the T roadster at the end of a tow bar, along with a bunch of hot rod stuff packed inside the cockpit, we found the engineless T hit the bumps pretty hard. One good bump tossed the adjustable pushrods out on the street. I saw it, my friend saw it, I hated 'em, so I just left 'em lay there, 16 adjustable Engle pushrods. Didn't care then, and truthfully I don't care now. I still hate 'em.

It has been a long story so far and just to get to the most interesting part, at least the most interesting for me. Sweetie and I moved about 60 miles from home and where we grew up, to a new and better paying job. I was able to get the coupe built up there. I ended up with a '56 324 inch Olds engine, bored .125" over which is about 335 cubic inches. It had a '37 Cad-LaSalle floor box, aluminum flywheel, #153 Engle cam, another big one with lots of lift and I bought the entire kit which included 1.8:1 rockers in place of the usual 1.5:1 rockers. These were adjustable and they had self locking adjusting screws. God was truly good. A set of Isky aluminum retainers and some good springs rounded out the package as far as the cam went.

The coupe got a set of home-made fenderwell exit headers, duals with Thunderbird mufflers, the performance muff for the time, a medium sized Holley four barrel and DuCoil ignition which, as the name implies used two ignition coils. This was in effect, two separate four cylinder ignitions and required a different firing order from the stock Olds. Heads were mildly reworked by just cleaning up the casting marks and a touch of port matching and we were in business. Later on a 6 x 2 barrel intake was added, but for now the Holley was perfect.

The engine swap and related equipment were like most things of the era, at least as far as hot rods were concerned. The main thing is that you made most everything yourself; motor mounts, headers, clutch linkages, traction bars, bigger floorboards, the required re-wiring and sometimes we made our own shifters, although if you were lucky enough to get a factory floorbox they were not necessary. When Hurst came out with their great little shifter, we found the side shift boxes with the

Hurst shifted quite a bit quicker than we could. Progress! Seems it's always one step ahead of me.

The part I really liked about this little coupe was its sleeper theme when initially built. It sported the Ford factory pea-green paint and had stock sized 6.70/15 whitewalls along with the small stock hubcaps. Only one tailpipe was exposed, the other was tucked under the bumper out of sight. The traction bars were removed for street running. The Sun Super Tach was way under the dash and darned near out of sight. It sat stock height and was not lowered. Only two things really gave it away. When parked, most rodders knew to look under the fender wells for headers and collectors and that's where mine were. The other thing that gave it away was the Dragfast collectors. These were an oval collector about 2-1/2 inches thick, 10 inches wide and eight inches deep. It had four two inch pipes going in and one two inch pipe going out to the mufflers. The collector cap was an aluminum casting retained by three bolts.

The car was quiet due to the stock T-Bird mufflers, but, the sounds emanating from the collector cans at idle could not be disguised. With the big Engle cam and the big header primaries this little car had a sound like no other. It was the baddest sounding car I ever owned. It was the baddest sounding unblown car I ever heard. There was simply nothing like it. It scared everybody away. That little car probably would have made Don Garlits nervous. Not much though, and maybe just on the street.

Cops used to pull up next to it at stoplights and you'd get a double take worthy of the three Stooges. Even at San Fernando drag strip, with the caps pulled and if we were pitted right behind the grandstands, we'd fire it up to warm it up prior to the time trials and people in the top rows would turn and look. It had the sounds and great ones they were, only trouble was, it didn't have the power to live up to the noise. 13.90s at 100 mph were all we got out of it. Not really such bad times for a street driven car at that time, although with what we all know now about gears, tires and suspension, and with some later experience factored in, it looks to me like the little coupe could have run high 12s. We were sorely hurting in the traction department and had to give a lot away during the start. In drag racing, as you know, that's what it's all about. Slow starts do not make for winners. Simple as that.

Since the car was a sleeper though, that was one of the very best parts about it. Three races I remember running with it, and I'll keep 'em short: A high gear roll-on, on a virtually empty freeway, against a brand new Olds. The Olds, driven by a couple of cigar smoking old codgers. Once the race started, and a bit after the roll-on, we were pulling away pretty good once we hit 65, which was where the Olds engined Ford coupe got up on the cam really good in high gear. The Olds driver was a touch PO'd, and the lady passengers were cracking up about the old Ford running away from his new car. The two old codgers, with a scowl on their faces, were in sharp contrast with their feminine companions, who had a big smile on their faces. The ladies were digging on a street race with an old Ford, The two old codgers weren't too happy, but the ladies were, they smiled and waved nicely at us when we slowed down and the new Olds slid past.

A run from a dead stop at a stoplight way out on the other edge of town. After the stoplight you entered the freeway. It was pretty empty most times as it was this time around. The opponent was an early model yuppie driving a brand new 289 powered Mustang coupe. Like most of the Mustang owners of the era, this was probably the most powerful car he'd ever driven and I imagine he felt pretty invincible. That was until he got swamped by the old Ford. He didn't like it though, he ended up sailing down the freeway giving us the single digit salute. Imagine his surprise when little brother and I ran into him at the golf course a couple of hours later. We didn't say anything, he didn't say anything. Sometimes I guess, those single digit salutes can come full circle and bite you on the backside.

The very best race was against a '51 Chevy coupe we met up with on a freeway in the San Fernando Valley. Since things were quiet traffic-wise and the freeway virtually empty, we both slowed to about 35, I slid the big old Cad-LaSalle box into second and we both nailed it. It was even for a bit, I shifted, the Chevy kept right on winding, shifted and just pulled away. Further down the road we both got off the freeway and stopped in a parking lot. He popped the hood revealing a nicely done small block Chevy engine swap. I thought the engine was one of the popular 364 inch strokers that CT sold at the time, and they were way popular in the Valley with the Chevy runners. He wouldn't admit to it though, just smiled, and in fact wouldn't really say much about his engine. Cool part was, his car was set up in the sleeper mode too. Seems only fair to have been cut down by the same method we'd cut so many others down with. Live by the sword, die by the sword .....

I ran the little coupe in the sleeper mode for quite a while, but the old yearnings for a hot appearing hot rod soon took over. The tach got moved onto the dash, a pair of cheater slicks were installed and a pair of Torque-Thrust mags went up front. The front bumper was pulled. This was about the time the jacked up drag race car look came into being and the little coupe fit right in. We put the coupe on a bit of a diet and a few things got removed in a quest for light weight. We'd been drag racing it at the track so much, that we decided it was a race car now.

Somewhere in here I bought a most cherry '57 Buick Roadmaster from WB's dad. It was white, with nice medium blue upholstery. It wasn't long before a trailer hitch was installed. It made a plush combo for going to the races. The Buick made a great tow car, with the only problem being its tendency to overheat now and then on the long grades when towing the coupe. We won't mention the less than great, prone to fade, brakes. Bad enough on the Buick when it was unloaded, I never had to really get on them when towing. A lot to be said for planning ahead.

"...We stood up and started pointing at the plane. By now the crowd had noticed and so had the starter. The starter put the hold on the junior fueler and turned to watch the plane. The plane flared nicely and set down right on the strip at the North end going South..."

CHAPTER TEN
AIR ATTACK AT THE DRAG STRIP
ONE OF THE REALLY GREAT THINGS ABOUT SAN FERNANDO WAS THE OPPORTUNITY TO WATCH OTHER CLASSES RACE.

The grandstands were backed up to the pit area. If we were waiting for the class to be called or had finished for the day, we usually went to the grandstands and watched the races. They ran the classes out pretty quick due to the noise curfew. Depending on the number of cars present that day, eliminations would be over in 1-1/2 to two hours.

San Fernando drag strip was also parallel to what I believe was San Fernando airport. (Seems obvious, but airports are not always named after the town they are in). We were in the grandstands waiting for C/Gas to be called. I noticed an airplane turning onto final for an approach to landing and pointed it out to my friends. He rolled out and was directly in line and on short final for the drag strip. (The airport was about 200 yards to his left). There was a junior fueler coming up to the line to make a single run. We stood up and started pointing at the plane. By now the crowd had noticed and so had the starter. The starter put the hold on the junior fueler and turned to watch the plane. The plane flared nicely and set down right on the strip at the North end going South. The starter gave the "cut-motor" sign to the junior fueler, the fueler shut down and his crew and some others shoved him back out of the way.

The plane turned out to be a Beechcraft "Mentor", a low wing military trainer that was starting to show up in private hands. The plane came to a stop and spun around in front of the grandstands about 200 feet from the start line. The pilot looked pretty calm considering what happened. After spinning around he taxied north, short of the bridge under Foothill Boulevard and spun around facing south. We weren't sure what he was going to do. Figured he would pull out of the way and shut down. Not this guy. The crowd was still standing. The starter was watching the end of the strip. The junior fueler was still sitting there. The revs came up on the plane and he started down the strip. This plane is a little larger than most of the light planes of the time, his left wing hung off the strip and the right wing was not far from the hedges on the riverbed side. He kept on coming, rotated and got off in plenty of time to clear the crowd by a large margin. The crowd still on its feet was whistling, smiling and cheering. It was totally unexpected and a great show. (Now it's easy to be critical here, but next time you're up in a light plane, take notice of how the airports blend in to the surrounding area, whether city or country. The asphalt paving takes on a washed out grayish/brown color and is well disguised. It's an easy mistake to make, especially then, and especially for a stranger to the area. Today, pilots have small books they usually carry that describe the destination airport quite well).

One other aircraft incident that occurred at the San Fernando drag strip was a little more serious. We had completed our runs in time trials; eliminations were about 1/2 hour away. I drove the coupe out the north gate to make a run to the Foothill Boulevard gas station. After getting several gallons of gas we returned to the strip. Just before turning into the drag strip from Foothill, we saw a low wing aircraft on approach. It seemed a bit high. The pits were near the south end. We drove to the

"...We staged, the amber light lit, she wrapped up the motor in the Olds, I promptly left, 'red-lighting' in the process. I had fallen for one of the oldest tricks in the book. This girl, as I was to find out later was a really experienced drag racer. My pit crew was laughing so hard they could hardly talk and could just barely stand up..."

pits and parked. A crowd was gathered at the fence bordering the entrance road and were facing the airport. A low wing, private airplane, (probably the same one we saw a few minutes earlier) was facing away from us, 90 degrees to the airstrip. The left wing fuel tank was on fire and burning at a pretty good rate.

This really big guy came running down the airstrip, climbed up on the right wing and was looking in the plane. He didn't know the couple flying the plane had gotten out and away from the burning airplane. Airport personnel were hollering at the guy to leave and that the people were out. He took his sweet time and finally got away from the plane. A few minutes later something under the engine compartment caught on fire and the plane was really burning good now. The San Fernando Fire Department showed up and had the fire out in just a few minutes.

No one was hurt in this little escapade. It seemed the plane made a very high approach, landed too far down the airstrip, locked up the wheels and slid into a power pole with the left wing which ruptured the fuel tank. For those of us in the pits it was quite a show. For those in the grandstands, it was drag racing as usual. Racing never even slowed down.

CHAPTER ELEVEN
THE STARTER'S WIFE
MORE STORIES FROM THE SAN FERNANDO DRAG STRIP

Time trials at the San Fernando drag strip were a lot of fun. Usually you could get two to four runs in before eliminations started. (Time trials ran 12:00 noon to 1:30 pm – eliminations ran 1:30 pm to 3:00 pm due to the open header curfew). There were a couple of interesting guys that were the starters. One worked at CT Automotive. We always enjoyed talking to him when at CT; he had a raft of stories, had seen a lot of hot rod history and was pretty knowledgeable about engine building. The other guy we didn't know well, but admired his late model Olds that ran about the same numbers we ran in our C/Gas '50 Ford coupe.

The staging lane guy would put together some interesting match ups depending on how the cars were coming through the staging lanes. A/Gas vs. Altered roadster, C/Gas vs. Stock Car etc. Our first time trials 'match up' for the day was against the starter's Olds, driven by his wife. Being a somewhat mellow 'male chauvinist pig' I thought; "piece of cake – powder-puff racing". Being relaxed and confident (you see this one coming – right?) she put a hole-shot on me that left so much daylight that the sun still shines on that very spot. My unofficial ragtag pit crew razzed me unmercifully. (This was worse than second grade when the girls used to beat hell out of the boys with depressing regularity).

Our second time trials 'match up' was against the same car, same girl. (Who says fate doesn't have a sense of humor). Being a pretty calm guy, I'm not mad about this, just determined to beat her to the finish line. (The starting system was the infamous Leaver/Loser system with one amber light and then green). We staged, the amber light lit, she wrapped up the motor in the Olds, I promptly left, 'red-lighting' in the process. I had fallen for one of the oldest tricks in the book. This girl, as I was to find out later was a really experienced drag racer. My pit crew was laughing so hard they could hardly talk and could just barely stand up. I don't remember how we did in C/Gas, but I remember these two races quite well. I learned something that day.

"...I gave up my starter career after setting off an Olds powered '40 Ford coupe and a 409 Powered Chevy coupe. These cars had some serious horsepower compared to us. After I waved them off, both cars with tires spinning started drifting toward each other. I was a skinny kid, standing there in the middle thinking skinny thoughts with both arms at my sides watching tire smoke go by my feet..."

CHAPTER TWELVE
LEAVING MISS LILLY
NINETY-NINE PERCENT OF THIS TRUE.

Names and locations have been changed to protect the guilty. In order to set the scene you should know one of the great revelations that struck us in the late fifties.

A somewhat loose knit group of us were running '40, '48, '49 and '50 Fords. A few of the group ran Chevies but most of them were simply nice cars with twice pipes, tuck and roll and at times a pretty fair paint job. (Have to admit – the girls loved 'em). The Ford group tended to spend most of their discretionary income (and whatever else they could get their hands on) on performance mods. We had some really ferocious engines in these cars. (Well, we thought they were ferocious). Most of us had multi-carb setups and dual exhaust, some had aluminum heads, a couple had hot cams and Fenton headers.

Our official top dog though, was a '49 Ford sedan with a full-race 3/8 by 3/8 flathead with everything. I never heard a car that sounded that great before, and just recently heard a newly constructed four carb full-race flathead in a '29 roadster. It's a sound you'll never forget. The full-race term may be obvious to most of you. It was also a designation for the cam grind. Grinders usually had a series labeled: Semi-Race, 3/4-Race and Full Race. Isky cams were generally the cam of choice. Isky's famous 404 jr. cam was available at the time but was deemed too radical for our cars – and rightly so. (Iskenderian had one of the greatest speed equipment decals of all time in the 404 jr. design)

Everybody's saying, "SEE YOU IN OAKLAND at the

FIRST ANNUAL

National Roadster

SHOW" JAN. 19-2

THURSDAY THRU SUND

World's largest trophy is okayed by Barbara Britton, starring with Ronald Colman in "Champagne for Caesar"

America's finest hand-built cars for track—street—a lake—many shown for the first time under one roof.

Across the U.S. more than 100 sportsmen a prepping their roadsters for this spectacular e hibit-competition. It is the biggest event yet in t history of the hand-built sports car. Don't miss it

Besides big-time entertainment at the National Roadster Show, you'll find fun aplenty in the fabulous S Francisco Bay Area. Better make hotel reservations no

Wire or phone for ROADSTER ENTRY BLANKS

NATIONAL ROADSTER SHOW. 918 FALLON ST., OAKLAND 7,

Most of the Ford guys could out-run the majority of the other kids in town, except for a couple of '50 Olds coupes, with basically stock motors and a '40 Chevy coupe with Jimmy six. The Chevy coupe was owned by an older guy (at least 25) from the neighboring town. He was one of the locals that really knew what he was doing. He stuck with this engine for several years and just kind of disappeared off the streets. The Oldsmobiles had a four speed Hydro with a low gear ratio of about 3.45. These hydros combined with twin pipes and the favored 8.20 x 15s would just kill us off the line. The Olds suspension really planted the tires.

The great revelation came when a couple of sailors from the Navy base showed up with a channeled '29 "A" roadster with a '48 Merc engine that appeared and sounded stock. They took on just about everyone in town at one time or another and won just about every race. I don't believe that it weighed more than 1600 lb. Our cars probably weighed 3100 lb. The light dawns

Okay, now we jump ahead in time to about the mid-sixties. A guy named Bob ran a muffler shop/towing service in town. He had a nice wife that liked cars, was smart and had opinions of her own. There was also a guy named Lester that worked at the shop and he could gas-weld so good that he put other welders to shame. Lester's welds – well, we had simply never seen anything like it.

Bob and his wife were really nice people; they treated Lester like family. Lester looked on Bob and his wife like the brother and sister he never had. Lester was from the deep south, had a great southern accent and though small in stature, was every inch a gentleman from the old school. He always treated us well. Right after Lester went to work for them, he started addressing Bob's wife as Miss Lilly. We knew that wasn't her name, but we thought it was cool, (having nicknames and such) and we never called her anything but Miss Lilly after that.

It seemed to us that only the coolest guys had nicknames. For a woman to have a nickname was really cool. Bob was one heck of an engine builder as well as being a pretty good tuner. Miss Lilly was a good driver and an accomplished drag racer. She had a car of her own, built mainly by Bob and Lester with lots of direction from her. Her dad was a local machinist and an ex-motorcycle racer, (flat track & TT) and had also driven flathead powered midgets at the local oval with some degree of success. Miss Lilly's knowledge and expertise in the automotive field, we felt, was earned fair and square.

Miss Lilly paid attention to the weight/horsepower thing. (Remember our great revelation?) Most of our group had paid attention also and were running some of the same cars we had owned in the late fifties. By now most of them had OHV engines of one kind or another swapped in. Most of these engines were close to stock, but the cars still had good performance.

The kid with the 3/8 by 3/8 flathead? Well he was still with us and still outspent us in the car department and he still had his '49. By this time he had a strong running Buick Nailhead in it with a lot of speed equipment. The thing ran about 100 mph and high thirteens on admittedly poor (and hard) slicks. For our group, that was pretty good performance, although by now the '55 - '57 Chevies had been on the scene for a while and it was tough to beat the factory optioned cars, let alone the cars built by guys that really knew what they were doing. (You have to remember – this was before the really good chassis that had good handling and excellent traction were available)

Traction science at the time was either "Traction Masters" (like the lower part of a four bar – one bar on each side under the rear leaf spring, many times home-made using old shock absorber rings and bushings for the ends or the clamped leaf springs a-la the Chrysler Super Stockers).

Miss Lilly raced a lot of these guys at the strip and otherwise in her coupe (a fat fendered one) with small block Chevy. She won a lot of these races. The car would consistently run in the high 12s through the mufflers. This was really good performance at the time. Now we had seen under the hood of this car many times, and truth to tell, there wasn't much to see. One four barrel Holley, painted valve covers and headers. Bob and Miss Lilly didn't spend much money on appearance items although the little coupe was clean, straight, had nice paint, nice upholstery and was soundly engineered. It ran painted steel wheels and small hubcaps. It was a bit of a sleeper, if you disregarded the killer cam rattle in the collectors, and the nose-down attitude.

We sorta suspected they were running a stroker crank, probably one of the 364 inch kits that were popular in the small block for quite a while. Sounded like it may have had a roller in it also but we never did see the engine torn down. Bob, Miss Lilly and Lester wouldn't say much about the engine.

After a while most of the locals wouldn't race them. One of their ploys was having Bob drive the coupe into a local hangout in one of the nearby towns where fast cars were known to hang out. During the hemming and hawing and otherwise setting up a street race, Bob would offer to sweeten the pot by letting his girlfriend (as he called her at times like that) drive. If the locals weren't ready before, they were ready now. Racing a girl had to be like taking candy from a baby. Invariably when backing out, she would act like she wasn't familiar with driving the car, had difficulty shifting, turning the steering wheel and similar things. The locals would just smile and think what a fool was Bob.

Miss Lilly was really one heck of a driver and could outdrive most of the guys in town. (Of course, to a man, we each thought that we "our ownself" could outdrive her and secretly pitied the others. The truth was she could probably outdrive any of us!

Many times during the bargaining, finagling, looking for an edge and all that, some of the faster car owners would hang back and let one of their slower guys set up a race with Bob and Miss Lilly. A close race here or an outright loss would set the stage for another race with even more money wagered. (We didn't always know the exact figures, but $50-$100.00. bets were common with the more serious street racers – that was serious money at the time.)

With all the details settled, and after waiting a bit to let some of the crowd at the drive-in, gas station or wherever dissipate, the two cars would slide out one at a time, with maybe one or two cars at the most following at a distance. These cars contained the lucky few that would hold the bets, start and judge the race and just plain get to watch. We felt lucky if chosen to go along.

In reality we were all pretty stupid. We lived within 75 miles of three different drag strips. God smiles on fools sometimes. (Good thing for us.) In our area, we were fortunate to have a smooth, fairly wide piece of road about 3/4 mile long leading to the golf course. Usually we drove to the end of this road and raced in the out direction. Otherwise, if a sudden departure was required we would have to drive over several miles of dirt/soft sand river bed roads to get out. Most times we made it, occasionally we got stuck.

These things usually took place late at night. Some of the crazies would open their cut-outs, lakes pipes or collectors – whatever they had. Most of us didn't, for the simple reason, that once we left, in our nice quiet cars, we looked sorta innocent. (Of course we fit right in with the motoring public with our primered cars, lowered front ends, nosed and decked etc. The truth was, we stood out like a sore thumb.)

The spectator cars would park out of sight, usually one at each end. The race cars would line up with headlights off. At a signal, lights were on, revs went up and the starter waved them off. It was downright spectacular to see and hear two high-winding cars accelerating down the dark blacktop, tail lights receding (and rapidly) in the distance. The sounds carried for miles. It was a sight to behold.

For a while I volunteered to be the starter. This wasn't too bad, just stand between the cars, point to each driver, they would nod, the arm would come down setting off the race. This had worked for us most of the time, but I gave up my starter career after setting off an Olds powered '40 Ford coupe and a 409 Powered Chevy coupe. These cars had some serious horsepower compared to us. After I waved them off, both cars with tires spinning started drifting toward each other. I was a skinny kid, standing there in the middle thinking skinny thoughts with both arms at my sides watching tire smoke go by my feet. It may not have been as close as I thought, but the realization came, that standing between two strong running cars was not a really great idea. The few times I played starter after that, I stood to one side, with an escape route thought out. No one in our area ever got hurt starting street races. Pure, dumb luck.

A street race was set up between Miss Lilly and a strong running, 409 powered Bel Air. We followed the two race cars out to a long country road between a neighboring town and our town. This was in a citrus growing area and there was a lemon orchard on one side and a plowed field on the other. There were six of us in a '51 Plymouth and two each in the race cars. The plan was – the passengers in the race cars and the Plymouth would get out at the power station road, which was actually a gated, locked driveway. One guy would go with the race cars to flag 'em off. The race cars would go down about 1/4 mile, turn around, turn the headlights off and when ready would turn the headlights on. The designated starter would flag them off and the race would be off.

Our vantage point was excellent since we were right at the finish line. We would park the chase car (the Plymouth) back in the orchard and walk about 200 feet to a berm that overlooked the road and watch the race. Sometimes, since we were near the coast, the road surface would get a little slippery late at night due to the fog beginning to form. This was such a night.

The cars were flagged off and they both left hard. Miss Lilly's coupe got a little hung out in second gear and never did come back. It slid off the road into the plowed field. Quite a ways into the field as it turned out. There was so much dust, we couldn't tell what happened. The opposing driver saw what happened, kept right on going and passed us well in excess of 100 mph. We could see him way down the road with his brake lights on for the corner. He made the corner okay and the last we saw of him was a couple of rapidly disappearing tail lights.

The Plymouth driver who was by himself didn't ask anyone anything, pulled out of the orchard hiding spot and was headed to pick up his friend who was the starter in this little escapade. After a time the dust cleared up a bit and we could see the little coupe was upright. Miss Lilly was still inside, unhurt and didn't get out until the dust settled. (She was a pretty calm individual, why jump out and get all dirty?) About a 1/8 mile from start line was a "T" intersection. The Plymouth driver's plan was to get his friend and rather than do the back and forth turn around, simply go to the intersection and pull a 180 there. When he got there, he met a cop car, red lights and all slowing down for the stop. The cops gave him the eye. I'm sure they knew he was involved, but rather than stop him, they continued around the corner to where Miss Lilly and the coupe were. The Plymouth guys, no dummies here, innocently made the turn and drove out of the area. (The owner, a bit of a worry wart, walked and bummed rides for about a week before he would venture out in his Plymouth.)

Well – we weren't dumb either, spectators would get ticketed for participating in an illegal speed contest or whatever it was called. The remaining six of us laid low in the orchard. Miss Lilly walked out to the road and talked to the cops for a bit and then got in their car and headed for the neighboring town. (Not ours.) We figured, great, she got arrested. A reasonable thought for us, as we were hiding in the orchard with seriously guilty consciences.

The coupe had slid about 100 yards through the dirt and was high centered on a plowed berm. We had definite desires to get out of the area before any more cops came. We crossed the road (looking guilty as sin we felt) and ran into the orchard bordering the plowed field and started walking. We were 10 miles from our town and about five from the other. It was about a half mile walk to the main highway between towns and a mile to the 76 station on the corner. We scared up a dime and called my sister at the skating rink where she spent her time. She was about through for the evening, as it was near midnight. After a bit she showed up in her '47 Chevy coupe, we crammed six of us in, three in front and four in back and left for town. The poor little Chevy was sagging on the springs considerably.

She dropped us off where our cars were parked and went home. CK (my friend) and I gave Bob a ride back to his shop. When we got there, Lester had the coupe there and was unhooking it from the tow truck. We were surprised as all get out.

The Bel Air driver, although not from our town, knew where Bob's shop was. He got the phone number off the shop door and called Lester. It was Lester's week as tow truck driver and he had the tow truck at his house. He went out to the field and got Miss Lilly's coupe out. A tow truck from the neighboring town was headed up the hill to the "T" intersection as Lester and the coupe came down the hill. Lester got some glares from these guys as he was a bit out of his towing area and getting their business. Lester figured they should have got there sooner. I guess, where tow trucks are concerned – win some, lose some.

Lester gave Bob a ride home where he found Miss Lilly waiting for him. It turns out, she was quite an actress, as well as an excellent driver. She had convinced the cops that her husband's powerful little coupe had just gotten away from her and she didn't know how to handle all that horsepower. The cops, in their manly way, nodded and smiled and agreed that sometimes a high horsepower car could be a lot to handle. Miss Lilly had charmed the socks off these guys to such an extent, that they delivered her to her door step, and watched until she was safely in the house.

We didn't see the coupe for a long while after that, several years in fact. Bob and Miss Lilly gave up street racing and got pretty busy with the shop. They now have five employees and are widely regarded throughout the city as a good honest place to go. A high recommendation indeed. They still drag race, although legally at the strip. The coupe is still with them and has a built 350 and is pretty much in street trim. (And has been seen to run high 11s, through the mufflers, but with pretty good slicks.) They go to rod runs now and then with it, and pretty much just enjoy cruising in it.

Which brings me to the reason that I remembered all this. Our great revelation of "light cars went fast". It's still a lesson that each generation seems to learn the hard way. It seems some kids saw the coupe at the shop and started the; "My friend's car can beat that" mantra. Turns out their friend had a Charger with a good running 426 wedge. This car probably weighed 4200 lb. Miss Lilly's car weighed 2900 - 3000 lb. Bob, always patient, simply invited them to meet at the drag strip, weekend next, and to bring a $100.00 bill. This was more than okay with them. They had a serious case of what we used to call "GTO Syndrome". GTO Syndrome being: Kid got a new GTO. The GTOs ran low 15s high 14s right from the dealer. After stepping out of an 18 - 19 second car, the GTO felt pretty fast. (And it was.) These guys felt pretty unbeatable, until they ran up against some of the strong running hot rods in the area.

There were some close races with the GTOs losing a lot of them, especially after the owners had tinkered with them a bit, knocking them a little bit out of tune. They were easy pickin's then. (In fact, one guy that had one that ran, 100-101 mph, invested a lot of money in official hop up equipment. After a lot of time and expenditure he could just barely make 100 mph)

Anyway, the porky-weight Challenger raced the light-weight coupe and lost. Last we saw of them, they were talking about building up the motor even more. 'Course the car still weighed the 4200 lb, but that didn't bother them. I don't think these guys ever read Hot Rod mag. I believe Hot Rod has run two articles in the last few years where they took a heavyweight car, removed weight in stages to show the performance improvement with no engine changes. Didn't do us more mature guys any favors there. Most of the kids that can see beyond the bright paint and chrome are enthralled by the horsepower and not too interested in light weight. I wonder if they ever think about why roadsters, lightweight coupes and rails do well at the drag strip?

Lester is still at the shop. I think he's a part owner now. He always has a smile for us. Last time we saw him, he was doing the mentor bit to a new generation of drag racers/welders.

Life goes on ....

"...The simple truth was: The Hydramatics were very dependable. If your Hydro happened to break you got a lot of knowing smiles and looks. Funny part was, if the stick shift broke, or the clutch went south nobody thought too much about it..."

CHAPTER THIRTEEN
NOSTALGIA ENGINE SWAP
SWAPPING EARLY OLDS V8s INTO THE '50 FORD

Here's the details on a couple of early Olds (303, 324, 371 and 394 series) V-8 swaps into the '50 Ford. Major required items were: a starter changeover lower bellhousing, (made by Offenhauser) an Olds engine to Ford trans adapter, (also made by Offenhauser) or an Olds stick shift bellhousing, appropriate throwout arms and bearings, a stick shift flywheel, clutch pressure plate and disc, bronze pilot bushing, a dropped tie rod, oil filter bypass plate, remote oil filter, '48 Cadillac starter and one used shock absorber.

Also required is a lower bellhousing, cast aluminum, that moves the starter from the stock Olds location on the left where it interferes with the Ford steering box to the right where it's pretty much in the clear. A lot of guys simply cut into the frame weakening it a bit, but the accepted and safe way to do this swap was with the adapter. The Olds oil filter hanging from the lower right of the engine was required to be removed due to interference with the newly moved starter. Frame cuts, properly welded and reinforced, are plenty safe. Many of the ones I saw were simply cut. Have to admit I never saw any broken ones though. I'm guessing they went straight to the junkyard.

The trans adapter or Olds stick shift bellhousing, flywheel, proper clutch, pilot bushing, throwout bearing and arm are fairly obvious requirements. Most Oldsmobiles came with Hydramatics, but there were a lot of stick shifts factory installed in these cars due to many people still mistrusting automatics. The simple truth was: The Hydramatics were very dependable. If your Hydro happened to break you got a lot of knowing smiles and looks. Funny part was, if the stick shift broke, or the clutch went south nobody thought too much about it. Finding the requisite stick shift parts was not too difficult. Generally if we saw a stick shift Olds in the junkyard, we put out the word and it was soon gone. Guys were pretty good about sharing information, selling or giving away excess parts and didn't tend to hoard things.

The dropped tie rod was required due to tie rod to pan interference. The Olds engine was a rear sump engine as was the flathead Ford but the Olds pan hung down considerably lower. A dropped tie rod was obtained from Bell Auto Parts in L.A., one of the nations premier speed shops. Cost was about $35.00, a serious chunk out of a hot rodders wages.

The Saturday morning trip to some of L.A.'s and the San Fernando Valley speed shops was one of the highlights for many of us. Usually word would go around that someone was going to L.A. to buy a big time part and usually it caught most of us with our finances down. With the tie rod (in this case) being the main reason for the trip (and gas was .21¢ per gallon for regular) Bell was the first shop hit. Bell was a great place to go, they always had display engines set up on stands to show the latest and the greatest. They also manufactured many different hot rod parts, including the famous "Bell" helmet. When I took up racing dirt bikes, Bell was the place where we got our helmets. I never bought any other brand and I bought several over the years.

During the rounds of remaining speed shops in the area we always found some good used bargains. Many small dress up items and hardware pieces for the latest project were purchased on these trips. A lot of the time some of the passengers could barely pay for lunch. No problem for us, we knew we'd be in that boat next trip.

The oil filter bypass plate was made by Offenhauser and was usually purchased at the same time as the starter changeover lower bell housing. A remote oil filter was required due to potential interference with the newly located starter. These were purchased at the local auto parts house and were a universal oil filter with a replaceable filter element. Price was pretty low, Fram and Purolator made very nice ones, complete with pre-formed hoses. Changing oil could be a messy job with one of these if you didn't think it through. Same thing with the '49-'53 flatheads and their head mounted oil filter. Smart guys invested in a suction gun. We just used a lot of rags.

The '48 Caddy starter was required because the stock Olds starter, moved over to the right side, now had the solenoid on the bottom. This interfered with the tie rod. The Caddy starter when mounted on the starter changeover lower bell housing was mounted in the correct, solenoid on top position. The Caddy starter was a six volt one and worked just fine on 12 volts. I never heard of one failing. Spun the engine over pretty fair too.

Swap #1 used a '37 LaSalle trans, the Olds stick shift goodies and a rebuilt Police/Taxi 11 inch clutch. A Schiefer aluminum flywheel was also used. This swap worked well for me and I never saw another done that was similar to this one.

Front motor mount was simply the Olds center front mount utilizing the stock bracket mounted by four 3/8 inch bolts on the lower part of the timing cover and was the factory arrangement. The stock insulator was mounted on two holes drilled in the front crossmember and used about a 1/2 inch plate to shim the engine to the proper position. (We were pretty good about using factory engineering when we could.) This made life pretty easy as the only changes required were slightly longer bolts.

Grade 5 bolts were used because they were recommended by one of the older (at least 20 years old) hot rodders that worked in the parts house. (We didn't know about grade eights) Most of us looked up to him and paid attention to what he had to say. He had a beautiful Titian Red (it was a popular color for quite a while) '50 Olds coupe with pipes, white tuck and roll, '37 LaSalle chrome plated stick shift, frenched headlights and was nosed and decked. Not to mention it was quite low in front, ran the proper sized big and little whitewall tires and had the '56 Olds spinner hubcaps. It was somewhat rare as it was a finished car. His friend that worked across the street at the Chevy garage had a similar '50 Olds fastback painted metallic green. Two very nice cars. Both of these guys were very knowledgeable and good about sharing information with us.

The stock Oldsmobile rear engine mounts were mounted to machined surfaces on the bell housing with one on each side giving the required mount triangulation. Some guys, with access to welding equipment would simply adapt the Olds rear engine crossmember to the Ford frame and most of these were very nicely done. The better ones were even painted.

We had to keep welding to a minimum as most of us did not have a welder of any kind. A lot of our stuff got cut out and clamped together and it was a trip to the local muffler shop for the welding, especially the things that needed arc welding. Arc welding was a bit of a "black art" to us as most guys simply did not have access to one. Gas welders were obtainable, sometimes a friend or his dad owned one, sometimes we rented one. If that happened, we usually had a whole bunch of projects ready to go so we would get our moneys worth.

Most of us had learned welding in metal shop, but one of our group was very skilled and had actually taken night courses at the local JC (Junior College). He was our designated welder and didn't mind the work. He figured any experience he could get now would stand him well later.

In this swap the Ford transmission mount was removed and a 1/4 inch plate bolted to the crossmember as the stock Ford mount had been. This 1/4 inch plate was made long enough to go under the LaSalle trans mount and the LaSalle mount simply bolted to it. Some guys welded these in, we found that a properly made plate, suitably reinforced worked well and later changes were easy. The trans and rear end were well lined up as dad had taught us about the tailshaft, pinion shaft alignment requirements, as he had been involved in many engine swaps in oil company trucks and just knew one heck of a lot of stuff.

Okay – I know you're thinking; "Here's the engine center mounted and the trans center mounted". Either: "How will the torque be controlled?" Or: "I want to be around when this thing is started up". And I know you're wondering what the used shock absorber is for.

The shock absorber rings were cut off the ends with a hacksaw which is the safest and best way. A lot of guys simply cut them off with a torch, and invariably the heated shock oil would ignite and act like a miniature flame thrower when the main body was pierced, as it always was. The torch tended to eat up a lot of the ring too, leaving a minimal amount for making into Traction Masters and similar. I saw one shock absorber cut that started the workbench on fire and for a while I wasn't sure we'd get it out.

With the two shock rings in hand we got about a 3/4 inch diameter bolt and two nuts. A piece of one inch OD round tubing was obtained, the ID a good slip fit for the 3/4 inch bolt. A piece of 1/4 inch plate about 2 x 3 inches was cut out and had four 3/8 inch holes drilled in the corners. The last was a shock mount stud that came with the shock absorber. (Whenever we got a junkyard goodie we found we should take whatever was attached to it. The yard operators didn't mind as long as you didn't get too crazy.)

The 2 x 3 inch plate was drilled to size for the shock stud, the stud had most of the bottom threads removed and was gas welded inside and out to the plate. The plate was held up against the flat, vertical front left of the front crossmember and the crossmember was drilled to fit. Appropriate bolts, nuts and washers held the plate to the crossmember. (Access was from the large factory cut out holes in the bottom of the crossmember.) A piece of 3/16 inch by two inch angle was cut perhaps 10 inches long and was mounted to the head using the 7/16 inch threaded bolt holes in the left head and extended out to the left about three to four inches. This was drilled for a one inch bolt with aircraft style lock nut. (Don't know where this fine threaded nut came from, didn't care, just used it.) (Probably from the five gallon bucket that dad brought home one day. It was full of virtually new bolts, nuts, washers and many brass fittings that was left over from some major oil field plant project and had been tossed in the trash. I hardly ever failed to find what I needed in this and have a similar bucket today and is the last resort when bolts or nuts etc. are required.)

The torque arm was constructed from the one inch tubing that was welded to one shock ring on the bottom and a standard fine thread 3/4 inch nut, well aligned, was welded to the top of the tubing. The other shock ring was welded to the six inch long 3/4 inch bolt head. Installing a nut on the threaded portion of the bolt, spinning it on a ways allowed the threaded upper part to screw into the lower tube section. The torque arm was painted, new rubber bushings installed and mounted to the lower plate. Once the engine was levelled, the upper arm was adjusted to length and the top one inch mounting bolt was installed. The lock nut was tightened and it was complete. This whole setup was gas welded.

We did try to burn the plating off the bolts, but there were probably many impurities in the weld. I always worried about the torque arm a bit, but even drag racing (with admittedly poor slicks) never caused it to break. It looked a lot racier than the bolt-on chains that came along later. Racy was good. To our minds we were damn near on the road. Little did we know that the additional details such as exhaust, clutch and throttle linkages, partial re-wiring and similar would take just about as long as the basic swap, probably longer. Headers, exhaust system and traction devices were built as described in previous chapters.

One of the stumbling blocks for this swap was the clutch throw-out arm angle. The Olds was almost perfectly horizontal. (As viewed from the back.) The Ford was at about a 30 degree down angle. Simply hooking a clutch pull rod from the Ford pedal to the Olds arm created a bad pull angle for the throw-out arm. A length of 3/8 inch cold rolled steel was utilized to make both a pull rod and a push rod for clutch actuation. A 6 x 1 x 1/4 inch tab with several adjustment holes drilled in, was gas welded to a one inch rod about three inches long. (Call this the transfer tab – or in yuppie language the non-transversely mounted, vertically oriented, mechanically actuated, directional change unit. Do these guys get paid by the word or what?) A 1/4 inch plate was Arc welded to the frame underneath the column and behind the steering box. The transfer tab one inch rod was slid into the two pillow block bearings with the 6 x I inch tab sticking down. The two pillow block bearings were mounted on the bottom of the 1/4 inch plate, which had been drilled to accept the bearings prior to welding. The clutch pedal was altered to accept the 3/8 inch rod.

One 3/8 inch rod, the pull rod, was made with a 90 degree bend at each end and drilled for cotter pins. This was mounted to the altered clutch pedal and the transfer tab, second hole from the end. It was retained by cotter pins and had the appropriate washers. The other 3/8 inch rod, the push rod, was made with a 90 degree bend on one end and the other threaded to accept the Olds hemispherically shaped clutch throw-out arm nut and lock nut. This end went in the Olds throw-out arm. The result was to give a straight push to the Olds throw-out arm and the proper angle of pull from the Ford clutch pedal.

One of my worries was the lack of a clutch equalizer bar, but this linkage worked out really great, and the lack of the equalizer was not a problem or noticed by other drivers. Dad thought it was a cool solution to a problem. Best of all, it never gave us any trouble.

Throttle pedals were usually the '57 and up Ford. This was a nicely made unit that worked great and fit well in the '50 Ford. All that was required was a pair of mounting holes – about 1/4 inch and about a one inch hole to allow access for the throttle arm.

The bottom of the gas pedal hung from the inner firewall. The top fed through the one inch hole and remained within the engine compartment. The two 1/4 inch bolts held the whole thing on and you were in business. Precautions required were to drill the one inch hole with a holesaw in the proper location in the short vertically curved area of the firewall. The throttle had a bit of a bend to it and if care was not taken it didn't fit well. Done right, it looked factory, and the original '57 seal worked fine.

Throttle rods were usually salvaged junkyard items about 3/16 inch diameter cut to fit. Later on we learned about heim joints and how to thread cad-plated rod for a really classy throttle rod.

The radiator was simple. The lower right outlet and upper left inlet were removed and flat plates soldered in place at the radiator shop. Radiator shops at the time practiced what we thought were dark arts. I've since learned we could have done the same thing with a piece of brass, the proper solder and a propane torch. Live and learn.

Moving the generator turned out to be necessary, but a simple fix was discovered. On one of our many trips to the junkyard we noticed that Nailhead Buicks had the generator mounted on a simple bracket and it was retained by two special head bolts. These bolts were the same size and length as the Olds but had 7/16 inch fine threads on the top end. Two of the Olds head bolts in the proper location were removed and the Buick head bolts stuck in. A bit of drilling in the Buick bracket mounted the Olds generator in the right place and the Olds adjusting arm fit fine.

A small bit of cleverness for the two 3/8 inch rocker cover hold-down bolts was to get two of the "coin headed or butterfly headed" bolts from the tappet covers on Plymouth flathead sixes. These made rocker cover removal a simple "no tools required" operation. I was glad I had them when, at the races, and by myself, I had to run the valves while in line for C/Gas. I usually made a point to run them prior to the days racing and usually accomplished it a few nights before the Sunday drags. In this case I forgot and was afraid to run as I had found at the previous race a stock valve spring retainer that was allowing the valve lock to slowly sink in. I bought a set of Isky aluminums and good valve locks and that problem went away. I had installed them and run the engine but had not made final adjustments.

Driveshaft conversion was easy. The stock Ford driveshaft and rear u-joint were used. The open driveline La Salle trans yoke was used and the GM/Ford conversion u-joint was used to make the connection. The driveshaft work was done at a local machine shop. That pretty much describes the first swap.

The second swap was simply a conversion to street use with another '50 coupe including the addition of a T-85 OD trans. A set of Hurst motor mounts was purchased along with a set of '48 Ford rubber biscuits and these were installed. These were really well made. An Offenhauser Olds to Ford adapter was purchased and installed which allowed the use of the stock Ford clutch linkage, including the equalizer bar. (An equalizer bar adapter plate was made and installed on the T-85 with the pivot matching the '50 clutch pedal pivot.) The "Interceptor" trans (as the T-85 was known) mount was installed very similar to the 1/4 inch plate method described in the first swap.

A bit of wiring and a couple of relays made the OD operational, and with the 4.27 rear gears made the new coupe a really flexible car. A Hurst floor shift finished off the trans installation nicely, although I did miss the tall chrome plated LaSalle stick.

Stock Oldsmobile exhaust manifolds were installed and new exhaust pipes were built. The outlets on each side were perfectly placed for the Ford chassis. This went quite a ways toward quieting down the car.

The original coupe was mined of all the necessary items to complete the swap and was sold down the street where it eventually ended up with a Caddy engine. I saw it in a shed several years later, but have no idea as to its fate. It had been a fun car with a couple of different mildly built flatheads, a stock Olds and a built up Olds installed. At the end it was pretty much the racer, metallic green, no front bumper or grille. With the amber plexiglass windows installed it was an eye catching little car at the drag strip. (NHRA did not require clear ones for several years – a good ruling, and one I agree with.) Before the clear window ruling, some of the color combinations between paint and window colors were great. The dark tint was most popular, a lot of reds and pinks were done as well as yellows and ambers. Dark blue was also popular. You could get virtually any color of the rainbow at the plastics supply houses.

A gasser style, pipe rear bumper similar to the, one I have on my present day roadster was installed. Although I feel the roadster rear bumper is a little slicker. It's powder coated black with black brackets and has machined aluminum end caps installed. The second coupe was a lot of fun on the street for a couple of years. The crank finally succumbed to the ravages of high rpm and no bearing inspections after several years hard use. I stored it for about six years and being busy with family and other interests finally sold it to a bodyman from Barris. I saw it a few times in the San Fernando Valley, now running a small block Chevy, a very race interior and still the original paint job. You'll note that we went to great lengths to avoid Arc welding if we could.

Arc welding at that time was to us, as TIG welding is now, a bit of a black art, not to mention dragging the car to the shop and dragging it home. The welding companies did us all a great favor when the buzz box came out and sold for an affordable price. I guess the very best thing I learned from all this was that dad really was right. A guy can do anything if he has the proper tools.

"...Engineers were generally pretty p.o.'d and did a lot of waving and hollering. We couldn't hear a thing and just hung on. No one ever got hurt, but the engineers were probably more scared than us. We were just a group of dumb, but adventuresome kids..."

CHAPTER FOURTEEN
ONE DAY AT SANTA MARIA

AFTER GETTING THE '50 FORD COUPE RUNNING WITH THE BUILT-UP OLDS ENGINE WE TOOK IT TO SAN FERNANDO DRAG STRIP A FEW TIMES, DID OKAY AND WON A FEW TROPHIES.

That was mainly due to being regulars at the strip, and getting to race against cars that fell into the class thanks to engine swaps and multi-carbs, but basically running stock engines. Most of these cars were 1-2 seconds slower than our car and our car was about 1-2 seconds slower than the national record.

There were several 55-56 Chevies from the local engine building shops that would show up and when they did it was all over for us. These cars generally ran right on or exceeded the records. About the only way you could beat them was if they red-lighted and that wasn't often as the drivers in these cars were pretty good.

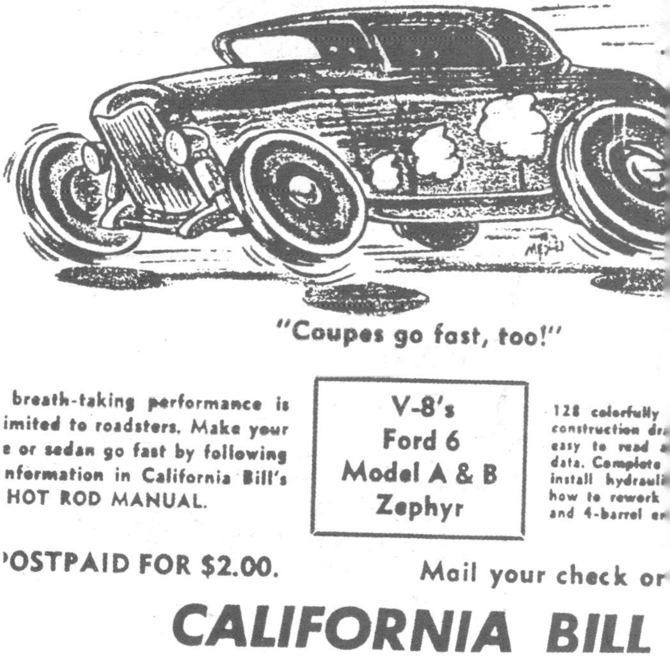

Now that we were drag racing regulars we decided it was time to branch out. We had been going to San Fernando quite a bit and had a couple of trips to Long Beach under our belt. Heck, I even ran the slightly built flathead engine at Santa Ana once.

Santa Maria struck us as a good place to go. We'd gone there several times while in high school and after as spectators. By this time the coupe had the front bumper pulled, the rear seat out and the exhaust system pulled in an effort to save weight. That was pretty close to what we could do in the weight savings department without completely stripping the car out. The option to return to street use later was always in the back of our minds.

"Coupes go fast, too!"

breath-taking performance is imited to roadsters. Make your e or sedan go fast by following nformation in California Bill's HOT ROD MANUAL.

V-8's
Ford 6
Model A & B
Zephyr

128 colorfully construction dr easy to read a data. Complete install hydrauli how to rework and 4-barrel en

'OSTPAID FOR $2.00.

Mail your check or

CALIFORNIA BILL

Lots of the Chevies were running fiberglass front clips, doors and trunk lids, not to mention the plexi windows that were getting popular. We eventually stuck in a set of these in the side windows. They looked most cool as they were amber in color and the car was a metallic green. NHRA at the time did not require clear windows and a lot of different colors showed up. Most popular were the dark tints, somewhat like the window tints of today. Other popular colors were blue and occasionally red. To our knowledge, no one made a glass front end for the 50 Fords, Anderson had fenders we later found out, but at the time did not do a hood.

With the coupe being pretty much a "drag racing only" car we built a tow bar (which I still have) and pressed the 57 Buick Roadmaster into service as the tow car. It worked out well, only real caution was to watch it on the down grades as the Buick brakes were prone to fade and adding the weight of another car to stop wasn't the most brilliant thing we did. Some of the steeper and longer grades called for someone to ride in the coupe and help out in the braking.

Santa Maria was an interesting strip. We heard that it was built as a training airport for the military during WW2. Maybe so. It seemed to me to be more of a typical crop duster strip. These were fairly common around California at the time and still are, in the farming areas. The strip ran a bit uphill and then ran downhill. (Times compared favorably with other drag strips.) With the military having Carte Blanche on just about anything they wanted during the war, there were other more desirable areas for airstrips. The military built a lot of defense related things along the coast during the initial stages of the war. After the Japanese submarine lobbed a few shells at oil storage tanks on the coast at Gaviota, just above Santa Barbara, small coastal gun emplacements were installed up and down the coast. There was one in the coastal town I grew up in and it was always fun to ride our bicycles down to the beach and check it out. First time I went, well after the end of the war, I was disappointed to find the artillery piece removed, but the remaining equipment was in place.

Just getting to the beach was a whole other trip. Getting there on that end of town called for crossing a railroad bridge perhaps a 1/4 mile long. There was a board walkway next to the tracks and we could ride on that. Of course there was a curve on the North side of the bridge and we could never see the trains coming and got caught out there several times. The drill was simple, stop, lean the bike up against the rail, climb over the rail and stand on the large timber cross-piece, drag the bike handlebar as far over the railing as possible and hang on while the train went by. Engineers were generally pretty p.o.'d and did a lot of waving and hollering. We couldn't hear a thing and just hung on. No one ever got hurt, but the engineers were probably more scared than us. We were just a group of dumb, but adventuresome kids. I even got caught on this bridge while crossing it on the BSA, but that's a whole other story.

Perhaps a little digression from the drag racing end of the story doesn't hurt. California, during and after the war years was a fascinating place to grow up. It had a lot of history no matter where you went. I was a little guy and had just started school when the war ended. One of the results of the tremendous war effort was the proliferation of war surplus stores that sprang up after the war in every California community. For us, it was about a six mile bike ride to the surplus store. Granted, not too far with the bikes we have today, but pushing a heavy-weight Schwinn or medium-weight Huffy, with only one gear and against the typical coastal winds was quite a job.

We could go in these stores with $2.00-$3.00, a lot of money at the time and come out of there festooned with back packs, canteens, first aid kits, webbed pistol belts, ponchos, helmet liners and best of all a machete. We must have been quite a sight with all the military equipment draped all over us and the bikes. We felt it was necessary for our weekly hikes into the hills. Being fully armed with single shot 22s didn't hurt either and many a day was spent traipsing around the coastal mountains, killing every tin can we saw.

As mentioned, Santa Maria was an interesting strip. It was laid out, oriented I believe running roughly west. Paralleling the strip on the South side was a line of Eucalyptus trees, a very tall native of Australia, that were planted as windbreaks in many areas of California. A small country road was on the other side. The pits were located to the south of this road near the east end.

I ran the little coupe in the sleeper mode for quite a while, but the old yearnings for a hot appearing hot rod soon took over. The tach got moved onto the dash, a pair of cheater slicks were installed and a pair of Torque-Thrust mags went up front. The front bumper was pulled. This was about the time the jacked up drag race car look came into being and the little coupe fit right in.

We put the coupe on a bit of a diet and a few things got removed in a quest for light weight. We'd been drag racing it at the track so much, that we decided it was a race car now.

Somewhere in here I bought a most cherry 57 Buick Roadmaster from WB's dad.
It was white, with nice medium blue upholstery. It wasn't long before a trailer hitch was installed. It made a plush combo for going to the races. The Buick made a great tow car, with the only problem being it's tendency to overheat now and then on the long grades when towing the coupe. We won't mention the less than great, prone to fade brakes. They were bad enough on the Buick when it was unloaded and I never had to really get on them when towing. There's a lot to be said for planning ahead.

The usual drill for many participants was to tow up in the cool evening hours and camp out in the pits. The tow up was usually done on a Saturday night and at times we went into Santa Maria proper, a nice little town that was loaded with nice hot rods.

Racing was always on a Sunday. Long Beach was one of the first strips to instigate Saturday night racing and it was quite popular. The old Saugus drag strip also ran Saturday nights, but it didn't have the draw that Long Beach did. The Santa Maria strip was not fenced and entry the night before was no problem. The county Sheriff s would stop in from time to time.

During an earlier time period I had been working in Santa Barbara and hung out with a bunch of Santa Barbara guys in a club called the "Chevrollers". Requisite for club entry was ownership of a Chevy or Chevy powered car. I ran a flathead at the time and was just sort of an honorary member and it was expected I would stick a small block Chevy in the coupe at first opportunity.

We had been there in the past as Saturday night campers and were watching a race for money between a couple of fairly fast Santa Maria cars. A Sheriff's car came in and a few of us started to run for it. A couple of the more experienced club members told us to stick around and watch. The Sheriff's car just parked and the race went on as if nothing happened. That was a totally new one on me.

After we had talked to the officers for a bit, the question was asked why the race hadn't been stopped. The answer was: This is private property and we have no traffic jurisdiction here. I think the simple answer was, nobody was getting hurt and the Sheriff's simply wanted to watch a good race.

My little brother, Louie – present day Henry J drag racer – had a good friend named Larry who came from Canada and had only been in the US for a couple of years. Larry would pitch in and help when he and Louie were at my house, and he would also get right in the middle of the work, lending a hand as required. He would get tired and filthy at the junkyard right along with us, whether for my car or Louie's. He never asked for a thing. A darned good kid and darned good company.

Little brother and I had invited Larry along. Larry was a good kid and fun to be around. He had the typical Canadian accent and it was fun to listen to him. He was pretty excited as he had never been to the races before. We towed up on a Saturday night, the Buick doing a fine job and even got over the grade out of Santa Barbara without a struggle. I was kind of glad as the Buick had a tendency to overheat and the cool night air did the trick.

Once at the track around midnight, we selected what we felt would be a good pit and settled in for the night. This was pretty simple camping, just sleeping bags and an ice chest. Little brother and Larry slept in the coupe and I slept in the Buick.

When morning came the strip operators would stop by and collect the entry fee from all the early birds. It was pretty cool to see a lot of guys and a few gals getting their cars set up for the day's race.

We got the coupe unhooked and fired the engine to warm it up. There were already a few diehards making single passes and it was only about 7 am.

As luck would have it, we popped the soft plug in the Olds water pump housing. It had a pinhole in it that was spraying water up on the left bank. We measured the soft plug as accurately as we could and I gave little brother a few bucks and the Buick keys and he ran up the road to a nearby gas station. He came back pretty quick with a couple of plugs that were too small and wouldn't fit. The gas station guy had told him there were no parts stores open in the area as it was Sunday and that probably no other gas station would have soft plugs, as he just happened to have these in a junk drawer. After taking a closer look at the smallest plug it looked like it would fit right into the leaking soft plug. We got the necessary tools out, and hoping that there was a shoulder behind the leaking plug, knocked the new one in place inside the old one. It went in fine, the leak stopped and we were in business. This soft plug arrangement stayed in the car until we finally blew the Olds engine and parked the car.

At the time we had been running low 14s at 99+mph. One of our goals was to break 100 mph, a barrier for many cars, as it was for us. Getting into the 13s would have been nice too, but I felt we wouldn't make it with the slicks we had.

First run out, the car felt strong in the cool coastal air. When I returned to the pit area little brother gave me a time slip that said 13.20 and 104 mph. I was elated and a bit surprised. Little brother and Larry were both grinning like idiots. Looking at the time slip again I saw that they had given me one they had found from a past meet and it was a motorcycle class. It was a good one on me, they sucked me right in. They gave me the correct slip which said 14.31 at 99+mph. This was pretty much what we ran for the rest of the day.

We did end up in D/Gas instead of C/Gas as the Santa Maria scales read out 200lb or so heavier than the San Fernando scales. It was okay as we still ran against the usual style of C/Gas cars that we always ran against. Of course we were all in D/Gas at the time. The killer Chevies that usually ran in D/Gas got stuck in E/Gas and so on. Just about everyone was knocked down a class, but still ran against the same cars as always. Eliminations started around 11 am and the classes were run out pretty fast as they didn't have the crowd of cars that San Fernando and Long Beach had.

One interesting matchup was a couple of flathead powered '29 roadsters. These were in a strictly competition class and were pretty stripped with only a simple roll bar for protection. One car was from the hometown and the other car was from Santa Barbara. The Santa Barbara kid tried to do a burndown on the home town roadster. Both roadsters had been set up in the waiting area which was across the country road from the pits and quite a ways behind the start line. Once the home town car was fired, the Santa Barbara car just sat there. Both of these cars did not have a radiator, just a closed water system with a surge tank and the standard water pumps. It was kind of a shock to us, we were used to good sportsmanship and had never run up against anything like this. Pretty soon, the crowd started hollering for the guy to start the car and the starter was also waving both cars to the line. The crowd wasn't partisan, there were a bunch of Santa Barbara guys that were p.o.'d too. In fact the Santa Barbara guys seemed to be the maddest group of all. In the end, justice prevailed. The hometown car pulled the Santa Barbara roadster on the top end and won the race.

We ended up running a black '57 Chevy two door for the trophy. As fate would have it these guys were from Santa Barbara too and had pitted next to us in the morning and had also borrowed our timing light. Their car was running pretty close to the same et's ours was, but the mph was down very slightly. The run for the trophy was kind of interesting. The '57 had better slicks than us and they just kind of bombed off the line at pretty high revs. Since the coupe had a fairly hard pair of slicks, driving technique was to stage, hold the engine at 2000 rpm and when the flag came down, dump the clutch and smoothly floor the throttle. It worked well if you stayed calm. If you nailed it too early it all went up in smoke. The car just kind of bogged off the line with minimal wheel spin and started pulling strongly right away.

Little brother and I both got fairly good at this and we could run the car within I tenth or so all the time. The coupe at the time ran 4.27 gears. We got a good start against the '57 and we were both dead even all the way down. About 200 feet from the finish line, the little Chevy just nosed over and the coupe, still pulling pretty well, pulled about a half length on him to win the race. We heard that they were running 5.13 gears and they simply ran out of revs on the top end.

The remainder of the eliminations were over shortly after that and it was still early in the afternoon. This was one of the fun things about Santa Maria. You could pick any car to race you wanted and simply drive up to the start area and the starter would run you through.

Which brings us to this part of the story. This was the first time we took the coupe – with it's Olds engine – to the Santa Maria, California drag strip.

With the turnout a little lighter than normal, the genuine racing was over with early in the afternoon. After that it was fun runs and grudge racing.

We had some great races against a 421 Pontiac Catalina hardtop and a black '57 Chevy two door mentioned earlier. Several times each in fact. Beating them both, each time, but just barely. The Catalina kinda ran out of steam at the top end and our little coupe with 4.27 gears drove right on by. The '57 Chevy was another story with his 5.13 gears.

Making it a very low geared car for the time. It was a dead even race until the little Chevy just nosed over about 200' in front of the traps and our coupe pulled him a half length every time. Fun racing for sure.

Louie drove the coupe a few times and was getting to be a pretty good driver. Near the end of the afternoon, I pulled back to the lineup area, ostensibly to make another run. I got out, stuck my helmet on Larry and we tossed him into the drivers seat.

We also turned the tach redline back to 5000 rpm as we figured he would go right past it in low as he'd never driven a strong running car before. Normal shift for the Olds engine was 6000 rpm and sometimes 6200. Louie and I had talked about letting him drive, but didn't say anything as I didn't want to give him time to get nervous.

We told him how to launch and that was about it, didn't want to confuse him with a lot of stuff. He did well, launched just as instructed, shifted about the right place and made a good run, maybe 3-4 miles slower than Louie and I normally did. He came back with a big grin on his face and it stayed there for the rest of the day. It was a good experience for him as he got to see just how it did go down.

34 years later Louie still sees him now and then and now and then when they talk about cars. Larry talks about how we let him drive the coupe at the races.

For him I guess, one of those brighter than bright life experiences that you never forget and remember in it's total entirety. I'm glad we were there to do it. I've had a few do the same for me.

Life travels in circles sometimes, but when the ends meet it's always interesting ...

"...All I saw of the Dyno Don car was that he was right next to Cook. The fire up road was probably 75-100 feet from the strip. When the S-W-C car went into fourth it started turning left, right towards where I sat in the little rail with the engine not running. Talk about nowhere to go and nowhere to hide!..."

CHAPTER FIFTEEN
THE LAST DRAG RACE
WELL ALMOST! ABOUT 1963 - 64

By now we had raced at a few of the So Cal drag strips. We started hearing about a new strip that had just opened at Irwindale. Having advanced beyond the mildly built flathead engines (real mild) we had by now, what we considered real race cars. Mine was still my '50 Coupe, 335 inch Olds engine, Cad-LaSalle trans, six two barrels, headers, traction bars, no front bumper as was popular at the time and slicks (hard ones). I still like the six two barrels, the three two barrel set up ran just about the same times but opening the hood at the strip and other places resulted in a lot of bugged eyeballs and dropped jaws. These things had major eyewash and none of that progressive linkage stuff, even when they were run on the street. In fact I never have run progressive linkage. A lot of them are just cheap junk.

Two things were now becoming popular as far as drag racing was going. B&M had been running their four-speed Hydro for a while. The wrinkle wall slicks had just started coming out. I wanted a set but couldn't quite swing it. Wanted a B&M too, couldn't swing that either! Probably a good thing, the wrinkle walls with their good bite would probably have torn the Spicer rear end right out of the car. As it was the car was running, 100 mph at 13.90 ets. A bit slow for the C/Gas class we were in, but we won our share of trophies. Cars equipped with the B&M Hydro and wrinkle walls were getting to be pretty much unbeatable for us. Besides the good bite the wrinkle walls delivered, the low gear of the Hydro was just killing us out of the hole. If I remember right the ratios were about: 3.45 low, 2.60 second, 1.31 third and of course 1-1 for fourth. Now these ratios may be off a bit. This is just from memory. (I'm real sure 3.45 in low is right).

One of my friends owned a '55 Ford pickup. We swapped in a 329 Olds with Hydro which turned it into a good strong runner.

What I want to point out here are two things. The 3.45 low, combined with a 4.57 rear and the wrinkle walls, would launch a car really hard. The ratio jump from second to third would really bog some of the smaller engines in some of the E/Gas cars. A typical E/Gas car was generally a '55-'56 Chevy with 283 motor, somewhat heavy compared to the same Chevies with 283 motors in D/Gas that had some items deleted for weight savings.

The Chevies with 327 motors fell into C/Gas. They were tough competitors! We generally did okay when up against the usual street driven hot rods, but when the B&M cars with the good slicks were in the class it was pretty much all over.

One of my friends owned a '55 Ford pickup. We'll just call him WB in this little missive, (WB stood for "Wonder Boy" as he was always doing something that made us wonder.) When the 272 inch Y-block went south, we swapped in a 329 inch Olds with Hydro (.030" over 324"). The Olds although stock, turned it into a good, strong runner. It was a nice truck, plain black seats, bright red paint and chrome wheels and of course twin pipes. That was almost always the first modification.

WB was a hard guy to figure out. Every once in a while he would do something really surprising. Not stupid, just surprising. He had a good buddy that he ran around with when he wasn't running around with us. We'll call him "Too Tall" here, because he was just plain tall. One day WB and Too Tall showed up at my house with a trailer in tow carrying an old dragster that was engineless, but in really good shape. I always thought it was a Kent Fuller chassis and aluminum body work. The car looked just like Tommy Ivo's Buick powered single engined dragster. WB and Too Tall came up with a well built, well equipped flathead motor from someplace. It was good that they had bought one already built. The last flathead they tried to put together for WB's '49 coupe had .020" rod and main bearings and a .010" crank. (Or as we called it in the parts house/machine shop I worked in, a 10-10 crank).

They dropped the crank in the block and torqued up the mains. It was done very professionally as they had borrowed my Grandfather's old beam torque wrench. (Which I still have and at the time, was the most exotic tool our little group owned). In fact, if anyone in our group had the money to buy either a piece of speed equipment or a tool required for installation of same, we always bought the speed equipment. Even if we couldn't install it, it looked great (and very official) sitting casually on a garage shelf. Of course the crank would not spin in the block, not even with a pry bar. Undaunted, our heroes proceeded to get the engine totally assembled and installed in the car. This engine was locked up tighter than a drum. We were flat amazed. Sure looked good though, shiny red paint and chrome acorns. The starter would not budge it. Pushing it with another car would not budge it. Pushing it and hitting the starter wouldn't turn it over. Many bad words were spoken.

They dinked around for two days until the awful truth dawned. They were going to have to pull the motor. The motor came out and they brought it to where I worked. When they told the old machinist what they had done, he started coughing and choking and had to walk away. I swear there were tears in his eyes. Every once in a while he would look at me, think about the two idiots and start laughing. This went on for several weeks. Of course after getting the correct bearings the engine went together okay, started and ran just fine. I'm not sure if they really understood what they had done. Now that they had tasted success, it was on to bigger and better things.

WB and Too Tall installed the already built flathead, with three two barrel intake and a two speed (no reverse) '39 Ford trans in the dragster. It worked out pretty good and actually ran fairly well. With the period perfect slicks (no wrinkle walls here), flathead motor and red paint it was a great looking little car. They ran it several times at San Fernando and it turned about 102 mph and low to mid 13 second ets. This was on gas. After a lot of talk they decided to join the big time and convert to fuel. They bought a five gallon can of alcohol and a one gallon can of Nitromethane somewhere. The car didn't run too well after that, they didn't realize they had to burn about twice as much alcohol than gas and their stock 97s just would not flow that much. They got to thinking and decided I must be a carburetion expert as I was running six two barrels. (Boy, were they wrong!) About all I had done to my setup (which was six Stromberg 48s – pretty much the same as the 97s except the 48s had slightly larger venturis) was some re-jetting and yanking the accelerator pump rods off the middle two. (In retrospect I probably should have left them on – what I thought was too much fuel when the throttle was nailed was more than likely a major lean-out until air speed through the venturis started pulling fuel from the main jet). Once the motor was revved up a bit it really ran good. Launch technique was to hold the RPMs at 2000, dump the clutch and hit the throttle. If you stayed calm and did it right, the car would launch with virtually no wheel spin from the hard slicks. At that RPM the main jets were pulling fuel okay. Actually it sorta bogged off the line. Do it wrong however and it was fuel dragster, smokin' the tires time. Most times we did it right.

This probably helped little brother on his way to being the very good drag racer that he is today. He was pretty good about following instructions. (It was that or spectate.) I had a four two barrel flathead manifold kicking around the garage at the time. We decided they should get another 97 and I would put the new setup together. Now I had been paying attention to a lot of the failed as well as successful things we had done. And I paid a lot of attention to other cars, talked to the owners who were usually the builders and found out what worked and what didn't. Most of the guys were pretty good about sharing information. The biggest speed secret was; bring money, lots of it, (still true today).

One of the most important lessons I learned was; either get a book about it if you can, or better yet, talk to a genuine expert. Since my work took me to the Valley a lot, I knew where every Speed Shop, big or little was located, (San Fernando Valley). It was usually me that picked up the goodies for the guys. (Which wasn't too often – genuine speed equipment cost genuine money). CT had some nice guys behind the counter and in the machine shop and I had been going in there buying mainly little things, but did buy an occasional biggy now and then. I was lucky enough to get hold of a guy that had run carbureted engines on fuel. He sold me four kits to convert the 97s over to alcohol and fuel and gave me some tips on how to do it. WB and Too Tall were a little stunned that I had spent about $45.00 of their money when they thought about $20.00 should have done it. As they were to see, it was money well spent.

We got the little flathead running okay on straight alcohol but decided we should take it for a test run before going to the strip with it. We trailered it to a little used road below a local dam. The dam tender came out to watch us unload and drove down the hill to where we were. He had thought that we were really gonna have a serious street race and was thinking of calling the Sheriff. After we explained what we were doing he went along with it and seemed to enjoy it. To him the little flathead dragster looked just like the real fast ones he saw on TV now and then.

We fired it on straight alcohol and let it warm up. Warm-up on an alcohol car takes a lot longer than you think. After a few second gear burnouts (two speed trans) we were pleased with how well it ran. We were ready. (When little brother ran gas in one of the Henry J's earlier incarnations we would tow him from the pits, through the staging lanes and to the front of the staging lanes. He would then fire up, burnout and go race. He shut the engine down in the shut down area retaining enough speed to coast off the track. The car was equipped with, and still has, a Sirocco radiator, a nice small one. We would then tow him back to the pits. The engine was always fairly hot. After switching to alcohol he could drive all the way to and through the staging lanes, do the burnout, race, drive back to the pits and not exceed 180° F temperature. It really makes a big difference).

I owned at the time a nice '57 Buick Roadmaster, white, with pipes (of course). We used this to flat tow the Coupe to the races. Of course, once at the track we had to install the traction bars and slicks. A trailer would have been great. (Some of the guys that ran automatics, lockers or welded spiders would flat tow with trailer hubs adapted to their rear axles. The adapter, complete with bearings, bolted to the original wheel studs and in turn had auxiliary wheels bolted to them. Generally the drill was to install it, lock the emergency brake and leave the transmission in gear which left the auxiliary wheels free to rotate without rotating the locker, diff. etc. These things with a street tire/wheel combo sticking out of the wheel well looked weird but worked well. Most serious race cars had radiused wheel wells for slick clearance. The narrowed rear ends were around but only on the most serious cars.)

Our little group of hard core drag racers, (at least we thought so) took off for Irwindale, leaving about 6:00 am on a Sunday morning. The L.A. freeway system was virtually deserted on early Sunday mornings. We were running along at about 65 mph on an empty four lane freeway with WB's '55 Ford pickup towing the dragster/trailer combo in the lead. All of a sudden the whole pickup/trailer combo started a mild fish-tailing. It got progressively worse until they were sliding back and forth across three lanes of fortunately empty freeway. WB was driving and looking straight ahead. Too Tall and WB's little brother were looking back with that sorta "Bug-eyed, I don't believe this is happening look".

WB was a pretty fair driver, but it didn't look like he was gonna save this one. We started slowing down so we wouldn't be in the middle of a rapidly developing wreck. From where we sat, it was gonna be a good one.

They never did slow down very much. Pretty soon the whole rig straightened out and started slowing down, the trailer was still swaying from side to side a bit. WB found a wide spot and we pulled off. WB had saved the day by just lightly staying on the gas and holding the steering wheel straight ahead letting the whole mess straighten itself out. Now this usually works pretty well when flat towing. Generally, flat towing can get away from you once the weaving starts as every time you input a steering correction, the towbar and car in back will input a force in the opposite direction than you want, trying to push the rear end out of line. The usual cure is just to remain lightly on the gas and hold the steering wheel straight. (My experience with trailers has been – it doesn't work every time!

When my roadster was under construction, but a complete car, engine and trans in, all bodywork on and generally looking like you could fire it and drive away. I bought a 6' x 10' single axle utility trailer to move from a rental to our new house. I got that size because the roadster would fit in (although the dropping tailgate remained opened and tied off level) and I could use it for other things. The '89 Ranger 4x4 turned out to be a pretty fair tow vehicle. I didn't think the loaded trailer was tail heavy, it didn't look it, but probably was. Anyway, it seemed to be handling well and being on a two lane country road at 45 mph I decided to accelerate to 55 mph. About 50, I entered a narrow bridge and the whole rig started the two lane boogie. One car had just passed and no more were on the bridge. It got progressively worse no matter what I did. I held the wheel straight, I accelerated, I accelerated harder, nothing helped. I finally decided to just let off the gas and ride it out sans brakes. We left the bridge and by now were headed down hill, sliding clear across both lanes and I was definitely having to steer now.

Pretty soon the truck started sliding too. Cars way down the road were stopping and pulling over. I was just hoping I could get far enough down the hill to crash in a flat orchard area and not go over the embankment into the river. Strangely enough, this California river had water in it. The whole rig finally gave two quick twitches and straightened out. I guess it simply slowed down enough to finally gain some traction. I was really lucky. (The use of a simple tape measure would have told us if we were tail or nose heavy – another one of life's little lessons)

Too Tall, brilliant lad that he was, had installed the two inch trailer ball just hand tight. In fact he didn't even latch the trailer hitch to the ball. (Sometimes we wondered about him.) The trailer ball was nowhere to be found. Being a resourceful group, we pulled one of the one inch bolts out of my traction bars that were in the trunk of the flat towed coupe. (They were too low to travel with.) The trailer hitch coupler was removed from the coupler which rested on a 1/2 inch or so plate. The one inch bolt, after some serious filing on the trailer tongue plate with a rat-tail, equipped with appropriate washers, was installed along with double nuts, one being of the aircraft variety. Now that it was too late, we were really being safe. During the hitch repairs I noticed that WB (a bit cheap sometimes) had installed a cheap piece of 1/4 inch chain retained only by a single dime store grade 3/8 inch bolt. (Grade 8? – whatta ya mean grade 8?). I couldn't believe it didn't break during our little escapade. (Sometimes when I took back on some of the things we did., we were either very lucky or somebody was really in good with God.)

We finally got to Irwindale. Little brother and I went to the regular pit area. WB and the dragster troops went to the "Hot Pits" where all the dragsters were. There was a pretty big crowd on hand in the grandstands and in the pits. One reason being; Dyno Don Nicholson in his SOHC Mercury Comet and Stone-Woods-Cook in their black '41 Willys that ran a Hemi about that time, were there for a match race. The match race had been heavily advertised in the LA area. (It was a surprise to us. We were doing well just to make sure the strip was open. Having Dyno Don and S-W-C was frosting on the cake.) Stone-Woods-Cook and Dyno Don were rumored to be running fuel. Maybe they were, I don't think so, but they were turning really good times. If I remember right S-W-C were running about 165 mph at 9.60 et or pretty close. Dyno Don was right up there with them and it promised to be one heck of a day. We got the Coupe set up and entered the staging lanes for time trials.

We had to wait three hours to make one run. (During the wait we wandered over to the Dyno Don pits and watched them replace a four speed that had let go in the first round. Didn't take 'em long. These guys really knew what they were doing.) The car ran about the same numbers it always ran so we parked it and walked back to the dragster area. WB's little brother was grinning like a kid loose in a candy store. It was his first time at the drags.

WB and Too Tall had gotten the car unloaded, fired and warmed up. They were ready, Irwindale at that time ran a Xmas Tree. I asked WB and Too Tall if they had ever run against a "tree". The answer was no. I could see this set them to thinking. About that time we got called to C/Gas. After a bit of a wait, we rolled up next to a small block powered '37 Chevy coupe. He drilled us off the start line. It was the old B&M Hydro/wrinkle wall slicks thing again. We had lost first round – again!

After parking the car we wandered back to the dragster area. WB and Too Tall were looking at me and talking to each other as we walked up. Now WB was somewhat shy and Too Tall was downright shy. Their greatest individual fear seemed to be that they might look dumb in public. (That never bothered me – heck, if Don Garlits asked me to drive his dragster I would have done it naked, set my hair on fire during the run and paid for the privilege – I really liked to drag race.) It seemed they were both afraid to drive against the tree. I tried to explain it to them, but they were leery of it. (I think too, the large crowd worried them.) They finally asked me if I would drive their little fueler. Well, I thought about it for a bit, (here boys, twist my arm – right here) and told them I would.

At that time about the only safety equipment required for the driver was a helmet, breather mask, goggles, gloves and a leather jacket. (Leather jackets being out of fashion at the time were available at local thrift stores for two or three dollars.) WB had bought a really great leather jacket for three bucks that any Harley guy would have liked. Having been around the car quite a bit I was familiar with the drill on running it. Besides the basics it had an ignition on/off switch, powered by a hidden motorcycle battery and a fuel shut off valve, oil pressure and water temp gauges. I had also been in the driver's seat, just for fun and when pushing it around the shop. This time was different. This time it was for real. It was a little bit strange.

The announcer called flathead fueler class to the fire up road. (The strip ran roughly east-west with racing going to the west and the fire up road going east. At that time it was only used to fire up the competition class cars, altereds, dragsters etc. (For the youngsters – cars such as these had no starters, no batteries and were push started with the tow vehicle. Some of the luckier guys had a friend with a really cool roadster or coupe that did the pushing. (Batteries were against the rules – we had ours well hidden – it didn't dawn on us that the tech guy could probably tell the difference between a magneto and a distributor – it was hard to believe how clever we were!)

There was no return traffic due to lack of a guard rail between it and the drag strip it paralleled.

This was to create an interesting situation. Being more than ready we were the first dragster in line for the fire up road. I was strapped in and ready. The crew pushed me out on to the fire up road. The fire up road co-ordinator (now there's a title) had us hold at about the 1000 foot mark. Dyno Don and S-W-C were fired up and rolling to the start line. We had perfect seats for the second match race of the day. The guys in the pickup had a really primo view. I could see pretty well from where I was sitting in the dragster. S-W-C was in the Left lane, next to the fire up road.

Now you've probably heard people say what evil handling cars these short wheelbase '41 Willys were. It sat pretty high according to the thinking of the day. Better weight transfer and all that. I had read that the way Doug Cook drove this beast (and beast is the right word) by selecting the B&M Hydro in the 1-3 position. The car would then shift through first, second and third automatically and he would shift into fourth himself. Sounds reasonable to me. The Xmas Tree came down and both cars left really hard. It looked like the 1-2-3 shifting was all done about 400-500 feet out for the S-W-C car. All I saw of the Dyno Don car was that he was right next to Cook. The fire up road was probably 75-100 feet from the strip. When the S-W-C car went into fourth it started turning left, right towards where I sat in the little rail with the engine not running. Talk about nowhere to go and nowhere to hide!

I got pretty resigned for a few moments. It looked like this black Willys was gonna run right over us. I figured this was as good a way as any and at least I would get famous. (Fat lot of good it would do me.)

Doug Cook has been touted as one of the sport's greatest drivers. You'll get no argument from me. There was no lifting of the throttle for him, he simply drove his way out of it, he had gotten seriously sideways for a bit, especially considering the speeds he was traveling, probably 145+ mph when he went by me.

One thing that may have happened to make this look bad, especially from my semi-permanent vantage point was; he was probably on somewhat of a ballistic course and I was never in danger. At the speeds he was traveling he probably couldn't have turned to hit me if he wanted to. I don't really know. I do know that I was seriously impressed with what I saw.

Once the excitement was over, I don't remember who won that match race, the fire up road guy told us to start 'em up. I didn't hear him the first time around as my heart beat was pretty loud. We fired and went to the start line where we were directed to the right lane. Burnouts and bleach boxes were not in use at the time, although some of the racers would pour bleach on the slicks and do a short little burn if allowed by the strip officials. Not always though.

We were up against the fastest flathead fueler there that day. As fate would have it he bogged, probably with a cold engine. We won that round. It was a bit surreal in that, being strapped in, wearing a heavy jacket, helmet and fire mask it was like you were watching a movie. You could see the scene outlined through your goggles, could see your gloved hands on the steering wheel and see your knees sticking over the rear end housing. It was like you were watching someone else. I simply wound up the motor right before the last amber lit and dumped the clutch at the right time. The car launched well and didn't spin the tires much. I shifted when it seemed about right, pulling straight back on the shortened shift lever, no tachometer was installed.

I was in the right lane and kept waiting for the faster fueler to pass me. He never did. Being strapped in tightly meant you couldn't turn and look around. I went through the traps, started shutting down and still didn't see the other rail. (Turn-outs were to the left.) I coasted down to the very last turn out. I was tempted to stop on the strip, but didn't. This was weird not being able to see your competition. Approaching the last turn off at about 20 mph, I hung a hard left and hoped for the best. The other fueler was nowhere to be seen. I was surprised to find that the little fueler actually cornered pretty well. I wound up the slightly zig-zagging return road toward the timing stand. (Timing was done in the tower and electronically duplicated at the timing stand at the bottom of the strip.) When I saw I couldn't make it I simply re-fired the engine and drove up. I beat the boys to the timing stand and was out of the car and had the time slip in hand when they drove up. When I showed them the slip, (we ran 112 mph and 12.92 et) there was a whole lot of idiot grins floating, around.

We won that day due to the remaining three flathead fuelers were run pretty much by amateurs like us. The bye run guy broke at the start line, (probably another failed '39 trans.) The other guy that won his race in the first round red lighted against us. (We ran 112 mph and 12.90 in the last race.)

Timing slips in hand, little WB went to collect our booty as Too Tall, little brother and myself loaded the little red dragster on the trailer. It being near the end of the day, and a lot of the cars were gone, little brother and I had hooked the coupe up to the Buick and parked in the dragster pits. WB and brother came back with a trophy, fairly nice one and a case of oil. (Cases of oil were popular prizes for the fueler guys as they used a lot of it.) We were really happy. We had spent the day with friends, we had done just about what we wanted to do and we had actually won. Right then – life just couldn't have been any better. I never did learn who won the Dyno Don, Stone-Woods-Cook match race .....

The one gallon can of Nitromethane still resided in the back of the truck, unopened. I don't think it ever got used, but it was one heck of a conversation piece.

An interesting little side note to all this: WB never did give me the four two barrel intake back. It stayed on the car when he sold it which wasn't a problem for me as I had borrowed his like new 2-1/2 gallon Moon fuel tank. I figured we were even. WB and I drifted apart, Too Tall disappeared, never to be seen again. The Moon fuel tank I have to this day and it sits on a shelf in my garage. It looks great there and brings back many memories. It's still in excellent shape with a couple of minor dings. It has an interesting history of its own. After being on the little red dragster early in it's life, it ran on my coupe for a while, at least until I sold it and converted back to street with another '50 coupe. It got loaned to little brother's friend and spent some time on a 10 second Pinto. It came back and ran on little brother's Henry J for a while. When he changed to alcohol, we built a five gallon tank for the Henry J. It then went on an alcohol dragster that started running low sixes and then they had to go to a larger tank. (Same couple that ran the Pinto, 2-1/2gallons just didn't quite make it on an alcohol car.) It got loaned to a friend of little brother's who ran a 10 second '56 Chevy until he could get his own tank. Neither brother or I would sell it. Loan, yes – sell, no. This little fuel tank could probably tell some amazing stories. It's been around a bit. It came with a pedigree. It has it's own history. And it's a part of the family....

"...All this time he'd been leaning back against the face of the rock cliff and just looking at the water. We had begun to have second and third thoughts about what we'd sent him to do. So it was, late in the afternoon, on a more than hot summer day, and without a word, little brother straightened up, glanced down and launched himself into space. It was pretty spectacular for sure.."

CHAPTER SIXTEEN
THE BIG PACKARD
OR THE MILD BUNCH!

I've seen, been around and even owned a few memorable cars. The owned ones at least, memorable to me, so I'll just mention one that belonged to a friend. This friend had emigrated from Kansas the year before, and was the owner of the Model A coupe that rolled on a city street in a very scary accident. No one was really hurt, except for one occupant that slid into some rose bushes, and he only bled for a little while.

The hardest part for LH, (the A coupe owner) was going home the night of the wreck and facing the music. Having been there myself due to my own foibles, I can tell you that playing the music is a lot better than facing it. But you knew that. We've all been there somewhere along the line.

After about 6-8 months of being grounded as far as having a car and driving it all by himself his mom and dad finally got tired of taking him places. He went with us a lot of the time, but his folks had to do the typical run the teenager around town for various things. I think too, they missed the handy part about sending the kid on an errand.

That was one part about driving I enjoyed, although mom and dad knew it would take longer than necessary, they usually didn't mind. If they were in a hurry, they told me so, and I went straight out and straight back, the smart thing to do if you had plans for the family car later that evening.

Somewhere along the line LH's dad found a '38 Packard four door, the long wheelbase model. The hood looked long enough to land Piper Cubs on and it had a ton of interior room. If it had been any longer you would have had to make appointments for left turns. In areas where our '49-'50 Ford coupes would swing a U turn, the Packard required a bit of back and fill to get turned around. On the really narrow little roads at the beach, it was a whole other project to just get the big Packard turned around. I always thought it was a bit of a limousine. Maybe! It had jump seats behind the front seat and part of the body was blanked off with sheet metal where the

small rearmost side window went in the shorter wheelbase models. It had the fender mounted spare tire, only one, and that was on the driver's side. It was big and had beautiful black paint, a stately old dowager of a car, not to mention low mileage and very cherry.

The interior was perfect and the chrome was great. It ran smoothly and floated down the highway in a most distinguished and stately manner. The only flaw was its tendency to overheat. That was our fault to a great extent, as we discovered that taking four couples and sometimes five in the Packard was more fun than taking two or three of our little coupes. And splitting the gas costs between several guys was no big deal. The Packard seated three in the front seat and four could get in there if necessary. Being teenagers meant that most of us were pretty slim. With three in the front seat, two in the jump seats and three in the big back seat it was a comfortable ride for four couples and there was enough room on the rear floor to seat two more.

Once loaded, it was a bit of a lowrider. Heading into the mountains on summer days would always make it run warm. Not a problem for us, we carried extra water and traveled next to a stream most of the way up. We made a point to stop at several good view spots on the way. Once up in the mountains, we went about 10 miles away from the highway, down an old paved road and onto a wide dirt road. The dirt road went back to a big swimming hole on a small stream and after a few miles the road narrowed down to a single lane with an occasional turnout. This was no problem for the big Packard, even hanging low it didn't drag as the dirt road was well kept and pretty smooth.

You had to cross the stream in a couple of places and early in summer when the snow-melt was still on, the water would get above the floorboards now and then. Usually not a problem as the Packard just slogged right on through. We did get stuck once and when we got out, water ran right through the car once the rear doors on both sides were opened. With four guys and a couple of the gutsier girls pushing we got the Packard rolling okay.

We did get more than a few double takes from the few jeep owners we ran into, I guess they figured they were way out in the country and in truth they were. 'Course once you got to the swimming hole, the road truly did turn into a jeep trail and the only thing you'd find there were hunters and fishermen walking and the occasional jeep venturing up the road.

Once there, the guys just stood outside the car and stripped down, no problem as we wore our swim trunks under our jeans. The huge Packard rear seat made a perfect changing room for the girls. Since we were gentlemen, we didn't try to sneak peeks. Well, not too much anyway, you just couldn't see inside the back seat worth a darn.

The swimming hole was a great one, especially since not too many knew about it and not too many of them wanted to drive eight miles down a dirt road, cross the stream twice and maybe get stuck. There was a sandy beach near the parking area with lots of shade trees to park under.

The very best part was the darned near perfectly sheer solid rock cliff on the other side of the big pool. The pool was quite deep on the cliff side and plenty safe for diving. The rock had a natural angled ledge to climb out on and you could walk up it and dive off with the diving height being anywhere from water level to about five feet up. Your choice.

Since part of being a teenager, for the guys at least, is the opportunity to show off for the girls, this place was tailor made. Along with the five foot rock ledge, someone, somewhere along the line had chiseled out steps leading way up the face of the rock cliff to four different small ledges where you could turn around and dive or jump off. The heights listed for the ledges are fairly accurate and conservative.

Along with "The Older I Get the Faster I Was" car bit, stories sometimes grow with each telling. No exaggerations need to made here. This was a tall rock cliff. Simple as that.

The first ledge, with room for two brave souls, was just about equal to the 12 foot high springboard at the High School Olympic sized pool at home. No problem in diving for most of us as we'd learned how to do it at school, the hard way in a lot of cases. You've been there I'm sure, just push off, stay kinda flat and parallel to the water and roll over at the right time.

Invariably there would be another group of kids at the swimming hole and sometimes some sailors or airmen from the local military bases, there being three of them close to our home town. We ended up mixing with and meeting some of these guys and made some good friends. These guys were usually dateless, they were far from home in most cases and didn't know a soul. But they had high hopes and always had an eye out for an unattached young lady.

After some of these guys had watched the diving from the cliff for a bit they would always give it a try. Some of them that came from the larger schools with pools similar to ours did okay. And some that came from the granite laden states back east had learned to dive off of high rock quarry walls. These guys did okay too. The ones that had problems at times, were generally from the flatlands of America and came from small schools with no pools in small towns.

Somewhere along the line they had gotten it in their minds that a successful and good looking dive was one where you launched, immediately rolled vertical and fell the remaining way perfectly vertical thereby making a clean entry. I'm sure you can see the flaw here, once launched and once rolled vertical they kept going right on over and there were some serious and painful back splats into the water. These at only the 12 foot level. The next couple of ledges were at the 25 foot and the 30 foot level. That was about the bravery limit for most of us.

I made one dive from the 25 foot level, as did the rest of the guys in our group, but after that one and because I went so darned deep I quit diving from there and simply jumped. Heck, the girls didn't care whether you dived or jumped; the points awarded for bravery in the face of stupidity were all the same. Most of us went to the 30 foot level, only five feet higher but for some, reason it looked a whole lot more than the five feet. Just the point of view I guess, although at this point the sideways trending steps carved into the rock cliff now had you above a point of rock sticking out a bit so you had to make sure to launch out far enough to clear the rock. It wasn't too big an outward leap, you just had to be sure to do it and no one in our group was ever hurt here. The 30 foot level was it for me. No dives from here, just jumps.

One of the sailors though, decided to dive from the 25 foot level and being a flatlander, not used to, or experienced in diving from high places, did the launch and roll vertical trick right away. Having consumed several cans of liquid courage didn't help matters much. Sure enough, he rolled over and hit the water flat on his back. The resulting splash put most "cannon-balls" to shame. He got to the surface okay, and his friends helped him get back to shore and laid him on a blanket. After throwing up a few times, he pretty much laid on the blanket for the rest of the afternoon but he seemed to be okay when he left. More than likely though, he'd given up diving as a potentially profitable occupation.

The fourth and last ledge was at about the 50 foot level, easily as tall as a medium sized power pole and quite a view once you were up there. Gauging the height of the ledges was fairly easy, once a couple of guys were on the rock face you could tell just about how high it was. I did climb up there once, once was enough, it was simply too much. We never did see anybody jump off the very top ledge, until we conned my little brother into doing it. He was about 11 at the time and since he was the unofficial mascot of our little gang he went most places with us and got away with more than a few things, like sitting quietly in the front seat of the Packard while the girls were changing in the back. When they discovered him, they beat on him a bit and flung him out the door. He ended up in the rocks and gravel and came up with a bloody knee, but I'm sure he didn't feel a thing. The girls were ticked off, but I don't think they were as mad as they acted. Modesty was a requirement of the times, and the girls made good use of it.

We picked up little brother and the girls indicated we should talk to him and show him the error of his ways. Little brother, being only 11 got away with a lot of stuff and he got away with a bit on this one too. We found it hard to tell him he'd done wrong, when to a man, we wished we'd have been there instead. He just had this big grin on his face for the rest of the day. Lucky dog. The girls soon forgave him because he was such a likable little character and they thought he was cute too. Man....

The end of the afternoon came and we were about ready to leave when we stopped for a while to watch a guy from another group on the very top ledge. He stayed there for quite a while, finally gave up and did the sensible thing climbed down to one of the lower ledges and bailed out. Nobody razzed him, as we knew what it looked like up there and none of us had jumped off. A quiet kid most of the time, he made a few quiet and disparaging comments about how the guy should have jumped off. Something he never should have said around us. A group that generally didn't take dares lightly.

We hadn't dared each other on the high ledge because we simply realized it was getting pretty serious up that high. And we'd all been up there and looked. All except little brother. He received more than a few choice comments from the guys and a couple of dares to do it himself. Pretty soon, money entered the picture. When the pooled money got to the astronomical level of three dollars if you do it, his mind was made up. Three dollars, especially to a little guy, was a serious chunk of change and I could see the wheels in his mind turning already. The girls, being the only sensible ones present, didn't want him to jump off and were very much against it, and told him so. Too late, the gauntlet was thrown, and it was way too late for any "real guy" to back out. I think we've all been here at one time or the other, something the girls had a hard time understanding. Doing the sensible thing is not necessarily in a guy's bag of tricks. Once you cross that line, there is no turning back. That wasn't a problem for us, we understood the "guy" rules quite well, we'd been there, done that, and only broken and bloodied a few things here and there. Heck, we kinda figured little brother to be expendable anyway.

Since it was late, only our little group and one other was still at the swimming hole. Little brother being smart, about money anyway, made us give the pooled money to one of the girls to hold. He swam across the pool and a couple of the guys went with him. Not to make sure he did it, simply in case he had to be dragged out of the water. We stayed on the beach for the same reason. Figuring mom would really be mad if we didn't at least bring the body home. They all got out of the water at the angled ledge at the bottom and dried off for a bit. Little brother started the requisite climb to the top. It didn't take long.

Once there, and it was his first time up there, he got a good view and a good idea of what it was all about. He started thinking about it a bit. That is what most of us had done and once the thinking starts, the bravery stuff goes out the window. He stayed up there for a while and after a half hour or so, we started calling him to give it up and come down. We were ready to head for home. After another 10 minutes or so, and at the urging of the girls, we told him to come down and he could have the money anyway.

All this time he'd been leaning back against the face of the rock cliff and just looking at the water. We had begun to have second and third thoughts about what we'd sent him to do. So it was, late in the afternoon, on a more than hot summer day, and without a word, little brother straightened up, glanced down and launched himself into space. It was pretty spectacular for sure. Everybody's heart had stopped beating for the few moments of free fall. The surprising part was the utter quiet. Not a bird was singing, not a person said anything, and everyone was quite stunned. This was just one of those moments when time stood still, for me, for the gang, and I'm sure for little brother. About half way down, it seemed to take forever to get that far, he started screaming. Too late now, the laws of gravity and acceleration are unforgiving and always in effect. He screamed the rest of the way down and right into the water. I don't know how deep he went, the pool was quite deep. About the time the guys on the other side could see through the bubbles, up came little brother with an ear to ear grin on his face.

It was not often that he could beat the big guys at their game and this was his finest hour. In one fell swoop, he became the hero and we became the dogs. The money was incidental, but gladly received. The best part for him was the care lavished on him by the girls who toweled him off, wrapped him up and put him in the back of the big old Packard. The girls, rightly so, were a bit ticked that we would so carelessly risk little brother's life. They cuddled up to him and treated him like a little king. They would talk to us, not much though, as we'd kind of put ourselves on the outside looking in, an interesting lesson for us in many ways. We not only lost the points we'd gained for taking the girls on a great picnic to a great place, we lost our hero points for, as the girls perceived it, the dangerous jumping and diving bit we did and put ourselves into the dog house for conning little brother into the big jump. We were to find later that this was only one of many trips to the dog house we would find ourselves embroiled in.

They say though, that every dog has his day. I'm ready to have mine if I can only get out of this little doorway ....

"...Dad had a pair of these on his '48 Ford sedan, a neat two door with milled heads, pipes, flippers, black paint and at times skirts. On a trip to Arkansas and driving straight through on a really rainy and pitch black night the headlights went out. A bit of a common happening with these cars with their cotton fabric wiring insulation..."

CHAPTER SEVENTEEN
SPOTS AND BOLT-ONS
APPLETON AND OTHER SPOTLIGHTS.

My opinion, and due to what I saw as a little guy, as far as the car end of things went, was that a lot of stuff like spotlights, skirts and similar things became popular because they were bolt-on items. Even a really built-up engine is still pretty much a bolt-on, or bolt together for most. Before, during and after the war, and pretty much true today, the builders and creators from scratch guys were pretty rare. My dad was fortunate to know a couple. My dad and my grandfather, were noted for being really good mechanics/machinists by more than a few. Either term pretty much applied to either one. If you were known as a good mechanic, more than likely you could handle the machine shop equipment quite well. This was especially true in the oil fields where they both worked.

Trucks and cars were only part of their duties. As you can imagine, working in the oil fields meant you got involved with a wide variety and differing sizes of equipment. Some large, some even bigger and some were simply large by huge. As long as I've mentioned the oil fields here's a little more on them. This is one piece of Americana that has some real artists, still true today.

The artists were/are in the machinist and welder category. I've seen some really brilliant solutions to problems done by the machinists. I've seen the same kind of brilliance displayed by the welders. The welders, at least in my opinion are the real artists in the oil fields. Some of the solutions to problems, both large and small are absolutely brilliant. Someone really ought to photographically document some of the stuff done by welders.

Welding really is both a skill and an art form. Much like playing a musical instrument. Let it go for a while and you can still do the basics, but it's not as good as you can do when you have been doing it for a while and are back in the swing of things, so to speak.

The two guys that Dad knew when he was a teenager and a young man were very forward thinking individuals. One built a Chevy bodied, lowboy style roadster that sat lower than anything seen before. That actually says quite a bit as Dad grew up in Southern California and even in the '30s it was a hotbed of hot rod activity. Said car had a chassis built from scratch, something virtually unheard of in the area and in the era as well. At least as pertains to amateur built stuff. The main frame rails were tubing obtained from the oil field scrap pile. Other tubing was used for crossmembers. This is a much bigger undertaking than it sounds as having access to a welder was pretty much something that no one had. The best that most could do was either fabricate something and take it to the welding shop or drag the whole darned car in and have it done.

It would be a different history than the one we know if the nice little MIGs had been available to the rodders of the '30s and '40s. This particular car was built with a view towards taking it to the dry lakes, but I don't think it ever got there as it was built prior to the war. It was reported to handle quite well, as it really was very low. The few things Dad talks about with this car are how you could crank the wheel hard over and it would simply switch ends. Try that with any other car of the day and you'd be lucky to only fall onto your side.

I think this little roadster was built by Dad's best friend that disappeared into the maws of WW2, never to be seen again. He was a P38 pilot in the Pacific and simply never came back from a mission and no one knows what happened. Dad doesn't talk much about him and I've never pressed him. Fifty-four years later it's still a painful subject.

His friend was another American hero, one among many, and many that we we all owe much to. The other kid was another one of those forward thinking guys. And I'm not sure when this one was done, but it was also prior to the war. I believe the car was a '35 Ford coupe. The flathead engine was built up quite a bit, but multi-carburetion was a pretty rare thing in those days. Realizing that the engine needed more breathing capacity the owner milled the top off the stock intake manifold, whittled up a wood pattern for two carburetors and had that cast at a local foundry. It was something along the lines of the Edelbrock slingshot two carb flathead intake. The new piece was brazed to the original manifold and it worked out fairly well even though it was now a large plenum style manifold as vs. the stock individual runner manifold of the day.

The car turned out to run quite well, although it was very overgeared. It pulled 112 mph in second. I don't know what it would pull in high, but it was nowhere near the 112 mph second gear speed. That kind of puts the lie to all those urban legend stories we've all heard about the Model As with two transmissions. One was reversed to obtain a very high overall gear ratio and go a "hunnert and ninety" with a stock Model A engine!

I have no doubt that a few tried this little trick, but in view of the torque tube drive and all the machining that would be required and keeping in mind that most machinists of the day were very astute, I don't think any but the most determined and non-thinking would have seen such a project through to completion. A lot of work could have been saved if these guys had read a book, talked to an engineer well versed in aerodynamics, or simply talked to a real dry lakes competitor.

Keeping in mind that few had the temperament, mindset or access to equipment required to do your own thing, it's easy to see why the bolt-on stuff was so popular. Some of the ones I remember were:

Bumper add-ons, wings, tubular grille guards and bumper

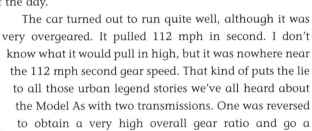

guard extensions. Tailpipes – fancy chrome tips. Pipes – a bolt-on in many cases or a trip to the muffler shop.

Skirts – an easy one for most, they usually required only setting in place and pulling the locking lever over.

Hubcaps – an easy one, just as our mag wheels are today. The most popular one was the single bladed bar flipper model. With skirts, only two were required. Lowering – not done by most, a few would use shallow lowering blocks on the cars that would accept them. Dropped axles were few and far between. Seems like these started showing up in the late '40s.

Chrome pieces – these went on the front edge of the rear fenders of some cars, ostensibly to stop rock chips, but mainly for the shiny bit. They were usually stainless or chrome plated.

Headlight eyebrows – in most cases just a bolt-on replacement for the stock headlight rim.

The famous blue dots – strangely enough, and in view of their popularity today, they were not often seen. The few that were got busted by the local gendarmes pretty fast. Aside from simply being against the law, the Police thinking was that only Police Bikes got to run blue lights. They didn't want anybody to mistake the blue dots for a Police bike. A bit bogus to me, the Police blue lights were visible for a long ways off and the blue dots weren't. Not to mention the disparity in vehicle size! I'm still amazed today at those who run these dim little lights. In view of the investment in time and labor in some of our cars it seems to be taking a bit of a chance. Different hood ornaments – the Flying Winged Female was popular. Some other styles were even lighted.

License plate frames – several different styles. A really popular one even into the late '50s were the square ones with glass over the license plate. After getting pulled over a couple of times, most guys removed the glass.

License plate reflectors – the coolest were the little US shield ones. They worked great on bicycles and since they came with wing-nuts they didn't stay on the cars too long. Even though a lot of bicycles ended up with them, if the wing-nuts were used, they didn't last very long on the bicycles either. Live by the sword, die by the sword. 'Tis only fair...

Interior chrome plated dash pieces – in most cases fitted to the Fords and these replaced the whitish-yellow plastic on the dashboards. Sometimes removed later due to reflected sunlight really blinded the driver.

Shift knobs – many times home made from layers of clear lucite and colored glue. An easy project and done in many high school craft classes.

Brody knobs.

Different style horns – my uncle had a three tone model that would play sorta recognizable tunes. Bermuda bells were popular and a few had the Wolf Whistle that ran off vacuum.

Whitewall tire paint, as real whitewalls were few and far between.

A popular trick was to reverse the Ford column shift with the shift lever ending up on the left side of the column with resulting reversal of the shift pattern.

Bolt-on portholes similar to the chrome portholes on the Buicks of the day. Generally these were looked down upon. Don't know why for sure, maybe because they required a hole drilled in the fender or simply because they were uncool. It does seem that they were more popular out of state than within. One reason I think, is the add-on portholes were the point where the bounds of good taste, at least for rods and customs, were exceeded. There does come a point where a car does earn the dreaded POS title, said title having nothing to do with condition, but more to do with style. No hard and fast rules, if you saw one you knew it. Easy as that.

Tall radio antennae on the rear bumper. The thinking here is that reception is improved due to the added height, but as most found, the reception went down the tubes somewhat as the tuning of the tall antenna did not match the frequencies involved in the AM band. (A small bit of trivia I used to listen to a stereo AM radio station in the early '60s. How do you think they did that one? The answer is simple and no electronic esoterica involved.) My Dad's friend had one of these on his '41 Chevy coupe, but it was soon pulled off due to it hitting the roof and trunk every time he stopped.

Foglights were a popular bolt-on. I heard many discussions of the merits between the clear lensed ones and the amber lensed ones. The real trick with these things is their accurately focused beam. Not much light spills off to one side or the other to create additional reflections in the mist. My choice for the Ranger were the amber ones. The Mustang has the factory clear ones, although they're called driving lights, probably due to litigation problems. Witness the bolt on roll bars for pickups are now called "Sport Bars". An old joke that makes the rounds every year is that you can always tell the cars and trucks from the San Joaquin valley. They're the only ones with fog lights. They are quite common in this Central California valley that I live in. An area well known for it's severe and long lasting fogs.

Southern California has basically two seasons, rainy season and brushfire season. Toss in a few earthquakes and mud slides and life gets real interesting real fast. Central California has basically four seasons: Spring, Summer, Rain, Fog. Sometimes we don't see the sun for a month straight and when we do, we may get another month of fog. That's one reason the foglights are big sellers up here.

And finally spotlights, a cool accessory on some cars and a useful one too. Easily installed with a bit of drilling, although you'd better be careful. Miss with the big drill and you've chewed up the front post pretty good. You just had to think about it for a bit, like any other hot rod project. Kinda like that old carpenter's maxim of – measure twice, cut once. 'Course, what happens with me is the: "I cut it off twice and it's still too short ......"

Dad had a pair of these on his '48 Ford sedan, a neat two door with milled heads, pipes, flippers, black paint and at times skirts. On a trip to Arkansas and driving straight through on a really rainy and pitch black night the headlights went out. A bit of a common happening with these cars with their cotton fabric wiring insulation. Driving straight through meant about 36 hours or so of driving and Dad drove it straight through a couple of times with only a bit of a break when mom took over a couple of times. No problem for the kids, we usually had a comfy bed made up in back and life was easy for us, aside from the requisite brother/sister in-fighting. Anyway, Dad flipped on the spots, aimed 'em down a bit so they were about equal to a low set low beam and kept right on driving.

The cops would give you a ticket for running the spots while driving, but at 3 am in a driving rainstorm and on a virtually empty highway, any thinking cop is gonna find a place to drink coffee and flirt with the waitresses. That's my theory anyway.

The spots were also used at the drive-in to play "tag". As soon as it got dark and before the movie started, somebody would shine their spot on the screen. Pretty soon somebody else got on there too and there were spots of light running all over the screen. The only rule being that when the movie started, you turned 'em off. 'Course there was always the fool that left it on when the credits started rolling and that started a cacophony of horns honking.

There were also baby shoes hanging from the rear view mirror on a few cars. Don't know much about that one, never did figure it out. In my era it was fuzzy dice hanging from the mirror. There were some definite, but unspoken rules about these. When they first started showing up they were hand knit from cashmere, in many varied and bright colors. Pep Boys was probably the first commercial one, and not being an outfit to miss any money-making opportunities, soon started making copies. It wasn't long before other stores followed.

The rules were simple. Purchased dice were looked down upon. Your girl friend hand knitted the dice for you. No girl friend, no dice. 'Course with some girls it was no dice anyway ....

"...We got a lot of usable parts from these cars and lugging a single overhead head back up the hill wasn't too bad. A few guys went so far as to drag a complete engine up the hill using two tow ropes and just pulling it up with a car or pickup. You could pull it 40-50 feet, stop, tie it off to the power pole, take up the slack and do it all over again..."

CHAPTER EIGHTEEN
SHOEBOX SERENADE
IN THE KEY OF C SHARP. OR WAS IT B FLAT?
I CAN NEVER REMEMBER.

Shoebox Fords. First off, there were no strong and precise points of delineation between the rod and custom versions. It was just kinda something you knew. Funny part was a rod could have quite a few body modifications, although not too much was done. The customs would have a lot more body modifications. The customs usually ran stock engines, or very close to stock. Multi carb setups were popular, usually a two carb flathead, most times with stock head and internals and sometimes with aluminum heads, but still with stock internals. The heads and multi-carbs done expressly to add detail to the engine. Kinda went along with the additional chrome and paint under the hood.

One of the real tell-tale points was the use of big and littles on the rod oriented cars. Usually 5.50-15s on the front and 8.20-15s on the back, sometimes the standard 6.70-15s front and 7.60-15s rear. Early stock wheels of choice were the four passenger Thunderbird 14 inch wheels and sometimes the wagon 15 inch wheels as both were six inches wide at the beads. A wide stock wheel for the time. Mixing the 14s and 15s was common as the 14s got the car another 1/2 inch lower in front and there's not much necessity for rotating big and littles anyway. Whitewalls were popular for both contingents for a while, but it soon changed to whitewalls for the customs and blackwalls for the rods. Since the larger rear tires geared the car up and the bigger tires got more bite we found out pretty quickly that the '49-'51 and even up to '54 drivetrains just wouldn't cut it. The reason it stopped at '54 was that was the latest car our little group owned for a while.

Shoebox Fords.......there were no strong and precise points of delineation between the rod and custom versions. It was just kinda something you knew.

Believe it or not, we found these same fragile drivetrains would live fairly well behind an overhead engine for a couple of reasons, mainly because we babied 'em a bit. The other because the overheads would get the tire spinning and the spinning tire is a safety valve. With the limited torque of the flatheads it took a more violent engagement of the clutch to get the tires spinning and many times the tires would bite good and drive train parts got puked out on the street, usually transmissions, although axles were next on the list. Occasionally a u-joint would let go and that was usually the end of your custom driveshaft, plus a few other things.

We got smart and started using the transmissions that came with the GM overheads or simply swapped in the Cad-LaSalle, Olds, Buick or Packard stick shift transmissions. Sometimes the guys with the non-Chevy engined cars would keep the factory four speed Hydro that came with these GM engines. In the case of the Fords the later three speed T-85 Interceptor heavy duty three speeds would be used or the Ford automatics would get swapped in. A much better way to go.

The Ford contingent soon learned to swap in the much stronger Spicer station wagon rear ends. These were a bolt-in and came with 11 inch brakes. After switching ends due to mismatched brake sizes after some serious highway panic stops, the station wagon front brakes, also 11 inch, were bolted in. Some Velvetouch lining, same stuff as the circle track guys used, and you had some really good brakes. The only disadvantage with the Velvetouch was a bit of morning sickness when they were cold. It was a highly overrated problem and we found that a couple of blocks driving and a couple of stops and they worked great. A lot of guys didn't like them as initially they didn't stop well until broken in. Break-in was simple and was pretty much 10 hard stops from 60 mph down to 15 mph, done in rapid succession. That and just driving for a few miles made 'em work better than any other drum brake linings in use at the time. At least amongst the stuff we knew about and could actually get our hands on.

We probably did pretty well here, we usually got our brakes relined at a small shop in North Hollywood right around the corner from CT Automotive, one of America's best speed shops and located near the Burbank Airport. They did a lot of Velvetouch linings for airplane brakes so we simply figured if airplanes used it, circle track guys used it and they worked much better than the fade-prone linings of the day, then it was definitely the "hot setup".

Aside from having a straight body, and probably a few primer spots here and there on the rods, the body modifications were pretty much limited to filling the holes on the front and rear decks where either the letters, ('49) or the plastic shields, ('50-'51) were, removing the bumper guards and bolting on a bullnose. The bullnose was simply a formed piece of stainless, sometimes a chrome plated piece, that went in place of the stock Ford hood ornament. Try to find one of those today!

I ended up running the stock piece for a while as I dropped the garage door on it breaking the plastic fin that stuck out of the hood ornament base. The fin, with the mounting holes broken off, then sunk down in the cast chrome-plated piece and kinda looked cool. There's a silver lining in every cloud right? Although in this case it was chrome plated.

A lot of rods ended up fully nosed and decked. Most times the front ends were lowered, sometimes a lot. Most times not so low. When the jacked up look came in during the early '60s some of us simply ran stock, uncut front springs and the stock sized 6.70-15 tires. Running skirts was de rigueur on customs and running them on a rod could get you drummed out of the corps. I believe skirts were popular on most cars in the mid-west and back east, but not so in California. Every now and then a new kid, from out of state, would show up in town and it wasn't long before the skirts were hung up in the garage.

One popular modification on the four door cars was the removal and filling in of the rear door handles. A few of the rods got frenched headlights and sometimes the taillights too. A popular modification for the '51s was the removal of the chrome windsplit for the larger '51 taillights and the bolt-in substitution of '49 and '50 taillights with the small quarter panel holes filled in. Sometimes the '49-'50 taillights would be frenched, most times not.

Another cool one was to lead the seam over the rear fenders which looked good on either a rod or a custom. A couple of neat little tricks I stumbled into with these cars was the split front seat could be replaced with the four door front seat. It bolted right in and was usable in the coupes and two door sedans. Never thought about it at the time, but the seat bottom was probably the same in all models. Since the seat back was mounted on the seat bottom pivots, it was a simple matter to remove the bolts that held the seat back solidly in place and you had a pivoting seat back. The four door front seat looked kinda cool in the coupes with the requisite TJ tuck and roll running all the way across. Rear seat access was a bit more difficult as the four door seat didn't go quite as far forward or tilt inward as did the two door seats.

That part was okay, as I was the driver, no problem for me. 'Course being a gentleman, I was always right there to assist the short skirted young ladies into the back seat. Many times ending up with a car full of young ladies as many times I ran sister's girlfriends and some female friends of my own across town and to the skating rink. Lothario I'm not, just a guy with a car in the right place at the right time.

The other cool one was the ease in removing the complete dash from these cars. Aside from either disconnecting the wiring or leaving it connected in most cases and leaving the components hanging, the dash was removed by simply unbolting two bolts from the steering column, two bolts from the sides at the bottom and removing about six sheet metal screw screws from the top where it went under the already removed windshield molding. This made life easy for a couple of reasons. Access for wiring and other things was great and it really made life easy during engine swaps as we had learned we could cut the transmission tunnel out of the '57-'59 Fords, taking a bit of the firewall and some of the floor and simply bolting, or better yet, welding it in. Bolt-ins worked well if things were trimmed back smooth and a coat of undercoat was applied top and bottom. Another part that was an advantage here, was to get enough of the donor car firewall so the hanging throttle pedal came with it. The '59 Ford throttle pedal was a good one for swaps as it did away with trying to adapt the clumsy underfloor throttle mechanism on these cars. All it took was an accurately placed hole saw and two drilled holes. It was a really good setup in these cars and went a long way toward making life easy during swaps.

Another little touch in the interior was to reverse the interior windshield molding, the center one. That placed the mirror down a ways and was a cool touch. We found that the slightly larger and semi-oval interior rear view mirror out of a '50s era Chryco car was a bolt-in and we much preferred them. Since we were young and flexible the passenger assist straps hanging from the bottom of the interior lights on both sides were quickly removed. For sure we didn't need that "old folks" stuff.

In my area we obtained some of the lighter weight parts for free at a couple of different locations. None of the Midnight Auto Supply stuff, just hitting a couple of areas where people dumped cars and one where cars really did go off the cliff. Although many times the wind machines in the orchards lost their carburetors when somebody got a new multi-carb intake manifold. These things were always a target for some. The wind machines almost always ran Ford flathead motors. Wind machines are used in citrus orchards to stir up the air when the temperatures get below about 28 degrees. That keeps the frost from settling on the fruit. Once the frost season is in, it's an all night and sometimes all day struggle to get ready for the next night's frost.

In the pre-smog era, smudge pots were also used. These were a device with round circular tank at the bottom and roughly four foot smoke stack. They were filled with crude oil I believe and the draft was set to make a lot of smoke. The smoke helped to heat the air and also helped keep the frost off the fruit. You could always tell when the frost was on, the whole countywide area would have a layer of smoke that took most of the day to dissipate. Since we were young, strong, determined and broke, we found that getting parts from the wrecked and abandoned cars was a good deal. Although sometimes you'd wonder while you were dragging parts up a steep dirt hill.

Our favorite place was a barranca where cars would get pushed over a 150-200 foot high cliff which really tore 'em up, or the more usual just shove 'em over the adjacent very steep hill and these weren't crunched up too bad. We got a lot of usable parts from these cars and lugging a single overhead head back up the hill wasn't too bad. A few guys went so far as to drag a complete engine up the hill using two tow ropes and just pulling it up with a car or pickup. You could pull it 40-50 feet, stop, tie it off to the power pole, take up the slack and do it all over again. Usually you'd find four guys or more and once the engine was up on top it had the heads pulled and it was manhandled up a ramp into a pickup. A whole lotta work. Heads and wheels were about it for us, although we did get a Plymouth trans out once. It was really easy as the car was upside down.

Dragging it up the hill was another matter though. With only two of us it was a struggle.

The toughest place was up in the mountains where cars slid off the road in one particular place and would end up 500-600 feet down a very steep hill. Said hill was about 1500 feet high, but the cars would get stopped by the large boulders almost half way down. We rolled a fully inflated spare off this hill once, with each bounce getting bigger than the last. When it finally went out of sight it was probably going 80+ mph, must have covered a quarter mile in the air on the last bounce and was crashing through the underbrush and down the river. Anybody fishing down there was in serious danger. We had no idea it would go so far, so fast and never did it again.

Getting parts off these cars was really a struggle and about the heaviest parts we got out of them were interior panels, trim, radios and that was about it. Once you got back up top with your little freebie, and after doing the three steps forward and sliding back two you were about done for the day.

A few other things we did with the '49-'50 Fords: (The reason I do not speak of the '51 Ford is that no one in our group ever owned one. No special reason, it just happened that way.) We removed the cigarette lighter and stuck in a two terminal GM style, marine starter button in the now empty hole. This was done for a couple of reasons. After an engine swap, almost always a GM engine, the original Ford starter push button on the left side of the dash was unusable. For Fords it simply went to ground to complete the circuit. For the GM engines, the starter button was used to energize a wire to the starter solenoid. It was cool in that, to start the car, you turned on the key that was still in the stock position to the right of the steering column and that put your thumb right on top of the starter button. Imagine, starting a car with one hand! The stock Ford starter button was left where it was and many times used to operate an aftermarket horn.

When the neato metalflaked clear vinyl, three spoked steering wheels started coming in, there were no provisions to operate a horn. The starter button was quickly put in service as the horn button. A funny one here was little brother's '54 Ford with built up Y-Block, automatic trans, 4.88 Spicer rear end, station wagon brakes all around. In fact, he's the one that discovered the easy swap with the station wagon brakes. After he'd done his '54 we found the '52-'53 wagon 11 inch front brakes were also a bolt in on our '49-'50 coupes. Anyway, he'd done the metalflake steering wheel bit to his '54 too and since it had a key operated starter switch he stuck a push button for the horn under the driver's side floormat right about where the clutch would normally go. Every damn time I got in his car to drive it, I went for the clutch, stickshift guy that I was, and promptly scared heck out of myself He did derive a great deal of enjoyment out of it. Paybacks are hell I guess.

Although I did drive his car quite a few times at the drag strip, and even though busy doing the Fordomatic shifter dance I never stepped on the horn button during a race. In case you've never heard of it, the Ford-'O' shifter dance went like this; keep in mind this is a three speed automatic with only two selections available on the shift column, low and drive. Low was low gear and drive took you through all three gears. Later versions would have three selections and these were low only, D1 which was second, and high. The car as you may have guessed started out in second gear and shifted automatically to high. D2 was low, second and high with the car starting out in low and progressing through the gears automatically and in order. The little Ford 'O' shifter dance was required with either style Fordomatic if you wanted to take advantage of the higher revving capabilities of a built engine. With the earlier style two selection type auto – stage the car in low gear, either power brake, (most popular), or flash the converter, (worked good if the carburetion was sharp and crisp and the car bit well – not many knew the flash trick) to launch. Shift to drive at the desired point. After the shift into second, pull the shift lever back to low. The trans would stay in second and not shift back to low until a fairly low rpm was attained. Shift to drive at the desired point whereupon the trans would go into high and stay there until the run was completed.

A few guys didn't know this method and would find if the trans was simply shifted to drive after the low gear launch and left there, the second gear shift would come before it was really wanted. The same basic idea for the later three selection type auto. Launch in low, shift to D1 for second, back to low and shift back to D1 for high when desired. Sounds a little offbeat and a bit difficult, but it was easy to do and you did have some time to pull it back into low after the one-two shift. It was always fun to demonstrate it to those that were unfamiliar with it. Got some interesting reactions at times.

In my little town, the 45 rpm record players were not to be seen. There were a lot of rods and quite a few customs, but the rear seat speaker and later the reverb unit was about it. One car that I can remember had a 45 rpm record player mounted on the rear package shelf, probably for the display value. I heard that it was not one of the players that you could actually use while the car was driving. These had a specially weighted arm among other things and generally wouldn't skip on a bump. The owner, a nice guy, also left quite a few of his records up on the package shelf too. Again for the display value I think. That came to an end when he returned and found the hot sun and the closed windows had made a nice little selection of pre-frisbee frisbees. Useless now as far as good sound qualities went, they sure did sail good when tossed.

Even though the '49s and '50s were very similar there were quite a few differences. The '50 really was an improved version and is the better car all things being equal. The '51 as far as I know did not have much changed from the '50 except for a few exterior changes in trim and grille and with a different dash and some minor interior changes.

I always liked the classy '49-'50 dash, but one project I never got around to was installing a '51 dash in my '50 coupe and loading it up with S-W instruments. I am a bit of an instrument crazy and have nine of them in my roadster. The basic five plus tach, vacuum, fuel pressure and trans temperature. I'm thinking that three more would be nice, including a voltmeter, why not? A couple of EGT gauges would be interesting, one for each bank. I also run a S-W vacuum gauge in my Mustang and Ranger. A most useful and highly recommended instrument. My dad used to run these and taught me quite a bit about deciphering them.

Some of the differences between the '49s and '50s: Bumpers – '49s are smooth and the '50s have a horizontal beltline rolled into them. Hood ornaments – the '49 is similar, but taller. The '49 says FORD in individual letters front and rear while the '50 has a plastic shield front and rear. Front grilles – the '49 has the smaller, more graceful and better looking teardrop shaped turn/park lights at the grille bar ends. The '50 has larger turn/park lights, rectangular in shape with a larger chrome surround. The '49 has wide V belts, the '50 and up flatheads, have the narrow ones. The '49 and '50 sway bars are different in size and method of attachment. The '50 has much improved door hinges, door latches, door handles, trunk hinges, trunk hold up braces and latch. The '50 has a gas door, the '49 has a chrome plated cap. The steering wheels are similar, but the horn rings are different with the '49 having a dropped horizontal bar and the '50 having it roll over the top, kind of like a rounded "D".

Dashes are similar, the '49 has a small vertical chrome bar close to and on either side of the speedometer and the '50 has a chrome plated cap at each end. Heater controls are different with the '49 having push pull knobs and the '50 having more modem side sweeping levers in a small nicely lit separate panel under the ignition switch. The '49 dash knobs are the desirable ones being fully round and chrome plated. The '50s are half round with a small concave stainless plate in the center. Interior door window moldings are plain in the '49 while the '50s, at least the Custom models, have a plastic badge with a very stylized car designed within. (When I say Custom, it pertains to the models offered. Basically the Deluxe, Custom and Crestliner.)

Not a lot of guys spent money or had the money to spend on too many other things. With a family and all, cars for most were basically transportation. But it was a whole other story for a single guy with a good job.

It seems the shoebox term came in around the late '60s and it also seems that it was perhaps used by Detroit factory designers as a generic term way before that. They probably used it in front of a magazine writer and it got into the language from there. I understood it to apply to the '49-'51 Fords exclusively, but it does turn out to be a good term for other cars too.

In fact, '49-'51 Ford shoebox fan that I am, it looks like a better name for the '55-'56 Chevies than Tri-Year Chevies. I'm not so sure about the '57, just callin' them a '57 Chevy pretty much says it all in my book.

Meeting people is one of the great parts about our hobby. It's a bit of a surprise sometimes to find that the old guy down the street was totally immersed in it at one time and has many interesting stories to tell. Sometimes, when they shut up long enough, their wives have some interesting stories of their own to tell. Not always about cars from either one, just interesting stuff, although the cars are my favorite stories.

There's a lot that just cruise down the ruts of life and don't have a whole lot, if any, interesting things to relate. But once you find the right ones, it's downright fascinating. Just gotta listen I guess.

The woodies in my small coastal town were mostly the '49-'51s. Some of the wood patterned later ones, usually Fords were also called woodies, as were the older Model A and up to '48s. As far as we were concerned, they were darned near all wood or looked it, so they were woodies. Bein full of surfboards, girls, food and beer sure didn't hurt. Just 'cause I was there doesn't make me right. Nor does it make me wrong. Every place and every time has their own rules and it's not always "set in stone" so to speak. Witness the pre-'48 argument. There's a lot of really great post '48s out there and where the heck do we cut them off at? Best one I've heard so far, was the post '48s are cut off simply due to lack of space. Any thinking promoter is gonna want to more than fill the venue with cars, his main interest is in making money. That's what business is all about. If I was a promoter and was looking out the gate at several hundred post 48's not being let in, for sure I'd have a few tears in my eyes. I for one like 'em all.

"...Virtuoso was the right word for this guy, we were just stunned at what he could do and in front of a crowd too. Not a problem for him. It was obvious to us that we had a long way to go. If we could ever get there was a whole other question..."

CHAPTER NINETEEN
IN BETWEEN THE RODS AND THE CUSTOMS

OR - PERHAPS ON THE OUTSIDE LOOKING IN - BUT WITH A VERY GOOD VIEW

We tend to group the enthusiast cars using somewhat tight definitions. We're not gonna get into the sporty cars, classics, race cars or resto's here. Simply the cars that made the street scene and did the occasional drag race bit. Rods and customs are fairly easy to tell apart, especially nowadays. Rods have a lot of variety, although they are usually powered by the ubiquitous small block Chevy. Customs have a lot of variety and almost all of them are powered by the small block Chevy.

It's easy to see why the small block Chevy is so popular, the rods have a lot of aftermarket "swap the engine in goodies" that make life easy and most of the customs can make use of a great deal of this stuff. There's never been an engine that had so much stuff made for it, both from the factory and from the aftermarket. Aside from the boredom factor with the small block Chevy on the street, they are an excellent choice and are a darn good engine. Go to the drag strip or dry lakes and you'll not find too many boring small block Chevy engines. These things can be made to run darned good and in a lot of cases better than good. I'm guessing here, but the small block Chevy probably holds more records in any venue than all the rest put together.

I look at my own rod, a '32 highboy roadster and think perhaps I should go no further. Pictures of it taken in the recent past show a simple, black, fairly typical roadster.

In the competition arena, there are a lot of different things to be seen on the small block Chevy. On the street though, they are normally stock and are just used to hold up the seemingly requisite Edelbrock valve covers and air cleaners. As noted, there are considerable differences today in the line separating the rods and the customs. I believe the Customs of today are much better thought out as far as design goes and for sure are better built. Rods of the past generally were built pretty good. They had to be, generally all the workmanship and parts were open to view. Not much stuff got hidden on the rods, one badly done and visible component was enough to earn the dreaded POS title. Not so with the customs. A lot of questionable engineering was done with them and generally speaking it was easy to hide, especially suspension components which were pretty much invisible. The out of sight out of mind theory.

Some of my friends bought these cars in later years. We were stunned to find some really amateurish, poor quality and downright dangerous work done on some of them. We'd seen these cars around for several years and figured they were most desirable and worth having. Generally they were, but a couple of them were a hard lesson for the new owners. What was the failing of most Customs in years past was the lack of a plan. Rods were easy as we were usually just copying a typical racer and that was an easy theme. Customs on the other hand had many modifications made, usually as the guys could afford them, and there was a lot of clashing styles and things that just didn't go together. That's why there are only a small handful of famous customs as compared to rods. The ones that are still famous today were put together in such a manner that all the design elements flowed together very well. They were, and in many cases still are, beautiful cars and excellent examples of the builders art. Others that remain famous generally broke new ground in the Custom ranks and made quite a statement. These cars were built by the Alexander Brothers, Starbird, Barris and others equally famous.

Barris did turn out some strange cars, but that was probably just following the desires of the customer. The customer's not always right, but the customer is always the guy with the money.

I don't know where Big Daddy Roth fits into all this. First time I saw him was on one of our many forays into the LA area, hitting all the speed shops we could, even when it was only one of us that had the money to spend on one piece of speed equipment. There were a couple of rod and custom type car lots that sold only these types of car. I believe one of them was called "Stick City" and I think that's the place where I first saw BDR. He was a big guy, and was striping a black '51 Chevy hardtop. The Chevy was a great looking car and we were amazed to see BDR laying on long and smooth lines with no guides at all. To say that he was skilled was a bit of an understatement. We had found a source for striping brushes and had done a bit on our own cars and those of our friends and fancied ourselves to be pinstripers. Seeing BDR pinstripe that Chevy was akin to being an amateur musician carrying a worn guitar down the street and stumbling onto a violin virtuoso playing on the corner.

Virtuoso was the right word for this guy, we were just stunned at what he could do and in front of a crowd too. Not a problem for him. It was obvious to us that we had a long way to go. If we could ever get there was a whole other question.

Interesting thing for me was that his patterns on each side of the car matched very well, even those that were not directly comparable. I see a few modern and famous pinstripers today laying on some very nice lines, but in many cases, in fact most, the patterns aren't really symmetrical. Their comment is that it makes no difference as you can only see one side of the car at a time. My comment is BS. Let's face the truth here. Some of these guys, and it only seems to be a few, are knocking out all the cars they can and the recipients of their labors seem to want the famous name on the car more than a good job of pinstriping. Take a stroll around both sides of a car done by a pinstriper, big name or an unknown. I think you'll find it interesting.

Maybe that's the best part about BDR, the only category he really fits into is the one of his own making. He's for sure, a one of a kind guy. I think he still has a lot to show us.

As far as lines of separation in the rods and customs of the past goes, there was a lot of overlap. Sometimes a typical rod, say a three window Deuce got so much custom bodywork that it really fell into the realm of the custom and was a long ways away from the rod. It seems to me too, that there is a definite place to stop the building and modifying on some of our rods. After awhile they just get too loaded down with stuff. The Model T roadsters are a good example. One of my very favorite cars, and I did own one, but that's a whole other story. To me, it seems the best ones are very basic. After all they are basically a copy of a genuine race car with overtones from both the circle track cars and the dry lakes cars. Do they really need all the extra stuff?

I look at my own rod, a '32 highboy roadster and think perhaps I should go no further. Pictures of it taken in the recent past show a simple, black, fairly typical roadster. Some things up close are more complex than other similar roadsters, but it's gotten to the point where it's close to looking "too busy". I think it happened when I decided to stick in a roll bar.

I'm pretty much a safety oriented guy and thought it would be nice to have a place to hide if it ever went over. Viewing the roll bars and typical heights of the occupants heads shows many roll bar equipped roadsters to have the bar much too low. Looks good when parked, kinda useless in a real emergency. Once the roll bar went in, a little measuring showed a top would go on right over it. And once the top mechanism and oak bows were obtained it was easy to see where the bows should be installed. The bows do go in a particular place, but the height is pretty much the customer's choice. There are a few inches of leeway. The roll bar fits nicely just under the top near the back, and you can see out of the slightly bigger than a mail slot window pretty well. Heck you can even wear cowboy hats in it with the top up. Looks cool, right up to the point where you get in or out, and knock the hat off on the top. Most impressive for the spectators. It's hard to be cool chasing a rolling cowboy hat down the street. Not that I've ever done that you understand. Ball caps are the ones of choice for most roadster occupants and for good reason. Wind being only one.

More than likely your top kit, (and that's probably what the upholstery shop will get if you have them install the top, very few shops will make them from scratch, although most will allude to doing so) will have the zip-out or unsnap larger rear window that snaps onto the top straps and holds the flap and the little back window up out of the way. This really helps in the ventilation department. The top does go down okay, it just takes a different method of folding it away. Namely, the angled side braces are allowed to lay down first which allows the top to point nearly straight up and then it will fold down around the roll bar. Doesn't look at first like it will do it, but it does. The normal fold it as you go method won't work here.

The top is a definite advantage and you have a lot of options with one. Removing the top entirely and pulling the hood sides gives the car a completely different look, one that's more competition and hot rod oriented. Strangely enough, the car is much quieter with the top removed. With the top on and everything buttoned up, I've been accused of driving a soft-top coupe. That's okay, because that's pretty much the way I like it. Coupes are my second favorite car anyway.

With this car, I am at a point where it doesn't need anything more than the fine tuning and tinkering we all like to do. Customs in years past blurred the line of demarcation too. Where we lived we found that the local customs were always easy pickings in a race as they usually ran a very close to stock engine, usually with a few dress up items and some pieces chromed. As with all rules, this was not a hard and fast one as some of the customs north of our little coastal California town had some strong running engines. At least the Fords and Mercs did.

Chevies usually stuck with the stock engine, nicely painted, chromed the valve cover and got a chrome air cleaner, sometimes had two carbs, but always had twin pipes. Some of the smoothest and best sounds ever came out of these twice pipe six cylinder Chevies. For just cruising around town the sixes had the "sound". Smooth and mellow are terms that fit quite well.

There were some great sounds to be heard when a good running flathead, built Caddy or Olds went winding through the gears down the old golf course road or blasting down the orange grove two lanes late at night, while you were just standing there watching the taillights disappear into the night. If you were part of an illicit street race, the sounds for the left behind spectators were really great. Most of us could easily recognize which car shifted when and pretty much what was going on. Mix in the chirp of tires when the next gear was hit and it was sweet music indeed.

Seems like the line of demarcation for owners, was that the customs were owned by really cool guys, some of them a little mysterious and some that didn't talk much. We got the impression that they didn't need to say much. They did know something we didn't though and we never figured it out, probably because they didn't talk much. Almost always they were accompanied by a lady friend or two.

Rods were owned by cool guys too. A different kind of cool, and for the most part they would talk to you provided the majority of your questions weren't totally dumb. We soon learned to keep our mouths shut and just listen. There were many gems of information to be learned, especially if one of the older guys was having a problem or building an engine and got to talking about it to the other older guys. Just listening taught us a lot. Sort of a "Learning at the feet of the Master" kinda thing. Now that I think back on it, I can see it was a Zen sort of an education.

Once in a while we got brave and ventured way out of town. Santa Monica, Long Beach and the San Fernando Valley. Guys there had cars similar to ours and sometimes they cleaned our clocks and sometimes we cleaned theirs. Trouble with running against an out of town car was you didn't really know what he had, whether he raised the hood or not. Most times he didn't. It was sorta like running up against a gunslinger that had a double barreled 12 gauge hidden behind his back. Surprise......

We did get an important lesson about customs though. We were in Long Beach one night when a very low un-chopped '50 Merc with dark blue paint came in. It was lowered, had skirts, lakes pipes, was nosed and decked and a club plaque in the back window. The back window was a good place for club plaques as the hanging them on a chain bit from the bumper was not used by most. In fact this is probably done today to copy something people think went on in the late '50s and '60s. The few plaques that did hang from chains dragged, got damaged and in many cases the cheap little chain broke and the plaque was lost. A club plaque was something to be proud of and was usually well taken care of. Next time you're at a swap meet, pick up a couple of the club plaques that are for sale. I'll bet that none of them have drag or scrape marks on the bottom.

We weren't actively looking for a race, as we had found that the LA and Valley cars could many times be very fast. With our mildly cammed, three carbed, aluminum headed, low geared '49-'50 Ford coupes we found ourselves in the dust more than once, although we still figured that most customs were potential victims.

The Merc got the hood raised after a while and we wandered over. A bit of a surprise. Sitting in the engine bay was a four carbed, Chrysler Hemi. We hadn't heard the quote in those days, being a scruffy and unsophisticated lot, but the line; "All things are not as they seem," sure did apply here. I think perhaps Shakespeare said it, if not, he probably ought to get the credit anyway. Old Will was a smart guy.

We wandered away, got in the car and left, sorta feeling like the Gazelle that stood very still while the Lion walked by. We would have been an easy one for sure. It wasn't too much longer that we noticed the custom guys were starting to swap in overhead engines with the Caddy, Olds and Nailhead being the most popular and about in that order. A few Y-blocks got in there, but not too many. What all that meant was, the customs were no longer easy pickin's.

I see that I have wandered a bit from the original premise pertaining to In Between the Rods and the Customs. That's okay. One nice thing about writing these little stories is you get to write what you want and it's kinda funny how wandering down memory lane sets you to thinking about other things that went on at the same time.

There was another group or class of car driven by the younger set that didn't fit into either rod or custom. Generally, they weren't wannabe rod or custom owners, just kids that liked cars, but didn't spend every last dime on them like most of the rod or custom guys did. We just called them "Nice Cars". Usually these cars were the popular models of Ford or Chevy. In a lot of cases they had nice paint, TJ upholstery, nice hubcaps or wheel covers, sometimes chrome wheels, most times pipes and always stock running gear. These guys enjoyed a good looking car and kept them up well, but their main interest was simply good looking transportation. In many cases they were two doors and coupes handed down from somebody in the family. In a few cases they were four doors, but the hot set up done by many and done by one in particular '49 Ford four door owner in our group was to do the nose and deck bit and smooth off the rear outside door handles. The fronts were left as is. This made a good looking car, almost like a two door. They were easily identifiable by a real two door owner, but were readily accepted by us.

'Course, what really clinched it for this car was the good running 3/8 x 3/8 flathead that would just walk away from our cars. Later on he stuck a Nailhead in it and we pretty much never caught up to him. At least on the street. For us, being able to buy one of these "nice cars" when they became available was a great score. The whole car was there and finished. All it needed, at least to our power hungry little minds, was a good engine/trans swap. Some cars even got a whole new junkyard Spicer rear end bolted in.

Cars driven by those in our age group had a wide range of styles and types. There was the "daddy's car", usually a four door sedan, Ford, Chevy or Plymouth and in a few cases some other make. These were also known as "mommy's car". Either name was quickly applied, and the hapless driver just had to grin and bear it. These cars were driven on dates at times, but most times just driven to a central meeting area and soon abandoned for the shotgun seat, or even the back seat of a rod or custom. Heck, a guy's gotta look good when cruisin'.

Sometimes dad's car was a real classic. One rather offbeat friend regularly drove his folks Franklin sedan all over town and at all hours of the night. It was the family car and had been for a long time. His folks had him late in life and were retired when he got in high school. They went to bed early which meant that he had lots of freedom and made considerable use of it. To his credit, he didn't get into trouble, not so much that he was a good kid, he was, but he was smart and managed to stay out of trouble.

Sometimes dad's car was a really cool one. In the early days of going to the Saugus, California drag strip, one friend's dad bought a new '54 Olds hardtop. He and his dad had a good relationship and dad was more than generous with the car. The kid soon had pipes and chrome plated cut-outs on it and shortly got permission to take it to the Saturday night drags at Saugus. Dad was cool and even went along second time out. Dad turned out to be fairly knowledgeable and pointed out several areas for improvement in the driving area. The kid took the advice and they were running near the front in their stock class several times out.

Of course, there were dad's that bought the kid a brand new car, in some cases really great ones. One I can remember was a nice white '56 Chevy convertible. How would you like to have that one today? It wasn't long before it showed up with pipes, chrome wheels, a dropped front end and the best looking girl in school. The owner was a friendly guy and still had the same group of friends after he got the car as before.

And then there were dad's that supplied the kid with a restored older car. Usually dad was a resto enthusiast and would put a really great car together for the kid to drive. One girl I remember ended up with a beautifully restored Model A sedan. As far as she was concerned it was a real car and she took it everywhere. Much to dad's credit and perhaps a bit to the Ford Motor Car Company it was pretty dependable and never let her down as far as I know.

Sometimes the girls ended up with a really neat car. The girl down the street ended up with a most cherry '50 Ford coupe that I tried to buy, but missed it by five minutes. The girl and dad were going down the walk as I was going up. It was owned by the proverbial little old lady and was absolutely perfect. The car died a sad death. The girl thought of the car as simply transportation and left it parked in the street all the time. There was room in the garage, but opening the door was "too much trouble" so it sat out in the salty coastal fog, got filthy dirty and was eventually sideswiped, totaling it out and rendering it undrivable. It went to the back yard and after a couple of years got a bit rusty and was hauled off to the junkyard.

My little brother is seven years younger than me. A strong enthusiast of drag racing. You can tell simply by looking at his race car. A tube framed, DRCE engined, 8.31 seconds, 166 mph Henry J. I think he got a taste for it when I used to let him drive my Olds engined '50 Ford coupe at the races. His era had a further splitting of car owners. There were still the ones as listed above, but there was now a further division and these were the greasers and the surfers. These labels had nothing to do with any particular ethnic group as both the greasers and the surfers had kids from many different ethnic groups in either camp. Since we lived on the coast, both sides were well represented. The greasers were simply the car oriented guys. Those that actually got dirty and built cars. The faster the better. Plus those, that if they didn't get especially dirty, loved cars anyway, the faster the better. The surfers were just what you think. A loose clique of beach rats that surfed every chance they got. It was amazing how many of them got sick and couldn't make school if the surf was up. In fact, many times when the winter surf was up, the school was a bit deserted.

In our town, surfers and greasers were just friendly jibes and nobody was insulted by either label. Not so in other areas. You had to choose your group and stand by them, either that or you got to bleed a lot. 'Course there were crossings of the lines by the greasers and the surfers just as there was by the rod and the custom owners. Many greasers owned surfboards and many surfers owned really neat cars. Spending a day at the beach when there was good surf, a cooler full of cold drinks and food and a gang of your friends, both girls and guys, was a pretty good deal in anybody's book.

This is the time period when station wagons became popular. You could haul all your buddies, all the surfboards, several girls and several coolers. The surfers that scored woodies early were the lucky ones. It didn't take long for the woodies, a car generally loved only by a few hardy and willing to work hard restorers, to have the prices skyrocket. Surprisingly, most woodies that showed up at the beach were in pretty good shape as in most cases they had been stored indoors and were well taken care of. I never saw one at that time that needed wood replacement. A little varnishing perhaps, but that was about it.

Hearses as well as ambulances got popular with the surfers too. Prices on these stayed within reason, but they were still neat old cars. We did the surf bit in my era also, but surfboards were few and far between. Surfing with a surfboard was pretty much unknown to us until the first Gidget movie came out. Then it took off and just about anybody that could carve wood and work with fiberglass found themselves in the surfboard business. Garages and shops along the coast that sometimes went begging for tenants were soon full of small time surfboard manufacturers.

For us, prior to the surfboard craze, and it was a craze, it swept up and down the coast like an epidemic, bodysurfing was the main interest, sometimes with fins, most times without. That and skimboarding were popular activities at the beach for us, during the daytime anyway.

Nights were another story and grunion hunting was a popular activity. A lot of people that went grunion hunting put it on a par with snipe hunting, although if you lived on the coast it was called "Going to the Submarine Races". There really is such a fish as the grunion and the trick was to hit the monthly high tide just right, remain in the dark and wait for them to come ashore and lay their eggs. Sometimes there are none and sometimes there's a few. Every once in a while, the beach would be totally covered in silvery fish bodies as the grunion washed up on the extreme high tide. Almost always very late, midnight to 2 am were not uncommon times for the grunion to run. The grunion always seemed to come in on a full moon, so flashlights weren't needed and in fact weren't wanted. Campfires close to the water were verboten also, as the grunion generally would not come ashore where there were lights. It didn't take long for a five gallon bucket to get filled with these fish. No poles or gear required, just pick 'em up and toss em in. Then the work began, cleaning them took a while, but there was some good eating to be had.

What usually happened though, we would simply go to the beach, the more deserted the better. There were many totally deserted beaches in the late '50s early '60s both day and night time. Since we had girls, beer, marshmallows and hot dogs it wasn't always grunion that was our main interest. A small bonfire would be built, ostensibly for cooking, but the light and warmth it gave off, a blanket and girl to share it with pretty much made life worth living. Add to that a burned hot dog, a cold beer and a rod parked just over the dunes and it just didn't get much better......

A few explanations about California and it's kids. TJ upholstery – just slang for Tijuana upholstery from Tijuana, Mexico, south of San Diego. A rite of passage for some of California's young men, heck you could buy beer there at 18. The key thing for us though, was the opportunity to get really good tuck and roll upholstery for very reasonable prices. Costs to completely upholster a '50 Ford coupe in high quality US made Naugahyde and Dupont thread ran about $100.00 - $120.00 complete. This included carpets, door, kick and side panels, seats front and rear, sun visors, package tray and headliner. You had to pay a 10% tariff crossing the border back into the US and that was about it, except for the part where you got the car in at 8 am and it got shoved to the back of the shop and you didn't get it out until Midnight or later.

The Mexican workers were skilled, worked hard and turned out a good product. Horror stories about cow dung in the pleats and poor quality materials were just that, BS stories. Cotton was used in the fifties for padding and in later years foam. These jobs were as good as any good car upholstery shop in the US. A similar tuck and roll job done in the US ran in excess of $400.00.

Skimboards: A term generally unfamiliar to anyone that didn't spend time on the coast and they're not seen too much today. Heck we got surfboards, boogie boards, wake boards, wetsuits, so who needs a skimboard? Thing with a skimboard is, you don't need much, a piece of properly shaped plywood and a pair of swim trunks. The skimboard was made of 3/8 inch plywood and sometimes from a perfectly round table top, usually from a smaller table about 2-1/2 to three feet in diameter. The right sized table top made a really good skimboard and some guys showed up with some that antique collectors would love to have today. They were usually made from 3/8 inch plywood about two feet wide and 4- 4-1/2 feet long. The nose was gently rounded and all sharp edges taken off. A cool design was painted on if you or your friends were a bit artistic and then it was painted with a varnish that hopefully wouldn't melt the paint. Sometimes guys would coat them with resin which was a waste of money, as the skimboard flexed and the resin soon cracked and let water in and dry rot was on the way. Regardless, they had a short life, maybe one or two summers and it was time for a new one.

Using them was simplicity itself. A bit of travel to the flatter beaches was required, but usually not far. You could use them on just about any beach, but the flat beaches were the best. Show up at the beach anytime, although high tides were always the best, especially if they were receding. Just stand there as the wave washed up on the flat beaches and when it started draining back out, watch the water depth until it was an inch or so deep and then run parallel to the water, gently drop the board and flop down on it. The best rides were when you timed it just right and the receding water had turned a bit dimpled looking which meant it was almost all gone. Lying down gave quite an impression of speed and it wasn't long before we were standing on the boards and sliding down the beach for well over a hundred yards in some cases.

Best beaches were winter beaches where the surf had chewed a bit of a drop off into the sand making a rounded, somewhat steep drop back to the shallow water. If you did it right, you could ride along the flats in a subtle curve and when you got to the little hill back to the water, sail right down and out into the small incoming waves into water about three feet deep. A good ride indeed.

A couple of other definitions:

Older guy – usually a guy two or three years older than us. Some of the guys that occasionally showed up at the rod runs were really old timers, veterans of WW2 and the Korean war. I say rod runs, but these were just not organized at all, Saturday night parkin' at the drive-in. Burgers, stories, friendly insults, outright lies and sometimes a street race would be set up. These guys were anywhere from 25 to 35 years old. Really old guys, at least from the vantage point of an 18 year old. From the vantage point of today, it looks considerably different.

DRCE – An acronym standing for Drag Racing Corporate Engine. An iron or aluminum block, aluminum heads engine with the block based on the big block Chevy engine. Heads were usually supplied by the marque involved; Pontiacs, Chevy, Olds. Little brother's engine is an Olds, 500 CID, dynoed at 1040 hp on gas with twin dominator carbs only, no nitrous, no blower.

Lakes Pipes – or lakers as they were commonly called. These were a long chrome plated pipe mounted under the rocker panel. It started right under the rear of the front fender and ended just in front of the rear fender. There were shorter ones that got popular later on as they were quite a bit cheaper. These ran from the rear of the front door, maybe a little bit forward of that and stopped in front of the rear fender. Sometimes they had a two bolt cap and were used as cutouts. Sometimes they had an angled turnout and were used as the exhaust pipes replacing the tailpipes. When they were used to actually carry exhaust they usually had a short piece welded in about two feet from the rear where the exhaust gasses entered. Some times guys did the whole magilla and ran a pipe forward from the rear of the muffler to the front of the lakes pipe and exhaust ran the entire length of the lakes pipe. The best setup though was simply using them as cut-outs and retaining the twin pipes under the rear bumper. Sort of a having your cake and eating it too.

Well, all things come to an end, and perhaps that's another line from Shakespeare. California was a most interesting place to grow up. Depending on the season we had anything from snow skiing to surfing to drag racing to motorcycle racing, and most any other thing you could think of. Most times no more than an hour away. Summers were mild and the beaches warm and inviting. We spent many hours there. The remaining hours were spent at work, school and with our cars. I'm just an average guy, I've done a lot of interesting things, mostly with people, family and friends, but a lot with cars. I wouldn't trade the memories for all the money in the world.......

"...He lost interest in the car and gave it to me. I dragged it home and realizing that the repairs would have taken a considerable amount of work and owning the coupe and the Buick, I just didn't have the time. We pieced it out and took it to the junkyard. A sad end for a nice little car..."

CHAPTER TWENTY
OLDS VS FORD
OLDS ROCKET VS FORD Y-BLOCK (AND OTHER TANGENTS).
LOST IN THE SIXTIES (AND OTHER PLACES)

Little brother's first car was a really cherry '54 Ford two door sedan. Grandfather bought it new. Our dad bought it from him. Little brother bought it from Dad. (I missed out every time it got sold.) Little brother ran it for a while in stock condition. He eventually got into fixing it up. He made some nice veneer wood panels for the doors and side panels that accentuated the stock door panel upholstery nicely. This little mod became popular locally and he did several cars for his friends. When he wanted the interior painted he asked me to do it as a few of my paint projects had turned out okay. The car was originally a light metallic green, as was the interior. We shot the dash and the window frames in a black lacquer. It turned out to be the best paint work I had done yet. They were so glossy and smooth, rub-out was never required. (And I still don't know what I did right!) At the time I had been running my '50 Ford coupe with the first Olds engine for about a year.

Little brother's first car was a really cherry '54 Ford two door sedan. Grandfather bought it new. Our dad bought it from him. Little brother bought it from dad. (I missed out every time it got sold.)

Brother liked the hot rod thing and got a 312 Y-block to hop up and install. Some of the similarities between these cars were surprising once we started thinking about it. Bore and stroke; Ford = 3.860" x 3.44 – A 312 bored .030" over. Olds = 3.875" x 3.412" – A 303 bored .125" over. CID; Ford = 322" - Olds = 324". Intake and exhaust valve diameters were just about the same. Compression ratios were similar. Ford = 9.0:1, Olds = 9.25:1. Intake ports were arranged differently with the Olds ports being larger. Exhaust ports were similar in size, although the Olds had 'siamesed' center exhaust ports. We both ran Engle cams with just about the same lift and timing. The Ford ran 1-3/4 inch header tubes, Tri-Y style into about a three inch collector. The Olds ran two inch header tubes, four individual tubes into an oval collector about 2-1/4 inches by 10 inches. Both cars ran two inch exhaust and tail pipes with Thunderbird mufflers, same part number.

Both cars had a factory four barrel intake with the same small Holley four barrel carb. (I had bored mine out, primarily to clear the Holley butterflies, and ended up with an open plenum chamber) Both had Mallory coils and the same air cleaners. Both ran the Ford station wagon Spicer rear end with 4.27:1 gears. Eleven inch Station wagon brakes were on the front and rear of both. I ran home made traction masters. He ran the stock springs for a while and eventually went to the clamped spring set-up. (As I did when the 'CHP' stopped me for the 'too low' traction bars. (They had a double bar setup and looked like ladder bars at first glance. We weren't trying to copy ladder bars. The material we had on hand to make these would not have been strong enough with just one bar.)

Tire sizes were the same, front and rear. The Ford ran a rebuilt Cruise-O-Matic while the Olds ran a Cad-La Salle stick shift. Had Sun 7000 RPM range Tachometers in both and both cars were similar in weight, his perhaps 100lb. heavier. Both were metallic green. Mine dark, his light. We didn't set out to consciously copy one another, it just seemed to work out that way.

The interesting thing was – he could never beat me in a drag race. My car ran mid to high 90s and mid to high 14s. His car ran low to mid 90s and mid to high 15s. Driving skills were about equal. Both cars launched equally well. He eventually got some 4.88:1 gears for the Spicer (from a Jeep dealer). The 4.88s didn't help that much as the car was somewhat traction limited with the tires we ran. (Used to get a lot of strange looks on the freeway though. Car always sounded like it was in second gear.) I think the main disparity was that his car may have weighed about 100lb more. The Y-block intake port arrangement was: On each side, the front two cylinder intakes were stacked one above the other. Same thing with the rear two cylinder intakes. I always felt the Olds had better breathing capabilities due to a straighter shot into the cylinders and the slightly larger port size.

He eventually painted the car a nice dark metallic green similar to that on modern Ford Explorers. It was a good looking little car. Later on we built a nice twin four barrel set-up for it using some little AFBs we got at the junkyard and rebuilt. Ran some nicely bent, polished copper lines for fuel and he got some nice air cleaners for it somewhere. Eventually it dipped into the high 14s. (He still couldn't beat my car. He sold the car to a friend, keeping the tachometer, and bought dad's '62 Plymouth. He also bought a Harley Sportster, in a basket, that turned into a nice running bike.

I bought the '63 Chevy pickup from little brother in 1974 and installed a Corvette four speed, mag wheels and painted it Porsche Red. It was a looker and I drove it everywhere.

The friend that purchased the '54 was kinda new to fast motors. Usually you could hardly hurt the Ford flathead or the Chevy six by over revving the engine. When stock, the small carburetors somewhat limited the rpms. He used to shift it by sound as he had with his old Chevy six. It wasn't too long before he blew the Y-block into many little pieces. He pieced out what was left and bought a 389 Pontiac with Hydro. Now a Pontiac rear pan sump motor would have been a tough swap into a Ford front pan sump chassis. He was not to be deterred. That was about the time the jacked up look was popular. 10% engine setbacks were also popular at the drags. (Measured from front spindle centerline to the first spark plug. Eg: 115 inch wheelbase, engine set no further back than 11inches utilizing above measurement technique.) This was a legal setup for the gas class cars. He cut the firewall and part of the floor out, way too much, and stuck in the Pontiac. It only went in far enough for the Pontiac pan to clear the Ford crossmember. They made up some kind of a gas pedal bolted darn near under the brake pedal and drove it for a very short while on the street with virtually no firewall and not much floor.

The Pontiac self-destructed shortly thereafter, (with a little help from a heavy throttle foot and no tach.) He lost interest in the car and gave it to me. I dragged it home and realizing that the repairs would have taken a considerable amount of work and owning the coupe and the Buick, I just didn't have the time. We pieced it out and took it to the junkyard. A sad end for a nice little car. (For me too – I always wanted that car, when I got finally got it, it was pretty destroyed) Little brother got drafted. Sold the '62 Plymouth. He kept the 'Sportster' (which he still has under a cover in the garage, it's still a cherry).

Little brother went to Vietnam and he came back with some saved up cash. Somewhere along this time he bought a really clean '63 Chevy one ton pickup. He was the second owner. The original purchaser optioned it out a little strangely we felt. It had the 'Fleetside' bed option and the large rear window. The running gear was V-8 motor with 3-speed stick; (he had deleted the heater and radio and stuck in a cheap Sears heater and radio). It was basically a deluxe truck with no options – weird!

Little brother and dad rebuilt a 327 after wearing out the original motor and stuck it in. It was a strong runner after that. I bought the truck from little brother about '74 and found the heater would not cut it in cold weather. I know, it's California, but occasionally one of those California Fall cold snaps with the daytime peak in the low 90s and below freezing at night would drift into the area. Returning home after a late swing shift about 2.00 am it was 27° F. and I had only a T-shirt. I figured, if this little truck quits on this lonesome road (22 miles from home) I'm gonna freeze to death. I started taking a coat to work, no matter the weather after that. Eventually put a cut-down Pinto heater into it and that worked great. I installed a Corvette four speed, mag wheels and painted it Porsche red. It was a looker and I drove it everywhere. (Between the two of us, and only two engines, we put over 250,000 miles on that truck and it still ran great when I sold it).

"...Fortunately the drive train held together and he came boiling by in low gear, engine screaming, pipes roaring and the right rear tire smokin' like a fuel dragster. He hit second gear right in front of us and the tire still smoked it for a bit. The troops were stunned, they all knew Skip ran a stock engine. WB and I just smiled and wouldn't say anything..."

CHAPTER TWENTY-ONE
THE COUPE GANG
ADVENTURES WITH CK AND ME.

The first time I met CK was when WB took Skip and I over to his house where we found CK, a couple of his friends and this nice little '35 Ford coupe sitting half way out the driveway into the street. We helped them shove it back into the garage.

The little '35 was a pretty neat car. Never had seen too many of them, guys usually preferred the before and after model years, and pretty much skipped over the '37s and '38s. Look at all the great '37s and '38s now, where the heck did they all come from?

CK had owned the '35 for a while and had driven it a bit in stock form. The hop up bug had bitten him and a few parts were collected. At the time, all most of us had done to our cars was fit twin pipes, multi-carbs and shaved stock or aluminum heads. A few actually had the Fenton cast iron headers. All bolt on stuff as you can see.

CK, a guy that was not afraid to tackle just about any mechanical job, had thought it over and decided the way to have a hot car was to start from the inside and work out. Instead of spending his money on external goodies as we had, he had purchased a cam and adjustable lifters, with the thought that the intake could be added later. The '35 already had twin pipes. I believe the cam was an Isky, grind unknown.

This photo really catches the flavor of the times and the car is a good representation of all our flathead powered, black primered '49-'50 Ford coupes. This one was CK's and the photo was taken about 1958-59.

Isky was the cam of choice for just about all the novice flathead hot rodders, probably due to Isky's high profile advertising with large ads appearing in Hot Rod and all. Other cam companies such as Potvin, Weiand, Winfield and a couple I don't remember were many times the choice of experienced hot rodders. This is not to say the Isky couldn't put out the horsepower, it's just that the more experienced guys knew what to pick and choose for what they were doing and they picked Iskys just about as often as the others.

CK got the cam stuck in the car, but did not know to check for valve to head clearance. The usual drill when camming a flathead with stock heads was to flycut the heads for clearance. Of course the engine would not turn over with the starter. CK and friends simply pushed the car to the end of the slightly sloping driveway and popped the clutch with the trans in reverse and got one really loud pop out of the engine. That was all she wrote. The cam was broken into three pieces and several valves were bent. As CK and friends were a bit busy WB, Skip and I soon left.

That was pretty much the end of the '35. After it took up garage space for a while, CK's dad made him sell it. Somebody got a righteous little coupe for $50.00.

Driveway destruction happened to Skip too. He had a cherry little '41 Ford coupe, short roof, one seat model, with flathead six his mom had bought for him when he was 14. The idea was, Skip would fix it up and start driving it when he was 16.

Skip was pretty talented in the mechanical department and no dummy. When he had a question or was stumped, he would go to the library with us, or simply ride his Schwinn "Corvette" bike up there and read up on it in the available manuals. (Later in life, he would work as a mechanic for the local Ford dealer and built a fairly successful Mustang drag race car.)

I recently ran into Skip at CK's house during an engine swap in CK's pickup. I hadn't seen Skip for about 25 years. He told me he had calmed down a bit, overhearing this, CK rolled out from under the pickup, looked at us both, shook his head and rolled back under the truck. He never said a word. Skip just grinned.

Skip was a bit of a terror in the neighborhood, especially to the neighbors whose house was next to Skip's narrow driveway. Skip's mom was a divorcee and a really cool lady, the house was full of kids all day long and she just went along with it all unless it got too noisy, then she would toss us out. Not often though.

Skip's mom worked, which meant he had a lot of un-supervised time at home. We were all a little envious. At times when she wasn't home, he would fire up the '41, back up the long narrow driveway, put it in low and burn rubber as far as he could and then slam on the brakes sliding to a stop in the garage. After a while the neighbors wouldn't even come out and glare at him over the fence, they just gave up.

Skip discovered that the old 6:00/16 tires on the little coupe would bum rubber really well if they had a lot of air pressure in them. He would take both rear tires off occasionally and roll them to the Chevron station on the corner and put about 60 lbs. in both. The driveway drag racing came to end when he pulled a couple of good ones. With the 60 lbs. pressure in the rear tires, the coupe would burn rubber forever. He finally blew it when he overcooked it, and slid into the garage taking out the back wall a bit. That really made him mad. He backed out and really got the tires frying when the trans let go. He got out and didn't say a word. I had never seen him so mad before. Without a word he went into the house, not even slamming the door. We got in WB's coupe and left.

I later found that WB and a couple of others returned in the afternoon with some old 2x4s, saw and hammer and repaired the garage wall as best they could. Skip's mom never noticed the break lines in the ship lap siding and where the repairs were made. At least we thought so; she probably just didn't say anything, because she didn't want to know.

Skip did make an attempt to repair the trans. As you know, the old torque tube Fords required either the rear end rolled out from under the car or the engine pulled to get at the trans. Skip had the car up on some big sturdy wooden blocks in the garage, had the rear end rolled out in the driveway, and the trans pulled. Oil was everywhere, he and the garage floor were covered and the trans was partially disassembled. Skip came home after school one day and found the little coupe had been towed to the wrecking yard. Resigned, he cleaned up the mess and life returned to normal for a short while. Skip's mom was really a good lady, as I mentioned. When he turned 16, his mom bought him a cherry little '49 Ford coupe, dark blue in color. He probably had it about a month before it was lowered in the front, had 15" wheels and whitewalls replacing the 16" blackwalls and had twin pipes installed. It took another couple of months before it ended up in black primer.

Black primer was the color of choice for many of us. It was easy to shoot at home, looked fairly good and showed all the other hot rodders we were on our way to building a neat car. Skip's car ended up in primer on the way to a good paint job. Or so he thought. Sandpaper, tape, a gallon of primer and thinner, a gallon of paint and thinner would strain the budget of many a rodder. A gallon of primer and thinner by itself wasn't too bad and was as far as many of us got.

I didn't see CK for about six months after that first meeting. Next time I saw CK, WB was hunting for him with the intent to do some serious butt-kicking. I don't remember exactly what WB was mad at, but it wasn't much. Truth to tell, I was a bit surprised WB would be hunting anybody down. Nobody in our little group thought of themselves as "tough guys". WB didn't even come close to being a tough guy. He was a skinny kid, about 5 ft 9 in. at the time and I sorta felt that if we sicced my sister on him, he would soon be running for his fife. Heck, I was bigger than WB and I didn't antagonize my sister.

She was 54 inches, a really good freestyle skater and strong as heck.
Our last fight was when she threw a living room chair at me and it hit the wall half way up. Me, no dummy, left right away and gave sister the respect she deserved after that.
Anyway, we found CK and his little brother Bud driving a black primered '49 Ford coupe, one afternoon. WB was driving his black primered '49 Ford coupe and stopped to talk to CK on a side street to the large housing tract we all lived in. (Except for Skip.)

I noticed WB didn't talk to CK as tough as I thought he was going to. I hadn't seen CK for a year or so, and he had gotten taller and gained weight. I sorta felt I would be driving WB home, a bit battered and bruised. CK was always patient, still is, and they parted on good terms.

I ran into CK a few times after that at the local drive in or the Frosty Shop across from the High School and we became good friends. They were both great places to hang out in cars, talk cars and see cars. Many a street race was set up at the Frosty Shop. The owner was pretty cool and didn't get too excited about a bunch of teenage boys and girls hanging out in the parking lot as long as they behaved. Anybody that drove through fast, burned rubber or otherwise hassled the public got 86d right away. He had a pretty good memory, and if you snuck back too soon, he would spot you and run you off again.

There was a stop light just 200 feet west of the Frosty Shop and occasionally a street race would start there and fly by the shop. Usually somebody would simply burn all the rubber they could and go blasting by. At times, some pretty fast cars would come in from a few of the outlying towns. If some of the faster locals were there, a street race would usually get set up for later.

Skip, now driving his '49 coupe and remembering his experiences with the high pressure tires in the '41, had saved the old 16 inch blackwall tire/wheel combo off the '49. These 16 inch tires were narrow and were starting to weather check a bit and were very hard, simply from aging. He had found the '49 would really burn rubber with the 16 inch tires mounted and would use them around town on occasion.

WB and I were with him one night when he went into the local Chevron station and pulled a pair of them out of the trunk. Chevron stations at the time had a really slick air station. It was next to the pumps at the end of the island and was operated by spinning a crank until the desired pressure was noted in the window. Pushing up on the lever would charge the air hose and you stuck air in the tires until you heard it chime which meant the tire was up to pressure. The machine would not go over the selected pressure and was an excellent system. You could dial up pressures in excess of 100 lbs. as trucks also gassed up and got air at the station.

Crazy guy that he was, Skip set the pressure gauge at 90 lbs. and started airing up the tires. WB and I, a bit afraid of the whole procedure wandered over to the coke machine about 50 feet away. I just knew the tires would explode and had seen the results of one truck tire explosion at dad's oil patch garage. The new guy had aired up a truck tire out of the safety cage, the tire had exploded and pieces of the split wheel were stuck in the bottom of the wooden roof. No one got hurt. The new guy got a rapid lesson in safe tire handling and dad's boss gave him such a chewing out, that most of the other mechanics decided they had business elsewhere on the lease, gathered up their tools and left. I heard that the boss told the new guy that if he ever did it again, he better be sure to die in the process or the boss would simply kill him his own self.

There was no "PC" at that time, you either had it all together or you were walked off the job. Skip got the tires aired up okay and we drove back to the house to swap rear tires. He lived a couple of blocks from the Frosty Shop and we drove over with WB and I wondering if we would have a blow out before we got there. Entering the parking lot from the side entrance Skip let us out and proceeded down the alley parallelling the main drag that ran in front of the Frosty Shop. There were a few guys we knew there and WB and I joined them. Skip in the meantime, had entered the main drag near the stop light just down the street.

When the light turned green he nailed the throttle and side-stepped the clutch. Not always a good trick with the fragile trans and rear axles in these cars. Fortunately the drive train held together and he came boiling by in low gear, engine screaming, pipes roaring and the right rear tire smokin' like a fuel dragster. He hit second gear right in front of us and the tire still smoked it for a bit. The troops were stunned, they all knew Skip ran a stock engine. WB and I just smiled and wouldn't say anything.

Skip had gone home and changed the tires back to the whitewalls and returned to pick us up. He did make a point to enter the parking lot with the choke pulled out so as to emulate a hot cam. After witnessing the huge burnout, no one even questioned the choke trick as we all did it now and then, but it was usually easy to spot, as a lot of black smoke came out the exhaust.

Skip played it cool and held his cards close to the chest. He wouldn't open the hood for the guys and for a couple of months most of the other flathead powered cars were afraid to race him. When we left, not a soul noticed how smoothly the engine ran, as the choke was open. It was a great gag and Skip had really put one over on them.

'Course being greedy, he went to the Drive-in and tried to pull the same stunt in front of some older car guys, that owned some seriously hot machines. These were cars that would regularly eclipse the 100 mph barrier at the drags, which was a bit of a standard for street driven cars of the period. If you could break 100, you were somebody.

One of the tricks that always worked well, but would only impress the younger set was to pass the drive-in on the north side going east, down shift to low, make most of the 140 degree or so tight turn at the end of the drive-in parking lot heading back west and then nail it. With the chassis unloaded you could get pretty good tire spin out of the deal and once the tires were spinning there was not too much danger of breaking something.

This wasn't good enough for our hero. He simply drove around the sharp turn, straightened out, wound it up and dumped the clutch. The tires started spinning good, got some bite and that was the end of it. The trans came unglued.

We took mercy on him and towed him home. This happened about 10 pm, by midnight he had the trans out of the car, ready for a new one he bought and fitted the next day. A couple of us were more knowledgeable than Skip, but no one could beat him in a one man trans swap. He had replaced so many of them that he could have it just about ready to take out by the time the helper had removed the driveshaft bolts with an end wrench. It wasn't hard. Four bolts removed from the crossmember on each side, usually he left two out to make future changes easy. Two bolts from the trans mount, two cotter pins from the shift arms, one bolt for the clutch linkage equalizer bar, the speedo cable, four trans bolts and of course the four driveshaft bolts. The crossmember was simply slid back on top of the exhaust pipes and glasspacks. He had so many broken transmissions laying around that occasionally he could assemble a new one and only have to purchase one or two items. His mom gave up trying to park her car in the garage and simply added washing it once a week to Skip's duties. It was okay with him, he always did his share around the house and a lot more than I did.

After a while, CK, WB, Skip and I all had black primered Ford coupes. (Mine were almost always '50s and theirs were '49s) There were also a couple of others in town and a couple more from the adjacent town. The cops had a hard time telling us apart.

Several times I got stopped in the housing tract that three of us lived in because WB or Skip had gone blasting through the neighborhood earlier. Never got a ticket I didn't deserve though. (Well, except once, I was running open headers through the neighborhood, drove by a detective's house under the speed limit. He stopped me and gave me a ticket for speeding. I guess I was paying for the transgressions of the others and a few of my own.)

About that time CK broke up with his long time girlfriend, a steady from early Junior High School. (We'll call her J in this little story.) WB took up the slack and started dating J and before long they were a pretty steady couple. I had been dating an English girl, not long in the country. (We'll call her D.) We dated pretty steadily, but never got real serious. I found her folks really interesting as they had lived through the "Blitz" and had a lot of interesting stories to tell. D and I were on her front porch early one evening and CK drove by in his little coupe. Recognizing my car, and seeing me, he gave us a wave and drove on by. D and I were simply good friends by that time. She had seen CK around and was a bit curious about him. I asked her if she wanted to meet and the answer was yes. I caught CK the next day and set up the old "Blind Date". (Not all of these were bad – every once in a while a good one comes along.) Needing a date myself, I called a girl from sister's circle of friends who was willing to join us. At the time my family had a female cousin living with us. This cousin was one year older than sister and one year younger than I. Sister and cousin had different friends. There were always slumber parties going on at my house and the house was always full of girls from one group or the other and sometimes both.

WB and Skip always liked to go home with me on Saturday nights as the house was loaded with young ladies in interesting dress. They weren't real excited about obtaining more modest outfits as it was just brother and his two harmless friends. It was old hat to me, but a real treat for VM and Skip. The folks were pretty good about letting these go on every two weeks or so. I was fortunate in that I got to know a lot of girls. Anyway, CK and I double dated, D and he were a steady item for a while. Eventually J could no longer take WB's lack of manners and social graces and split up with him. (WB had good manners, he just chose not to use them.) CK and J got back together and WB, Skip and I had no steady girl friends, but had a lot to choose from on Saturday nights. More than once, we loaded a car full of sister's and cousin's friends into one of the cars late Saturday nights and went cruising. At times two cars full. Gas station guys were always amazed when we pulled up with 4-5 girls in shorty night gowns and house coats late on Saturday nights. (Don't get your hopes up here, it was mostly just innocent fun, although we got one heck of a reputation at the Frosty Shop.)

CK, J and I double dated a lot, me with several different girls. I found out that CK knew a gorgeous brunette from High School and had been simply good friends with her for a long time. They had gone to Junior High school together, a different one from mine. The brunette, (call her GA) got to know CK by defending him from one of the teachers that liked to pick on him.

CK wore the typical car guy outfit. White T-shirt, Levi's and loafers. He really was a good kid, he got into trouble because he would stand up for himself when he thought he was in the right and ended up in the principal's office many times. Some times deservedly so, most times not. Same thing happened to him in High School and once again GA defended him. (Not that he ever needed defending, he was six feet and 175lb.) GA had a strong sense of right and wrong and this time she ended up in the Principal's office with him. A bit of a shock for her, as she was a straight A student and had never been in trouble. I had seen GA around town and was intrigued by her. She had a steady boyfriend so I figured that avenue was a closed one.

CK being good friends with GA and knowing GA's family well, had dragged me out to visit after her mom had come home after surgery. This was Summer and many of the local girls had dyed their hair blonde, probably in answer to the pool chlorine turning their hair a strange greenish blond color.

I met GA's mom and brother and was visiting when this good looking blonde walked in. I didn't recognize her at first, but I liked her looks and had always had a weakness for blondes. Of course it was GA, now with blonde hair. Did I mention she looked great? I thought about her for a week and asked CK to try to set up a date. By that time her old boyfriend was long gone. CK, a good guy, did so. (And CK always seemed to go on interesting dates.)

Our first date, was a double with CK and J. We took CK's dad's '57 Ranchero, a white cherry with twin pipes and strong running 312. The four of us crammed into the one and only seat, I know we couldn't do it now, mainly cause the guys wouldn't fit. We started out at 7:00 am, headed for the LA area from the coastal city 50 miles North. We stopped for a very short bit to drop something off at CK's relative's house and proceeded to Disneyland. After several hours there, we went to Knott's Berry Farm, another amusement park. After a few hours there, (it didn't have the rides and attractions it does now) we went to the Long Beach pike, one of California's oldest and most famous amusement parks. I think we closed down the place at midnight. Driving home, with the girls asleep, CK had me drive the rest of the way and we got the girls home about 2-3 am. Heck, just thinking about this little trip today wears me out. I get nervous just thinking about going to Disneyland let alone spending another day like that.

CK had joined the Army sometime prior to the "Killer Date" as we call it nowadays. This "trip" was done while he was on leave.

After CK went in, I had bought a BSA Gold Star, the alloy clipper model, which was a very rare motorcycle. Didn't realize it at the time, although I sure do now. It had the 500cc Catalina engine and was set up for the Six Days Trials. A bit like the enduro's. It came with a muffler, but no lights. I added a dry cell powered stop light and a rear view mirror and horn to make the CHP happy and the cops pretty much left me alone. It was enough to rip and tear around in the mountains and riverbeds, zooming around the streets was not required, and we simply rode our bikes to the dirt where we proceeded to go crazy.

CK's little brother Bud had purchased a Vespa scooter about the time CK went in the Army. Bud and I got to be great friends and spent the Summer together riding our bikes all over the county and more than a few miles on the then deserted beaches. Beach riding was against the law, but if you stayed in the empty areas and away from the beach housing areas no one bothered you. We had a lot of fun times and would swap bikes back and forth. Bud loved the BSA and I didn't mind traveling to the riding areas on the Vespa. Generally I rode the BSA in the dirt, but let Bud do some dirt time as well.

Bud darned near killed himself on the BSA. We used to ride down to the beach through the lemon orchards on a wide, paved single lane road. There were old, beat up no trespassing signs posted, but Bud, an affable character had paved the way by sharing some cold sodas with some of the regular employees and the boss who was probably the owner. We only used the road for a through trip once a week or so. The workers would simply wave and smile at us, as would I seeing a couple of guys headed for the beach on a weekday morning. Generally we hid the bikes in the dunes and body surfed for a while, winter and summer. No wet suits for us, (although we would have had 'em, had they been available as they are now.)

In the winter we surfed until we couldn't stand the cold any more and would go to the 3-4 feet deep tidal pools that were warmed considerably by the sun, even on hazy days and soak in them until we felt brave enough to body surf some more. Some of the areas we surfed in were next to the Coastal Highway and tourists would stop and watch and shake their heads at the two crazies in the cold water in the winter. The hardest thing about all this, was getting out and changing into dry clothes packed on the bikes. At times like that, we just about froze.

One of the best parts about the paved orchard road leading to the beach was the railroad track crossing. This is where Bud almost got his, or bought the farm, so to speak. The road leading across the railroad crossing was a perfect ramp, hitting it at about 50-60 mph would make you fly a very long ways until coming down on the other side. It was a lotta fun, and not too hard on the bike as the other side was downhill a bit. When I did this, Bud or someone else would always stand guard as you couldn't see the trains coming. Well, the inevitable happened, Bud was riding the BSA up from the beach and after making the last turn, got on the straightaway to the railroad crossing and gassed it. I was a little back on the Vespa and could see the train coming. Bud couldn't see it, and with the BSA noise and crash helmet he didn't hear it.

I nailed the Vespa, but it was hopeless, the BSA just pulled away. Bud finally saw the train through the Eucalyptus trees and locked up the rear wheel. It was sliding along, wavering a bit, but staying upright just fine. Bud was actually a pretty good rider. He never did touch the front brake. He and the train engine got to the crossing at the same time. Bud leaned the BSA over so far to the right to avoid the train engine, he almost fell over as by that time he was sliding no more and simply trying to make a very tight turn. It scared hell out of both of us.

Bud smoked, I didn't. We both sat down and had a cigarette!

After it was all over, we found the rear tire skid marks to be about three feet from the track. Bud had stopped 90 degrees to the direction of travel and almost laid it over. Good thing he didn't, he would have slid right under the engine.

GA and I got married. A bit of luck for me and I still think I'm lucky. She was an interesting girl then and still is now.

Bud, a bit of a salesman, and a charmer had convinced several of his friends to chip in and buy a bunch of beer for a weekend beach party. Beach parties at the time were a lot of fun, a date if you were lucky, alone if not, some beer and cokes and a bonfire. We used to be able to do that as there were miles of empty beaches in our area. Although I went to one later on that got a bit out of hand in the bonfire dept. There must have been a hundred kids present, I'm guessing there must have been a hundred tires or more that were tossed on the bonfire. When this thing got going, the flames were immense and could be seen for miles. The fire department Sheriff and CHP showed up and ran us off. Rightly so, this one was a bit much. 'Course all we did was split up and go to the north beaches in smaller groups and have a beach party there. Next morning the tire pile was still burning a bit and still giving off smoke.

Since Bud was about 17 and having no place to stash the beer, immediately thought of me. I was newly married and was just moving into an over garage apartment. Bud brought 11 cases of Coors by and asked me to store it for the weekend. The deal was, I could have a couple of cases for my trouble. The little Frigidaire was totally empty as this was to be our first night in the apartment. Since we had a poker party on for the night, I opened four cases of the Coors bottles and stashed them in the Fridge. I thought it would be a great gag when one of the guys went to get a cold one and found 96 bottles of beer tucked away. As fate would have it, GA's grandmother, a genteel lady who had gone to the proper schools and married a fine young man from New Zealand, came by to visit and see how the moving

The slim red headed young woman is CK's wife Jan. The car, her '57 Chevy sport coupe she owned at the time of their marriage. Note the dechromed hood and whitewall tyres.

was going. Wishing a drink of cold water, she opened the fridge and saw nothing but the 96 bottles of beer. She didn't say a word, simply closed the door and sighed. I wonder to this day what she was thinking.

Two years later when CK got out of the Army, he and J were married. I was proud to be the best man. WB married his long-time girlfriend, a little blonde girl from Texas. Skip was left standing there, wondering what had happened. This was about the time I got the Olds powered '50 Ford coupe running. CK still loved cars and does to this day. CK's wife owned a nice '57 Chevy hardtop when they were married. CK had a lot of electronics training in the Army and when he got out I tried to get him to apply at the power company where I worked. He liked communications and eventually went to work for the telephone company.

He owned a few interesting cars over the years. Right after the Army, he bought a '57 Dodge hardtop, painted it Titian Red and installed Dodge Lancer wheel covers which were just about as popular as the Olds Fiesta spinners. It had pipes of course and was really a beautiful car. With the good looking Dodge and the wife's metallic bronze '57 Chevy Hardtop, they had a couple of great choices when it came to driving somewhere. CK got new car lust, traded in the Dodge and bought a brand new metallic red Comet

The body for the roadster came packed in a crate which had to be cut open. The under construction photo is from 1987 and includes our long haired Daschund Muffet.

Cyclone with a white interior, 289 and factory four speed. This was a nice little car that was Mercury's answer to the Ford Mustang. CK swapped the mufflers for some good sounding glasspacks and drove it everywhere.

CK's dad, who was a bit of a character, drove the Comet and bought one for himself shortly afterward. His was virtually the same car except it was white with a red interior. Did they drag race? You bet, CK winning handily as dad was a bit out of practice and couldn't speed shift worth a damn. Somewhere along the way the '57 Chevy was sold, a move he regrets to this day. (Wouldn't we all.) The wife took over driving the Comet and CK bought a clean '55 Ford pickup running a stock 272

Y-block. It was a nice pickup, painted factory red. CK had pipes on it in no time and chrome wheels installed shortly thereafter.

As I had been pinstriping and flame painting off and on for a while we laid some white pinstriping on it, front and rear and inside. We even put some on in some strange places. The rear door jambs, glove box lid interior, under the hood in a few places, the air cleaner, rear of the cab under the window, the rear end housing and probably a few other places I can't remember. I do remember CK had a lot of beer in the fridge when we started and not so much when we finished.

Little brother was with us that day. He had recently obtained his license and I had let him drive the coupe a bit. He was pretty stoked on it and kept insisting we finish up and leave. His plan of course, was he would drive it for me. After a while, his complaining started bugging us. We gave him $3.00 for gas, the keys to the coupe and told him to come back when the gas ran out. Big Mistake. Little brother was good about saving money and always had some stashed at home. He went straight home and picked up the money for more gas, and headed out to pick up a few of his friends. We thought he would be back around 3 pm.

We just kept pinstriping and decreasing the quantity of CK's beer supply. That's one reason so much pinstriping got laid on the truck. Looked good though. Little brother showed up about 8 pm when it was getting dark. He had three friends with him and a big grin. He thought maybe he was in a whole lot of trouble. CK and I were beat, it had been a long day. I simply got

Little '38 Morris 12 belongs to my good friend CK. This is his latest running project car, powered by 350 small block Chevy, Turbo 350 and Chevy S-10 rear end with Mustang 2 front end.

in the coupe and had little brother drive us back to the folk's house where we were staying.

After living for a while about 50 miles from the town where we grew up, the wife and I moved about 20 miles closer. After the move CK decided to paint the truck. I had done a fair paint job on a few of my cars and agreed to do his. We shot the truck outside with Titian Red enamel and it looked pretty good. Santa Barbara, about 50-60 miles away as the crow flies had a massive brush fire burning and it had been burning for 2 days. The timing was perfect. The fall out from the ash hit town just as we were finishing up. We rolled the truck into the doorless garage, but it didn't help. Ash got all over it and the next morning it looked like a Titian Red washing machine tub interior. It was sad to see after a couple of weekends of hard work.

CK took the truck home, had a sanding party and took it to a regular paint shop. They shot it a nice Mustang Orange and it really looked great. CK's little truck was a good one and we hit a lot of junkyards looking for parts and hauling same for the next couple of years.

CK and I didn't see much of each other for the next decade due to my job keeping us well separated for a while. We saw just enough of each other to keep up with family and friends. By this time he had been through several Ford 3/4 Ton pickups and was into desert riding on off-road bikes. After they had been doing off-road for several years I bought a new dirt bike and joined them. We did this together for about eight years before our group folded. CK had sorta been the unelected president, had everyone's work schedules and coordinated all the big rides with friends and family. Eventually we ended up with four dirt bikes and the whole family rode. Younger daughter turned out to be a very good rider and could beat most of the boys in the group. We had some big turnouts at times, with more than 60 people gathered around the campfire for the weekend.

With the dirt bike extravaganza over, CK and I turned back to hot rods. I was able to buy most of the parts for my roadster at one time and after a good start, it ended up sitting for awhile. CK found an interesting little car, a 1938 Morris 12, four door. A bit like a slightly scaled up Anglia. A lot of the body work had been done, a Mustang front end and S-10 rear stuck under, and a good running odd-fire Buick V-6 fitted. The guy that built all this originally was a drag racing friend of little brother's and sold out simply due to lack of time. CK, always a hard worker, had the little car running in primer in about 10 months while still operating his small welding business.

CK got the Morris painted and upholstered in short order. It was a pretty good performer with the little Buick V-6. and a great looking car. My roadster was complete with all major work done and looked like you could drive it away. CK's getting the Morris going kinda got me rolling also. About 12 months later I had the roadster completed except for upholstery and was driving it on the road.

CK came up to visit right after I had stuck a cam and dual quads in it. It was started up and first driven with a stock cam and single four barrel, I thought it would be easier to work out any bugs with a non-temperamental engine. As it turned out, the cam and dual quad are not any fussier than the stock cam and single quad were and the car turned out to be pretty much trouble free. (It's an easy car to work on, so swapping cams was no big deal.)

Of course we spent the day cruising the area in the roadster and had great fun setting off car alarms by rumbling by at 20 mph in high gear. Three in a row is our record. Since I wanted to hear it run, and see it go down the road, I got out on a quiet country road and had CK drive it away. He nailed it pretty hard on the way back and when he reached me he was smiling and I could tell he was thinking about something. He never did mention what it was though.

CK went home, 200 miles south. I heard through the grapevine that he had yanked the Buick V-6 and had built a mild SB Chevy 350, stuck it in, including building headers and modifying the firewall all in about two months of spare time. This was in a finished, painted car and I don't think he scratched it a bit. It's a good looking little car. It pretty much flies down the road now, lighting up the tires on demand. It handles pretty well too. Ergonomics are the only fly in the ointment. Moving the throttle pedal and installing newer bucket seats will be done shortly.

I helped CK move to a new home recently, 30 miles closer to mine, making it great for me as we visit back and forth a lot. One of the fun parts for me was driving the '38 Morris to the new home. Of course several applications of full throttle had to be made in order to get a good impression of the new engine. It passed with flying colors. It seems that, when the horsepower bug bites, it bites deeply ....

"...Sure is funny sometimes when some of these characters pass me and I catch 'em at the next light and roll right on by while they're just starting up again. They nail it, pass me, get way ahead and have to lay on the brakes hard for the next stop light..."

CHAPTER TWENTY-TWO
SUNDAY DRIVE
DID A COOL RUN RECENTLY. JUST ONE OF THOSE DAYS WHEN THE ROADSTER WAS BEGGING TO BE DRIVEN SOMEWHERE.

Sometimes it seems the '32 has a life of it's own and I'm just there to do its bidding. If it sits too long in the garage, I can tell it needs to get out and do a touch of cruising. Or maybe it's me. Who knows and who cares? Both of us get to go somewhere interesting.

I hadn't driven the car for a while as I had been doing some "backburner" projects on it, namely I finally got the brake pedal pivot zerk installed. A job that would have taken five minutes while under construction, ended up taking 3-4 hours, having to pull the header etc, etc. To top if off, there was still plenty of grease from the original installation. I thought I would end up with an egg-shaped bushing, but it was fine.

The recently installed Borgeson steering u-joints that took all the play out of the steering and the brand new, installed just that morning, polyurethane replacement bushings in the rear sway bar just begged to be taken for a test drive. Normally I like to leave in the morning on some of the longer trips, but once the pillow blocks were bored out, the new bushings installed and tools picked up, I was kinda through in the garage.

Sometimes it seems the '32 has a life of its own and I'm just there to do its bidding. If it sits too long in the garage, I can tell it needs to get out and do a touch of cruising.

There are still a few other backburner projects I want to do too. Probably the biggest one is re-insulating the firewall. It gets a touch warm in the summer so I always think I'll re-do it in the winter. 'Course, in the winter, it helps keep the interior warm so it doesn't get done then. Kinda like the guy with the leaking roof. Can't fix it during the rain, because it's raining. Don't need to fix it when it's not raining, cause it doesn't leak then. Sometimes life is simple and sometimes life is complex. The firewall seems to have a bit of each. Oh well, what else is new?

Sweetie had some projects of her own going on that she wanted to stick with and decided to stay home. It was just me and the roadster, not to mention just getting out for a while. Weather was warm, about 85 or so when we started out. Just right for the roadster once a little wind gets flowing through it. I headed south, running a lot of the little country roads that are in the area, going toward Strathmore, just above Porterville. Found more potential rodding material, '50s era stuff. Seems I always find something when cruising these back roads. Got to see a potential parts Plymouth, another '50, same year as mine. This time the for sale sign is gone and it's just sitting where it was a couple of months ago. I'll check it again at the end of summer and the price may be right. If not, well, there's quite a few of these mid '50s era ChryCo's sitting around this big farming valley.

Running south and dropping out on Highway 65, a bit of a freeway, wide four laner anyway, I ran the roadster up to 65 and just cruised along. Nothing fast, just rolling along, listening to the sweet running engine and thinking about things. Car stuff for the most part, just cruising the roadster kinda focuses the mind and I get a lot of things figured out just sailing down the highway.

One thing I do notice, no matter how fast I go, I still end up getting passed by everybody. Seems worse in the roadster than the other cars, but even in the other cars I get passed a lot. Everybody seems to be in a big hurry, maybe they know something I don't. Then again, maybe I know something they don't. Taking a bit of extra time has a lot of small benefits, ones I'm sure you know too.

Sure is funny sometimes when some of these characters pass me and I catch 'em at the next light and roll right on by while they're just starting up again. They nail it, pass me, get way ahead and have to lay on the brakes hard for the next stop light. I know a few people who drive like that; I make a point not to ride with them if possible. They do seem to be buying new brakes every year or two. The way people drive nowadays has gotta be a boon for a brake shop.

Turned off the highway headed for Strathmore. Drove through town, and got on the wide and fast two laner going east. You can really see why California is called the Golden State, the native grasslands are dormant now and the hills are covered with a lush golden shade of color. Some folks think the hills are simply brown. I'm here to tell you it's not so. They are many shades of gold, just depends on where you're at, what time of year, the weather, cloud cover and maybe even your frame of mind. Gold, yes, brown, never.

Since I was in the area and had never been there, I started looking for a friend's ranch. I do remember how he said to get to it and it sure looked like I was at the right place. Think I found it out near the old rock quarry. There was a long dirt road leading in to four houses, but the mailboxes out front did not have his name on it. Kind of a spur of the moment deal, I should have called first. I wouldn't have minded going down the long dirt road if I'd known for sure he was at the end. Ended up letting it slide till another time as the roadster was just washed and waxed. The low hanging fan tends to suck air through the engine compartment and right out the louvers if you drive slow on a dusty road. Not to mention that doing the little trip solo was kinda fun.

I left there and drove up the winding road into Springville, a small resort town at the base of the Sierras, fueled up and got a cold drink. The whole Springville area is beautiful, much cooler than the valley floor, maybe 10 degrees or so most times and they do get a breeze down the canyon. Springville is located at the base of the Golden Trout Wilderness. Some good fishing there for those willing to hike in.

Left Springville going north on Yokohl Valley Road. Lots of nice big and small ranches on the south side of the 3000 feet high ridge. A very twisty and winding road to the top. Narrow too. Not recommended for cars with trailers. I can see why, a couple of the turns took 1-1/2 turns of the roadster wheel and it only has 4-1/4 turns lock to lock. Bad place to drive off the road too, some seriously big drop offs. Some only 200-500 feet to the roadway below. (If you stopped there.) And some drop offs looked to be at least 1000 feet of sailing down a very steep cliff, not quite straight up and down, but close. Not cool in a roadster, and not so great in a coupe either.

After crossing the summit, great views in both directions, a bit more winding down the road and you get on the north side where there are bigger ranches. The really bad twisties open up quite a bit and you can run a little faster. Not too fast though, it's still a narrow road. Nice part is, it's used mainly by the residents and only by a few sightseers. I think I only met 5-6 cars and pickups apparently belonging to residents and only saw one car that was doing the sightseeing bit. The sightseers always wave and smile. Seems everybody likes roadsters. Perhaps seeing one that was totally unexpected come around the corner in an isolated area just adds to their day of seeing the sights.

I even ran close to a couple of turkey buzzards sitting on the fence. Normally you don't get very close to these guys, but at 50 mph leaving a turn, I kinda surprised them. Slowed down, pulled over and stopped. I watched them do a bit of wing flapping to get airborne, then they just settled into a glide towards the large meadow slightly below and a quarter mile or so away. Once there, they caught a thermal and just cruised lazily up into the afternoon sky. A bit of cruising for everyone. A good day for it, for sure.

About another eight miles or so of running along the big ranches, saw a few famous last names at the entrance to some of them. Hollywood type names, this area was known to be a retreat for many movie stars, starting about the '30s and it still holds true today. Not that I'm star struck, just interesting to see.

After some 50-55 mph running through the ever widening curves and finally on a few long straights, I ended up at the 198 freeway and ran for home. About an 80 mile round trip. The roadster handles so well and is such a pleasure to drive that it's the most fun car I ever owned. The big and smooth running engine is a decided plus as well. Just leaning on the throttle a touch, hardly ever more than half way, brings you right back to cruise speed after exiting the turns. No down shifting required at any speed. A strong running engine in a light car has got to be one of life's best driving experiences. Just nothing quite like it.

A nice enough cruise that I've got it plugged away in the memory banks for some cooler weather when sweetie would like to go along. I hadn't been down that way for 10 years or so and there's a couple of other interesting areas to check out once we're in the vicinity. This time though, I think I'll leave early in the morning to give us plenty of time to see what we can see.

There's been more than one cruise we've left on, usually with a particular destination in mind, but we don't always get there. Sometimes the trip is so much fun and we end up stopping at so many interesting places along the way, the day just seems to fly by. The good part is, we still have a good cruise destination for another time. Kinda like having your cake and eating it too ......

"...With the roadster full, I head inside to grab the credit card and CK takes over the question and answer session. He knows just about as much about my car as I do. In fact, if he's not careful, his little welding business is going to turn into a rod shop..."

CHAPTER TWENTY-THREE
ME AND CK HIT THE RACES
SOMETIMES THE BEST LAID PLANS DO WORK OUT.

And sometimes the best laid plans are no plans at all. CK and I have been going to the March Meet off and on since 1964. We made it when we could, and other times, other things. CK and I have known each other since high school. In fact he's the guy that introduced me to my wife. One I owe him for and in a good way. Sweetie's been a delight and has always been an adventuresome girl. Lucky for me for sure, as my life has taken me in many different directions. Most all of them interesting.

The last few trips to the March Meet and the Hot Rod Reunion for that matter have been an absolute three day blast. What made it so good was that CK owned a fifth wheel trailer that he brought up. We had it parked on the east side of the track at about the 800 foot mark with a great view. We parked next to the fence and had his pickup parked nose under the fifth wheel overhang, bed towards the track, good chairs within, a large shade over the bed, good food and cold beverages handy. Not to mention the great evening barbecues, meeting and visiting with some of the other rodders that ended up around our campfire.

It worked out great, as I usually drive the roadster down and we use it like a big golf cart just to run around the pits, the swap meet and to visit friends. Bad part for CK was, that since he was driving his pickup/trailer combo, his neat little Morris 12, small block Chevy powered, bright yellow, a neat and fun car, had to be left home. A bit of a bummer as having a rod there just adds to the fun.

Little brother's Henry J drag racer in its latest form with chopped top and DRCE engine. In this form it runs 8 second quarters in excess of 166 mph.

This year was a touch different. CK sold the fifth wheel and 3/4 ton pickup and had decided to return to either the pickup/camper bit or motorhome and tow the rod on the trailer with that. Nothing wrong with trailering the rod. For sure, a lot easier on the girls. Especially since neither my roadster or his Morris has A/C and let's face it, some of the runs we've gone to have been in fairly extreme weather. Extreme anyway for Sunny California, one trailered trip down south in mid-December had us climbing the infamous Grapevine (1-5 going into LA from the San Joaquin Valley) in strong headwinds with 50 mph gusts, and temperatures just above freezing. With the Ranger doing 50 on the flats and the 50 mph wind gusts, it blew the pickup mirrors flat against the door. Coulda been done in the roadster but we prefer to enjoy ourselves in it and not make a survival exercise out of it. Most times we're bringing hot rod parts back for somebody or taking them down. With the lack of available space in the roadster, it's a bit of a moot point anyway. The important part for me is seeing that sweetie is having a good time and is comfortable.

We decided this year to just make it a one day deal on Saturday. It was the usual pre-race drill on the roadster, wash it on Wednesday afternoon, late as always, as there's no shade until late in the afternoon on my east facing driveway. Wax it on Thursday, not too big a job as it's a little car and with umpty dozen wax jobs on it already, it cleans up quickly. Friday, check all the liquid levels and tire pressures and fire the engine to make sure it still runs after being washed down Wednesday. With a louvered hood, I usually cover the engine, but about twice a year it gets washed too. With things all set, just kick back and wait for CK and his wife J to arrive Friday afternoon.

Once they were there, we found ourselves enroute to a local restaurant. Brilliant us, meaning CK and me, we thought we were in for a great home cooked meal. Both of the girls are good cooks. At least that's our story and we're sticking to it. Gotta have some excuse for that touch of overweight that CK and I carry around. The girls, not being anywhere near dumb, and the truth probably is that either one is twice as smart as CK and I put together.

They had plans, fancy that! First step on their plans was dinner out. 'Course, the treat was on the boys, as it should be. With such fine company, how could we not treat them to a night out? Well, dinner anyway, most nights we just like to kick back and hang out at the house. It was a lotta fun this time around, it always is, but an added bit of interest was a nice old guitar CK had brought up for me to re-string. He'd talked about getting one and his daughter got it for his birthday. We're very much amateur musicians, but with two guitars and sweetie's autoharp it's a lot of fun.

Up at dawn, CK and I hit the coffee, the girls, are not far behind and we're treated to a great home cooked breakfast. I think the girls want us to hit the road, as they have some serious shopping in mind. Even if we were not hitting the March Meet, we'd probably hit the road anyway. Lots safer that way.

We roll the roadster out in the driveway and light it off. Usually I fire it in the garage, but it's usually parked nose in. With it parked nose out and fired in the garage, it sets off the garage smoke detector. I've done that one a couple of times. I have also set it off when brazing or welding. The roadster is a '32 Ford highboy, powered by a built for torque 462 cubic inch Buick engine. Black with black cloth top. And it even has a heater! Still gotta dress warm though, Levis and tennies for me, T-shirt, sweatshirt and jacket along with knit watchcap and warm gloves. CK turns down the extra watchcap and gloves and has a T-shirt and jacket, along with a most cool beret. Just the hat for a roadster guy. Not that he's so tough; the heater is on his side of the car.

Once you're settled in one of these little cars you're kinda set for the duration, especially if you're the driver. A whole lot like getting settled into a small airplane in the winter. Roadsters are a whole other world of driving. In a small way, like a four wheeled motorcycle. The wind is always there, and it's always looking for a way in. Not as bad as the bikes though, but it's still there.

Once you're up to highway speed, it's like being in a slow flowing and cold river of wind. It's times like this I'm kinda glad the hole for the throttle rod, although small, leaks a touch of warm air right on my bad knee. Maybe I'll do something about it this summer. Maybe....

The run to the freeway is just the right length to get the cold blooded Buick engine up to temp and get the oil warm. Even then, we're still running right at 65lb oil pressure. Interesting part about the S-W mechanical instruments, which are a particular favorite of mine, you can watch the thermostat open and close by the back and forth sweep of the water temperature needle, until it settles out at 182° F. One reason the Buick is so darned cold blooded is the heat passages in the heads are blocked. I wanted to run heat, but couldn't due to running an early style intake on late heads. For sure, I do recommend running heat on street engines, but you can live with the blocked heat passages on the street if you just pay attention. Running a choke, manual or electric helps, I've run both on this engine, and even had the dual quads set up with manual chokes operating on both carbs. The 750 Carter now on the engine has an electric choke. Just takes a little more warm up time on the engine in the winter. Summer, no problems.

One funny one I noticed when running sans hood sides with a Holley and then with a Carter, both carbs equipped with electric chokes, was that the Holley choke would cool off and engage the choke on a hot engine re-start where the Carter would not. With the hood sides on, which is the way I run it anyway, no problem with the Holley. Did have me wondering for a while though.

Since the freeway segment of the trip headed east is about eight miles, we get off at Highway 65, a two laner, and start running south down to the Famoso, Drag Strip. Down around Porterville there's a nice stretch of freeway and we're running at 70 mph real comfortably – and getting passed by everyone. I don't say it out loud, but I'm thinking to myself, this little car is really running good. Smooth too. It likes the 70 mph mark and everything seems to settle right into sync. That little thought is always in the back of your mind though – they always run the best right before they break.

At 70 we're clicking along at 2700 rpm or so, the tires are just humming along, the wind is flowing softly through the car, the steering is just a light touch and even with the limited suspension travel, it's riding along pretty smooth. Even the top quiets down at this speed. At the 2/3 point we stop for gas at the Texaco Mini-Mart about 20 miles north of the track. Since the roadster wasn't full when we left, and I've found it wise to top off, as cruising around the track and pits at idle last time used up quite a bit of gas. Course the fact that last time we were there for three days and went 20 miles inside the race park made a bit of a difference, not to mention almost emptied the tank.

One of the fun parts about these little cars is meeting new people. And like always, a guy stops by to ask questions about it. The younger guys are usually asking builder type questions and the older guys are taking a trip down memory lane. I like talking to either one.

With the roadster full, I head inside to grab the credit card and CK takes over the question and answer session. He knows just about as much about my car as I do. In fact, if he's not careful, his little welding business is going to turn into a rod shop. He's done quite a few rod oriented jobs, has fair prices and does good work. The word does get around. Better for him too I think. Working on the rods is usually lots more interesting than building another wrought iron gate.

"Racer" as the locals call him, runs a bright yellow '52 Chevy tube framed coupe that runs in the low nines. He's had a lot of different Olds engines in it and always makes 'em run good.

Back to Highway 65, we drop in with a pack of 70 mph runners and most turn out to be headed for the strip. No rods though, we left a touch late and that's usually okay. The gates are still crowded at 7 and 8 am and when we get there at a bit after 9 am, we drive straight in, pay for the rod show which includes my admission and CK pays his straight admission. We head for the show entrance lane and drive straight past it and disappear into the pits. Nobody there waving down cars like last time. Well marked though. We wander down the pits toward the top end and find little brother's friend and his wife from the old home town. "Racer", as the locals call him, runs

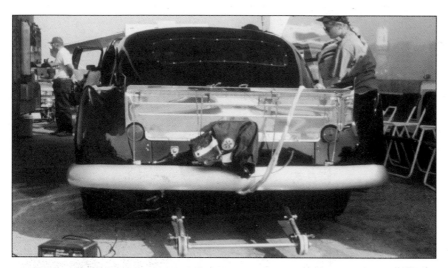

a bright yellow '52 Chevy tube framed coupe that runs in the low nines. He's had a lot of different Olds engines in it and always makes 'em run good. He did try a big block Chevy once, but went back to the Olds. I think he's running a 425 cubic inch one at present. One of the few free thinkers I ever saw at the drags. He's tried a lot of interesting things with the little Chevy. His wife runs a most beautiful '37 Chevy coupe that Racer painted himself and it looks great. The '37 runs a small block Chevy and runs in the high 11s through the mufflers. They drive this one on the street quite a bit.

The rear shot of the Henry J shows the width added to the body between the fenders and the body proper, a small detail not noticed by many. The interior shot below shows the Lenco shifter handles and the ignition system components that go along with the crank trigger ignition.

Racer's wife is one of the best drag race drivers I ever saw. She doesn't get rattled or nervous, she just leaves. Never saw her red light either. Racer's good on the lights too, in fact at one of the Palmdale nostalgia races about 7-8 years ago they took Hot Rod 1 and Hot Rod 2. Not too bad.

Racer runs an auto transmission shop and in fact built the trans-mission in my roadster. I told him what I wanted and it turned out exactly like I wanted. Basically a good performer, with some beefed up parts and a mild shift kit so the darned thing doesn't try to break your neck or chirp the tires during normal driving. His shop is 200 miles from my home and I made a special trip down there so he could do the roadster transmission. Gonna do the next one there too.

After finding out where little brother was parked, it was back to the bottom end and the "hot pits" for us. We found little brother parked in the wide lane entering the car show. Figures, we shoulda tried there first. There was room to park the roadster behind the Henry J and stay out of the way of the incoming show traffic. You couldn't have asked for a better place, they had chairs under the shade awning, and when not wrenching on the HJ they watched the car show go by.

Wrenching on the HJ has gotten a little easier for little brother as the youngest son has turned into a pretty good tuner and is usually interested in trying something new if a performance increase is in the offing. Even the hard jobs don't faze him. There is a bit to do on the HJ between rounds. It runs a 500 cid DRCE engine, Lenco and carbon fiber clutch among other things. Seems like the clutch gets adjusted now and then, the valve springs get tested while on the engine, and the valves get run every time. It still breaks a valve spring now and then, but nothing like it did at first. Seems these big motors with lots of lift and running at high revs are hard on the valve train. Shift points are right around 9000 rpm.

They were testing the Dominators (two), that had recently had the tops epoxy filled and the air bleeds replaced with small removable ones that look like little bitty carb jets. This car has way more adjustability available in many areas than I want to get involved with. For those that don't know about the DRCE engines, this is the way I understand it. DRCE stands for Drag Racing Corporate Engine, a GM designed product and with their penchant for corporate engines it works well. The block is based on a big block Chevy. Older versions such as little brothers have cast iron blocks, newer ones are aluminum. Since Pontiac, Olds and Chevy run these engines they usually have heads, billet aluminum in all cases I know about, supplied by the

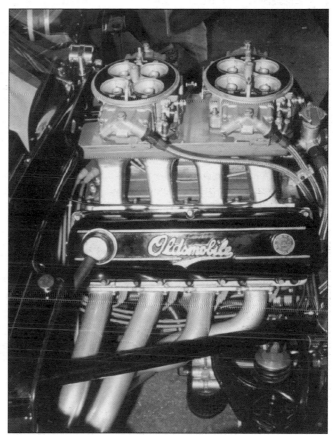

This photo shows the ready to run DRCE engine as it is now with epoxy filled block and Holley carb tops etc.

marque involved and rocker covers labeled with the marque name. I'm not sure about the intake manifolds, I think they are specific to the brand engine involved, ie Olds engine, Olds intake manifold for the DRCE. In little brothers case, the intake is welded sheet magnesium and the rocker covers are cast magnesium. The header flange bolt pattern may be different too. Little brother's engine dynoed at 1040 HP and running the numbers indicates it's putting out about 950 HP as it's now running.

We give little brother the extra roadster key that I always give to CK in case he has to move it and CK and I take off for the swap meet. We had a list of stuff, but found nothing. Well, I found one item, but I'm not giving a vendor $37.00 for a list price $22.00 item. And I'm still looking for a pair of 15 inch Moon spun aluminum discs. These measure 16 inches in diameter and have the Moon logo stamped near the drilled holes. Seems like these got popular a couple of years ago and they're getting hard to find at swap meets.

The manufacturers midway didn't seem to be as big this year, but maybe I'm comparing it with past Hot Rod reunions where everybody seems to come out, so we didn't buy much there either. Just a couple of event T-shirts. We asked for XL four times and the guy stuck large ones in the bag. Our fault for not looking I suppose. Although daughter is now enjoying my ex T-shirt.

We got back to the pits in plenty of time to move the roadster out so little brother could go to the A/Gas staging lanes. Then we parked way in front, where it was blocked in, but what the heck, we were there for the day.

With the Suburban full of the pit crew, CK and I walk over to the stands to watch the HJ's first run. What a ferocious little car. It just sits down, goes straight, pulls hard and makes a lot of great noises. Best viewed from about the 1000 foot mark and up in the stands. It ran an 8.56 and 161 mph.

People at the drags are funny. Seems they all want to be at the start line. There's a lot of action and noise there for sure, but over the years we've found that the 1000 foot mark gives the best overall view of the whole race track.

A bit more wandering of the swap meet, just to make sure we didn't miss anything. Did see a lot of older Chrysler Hemi stuff, most all slated for the fuelers. The front motored nostalgia fuel guys, most of them I think, have been lobbying for some changes, specifically to use the later 426 Hemi. It's obvious the parts supply for the older motors is getting pretty slim.

CK does find a couple of Model A coupes for sale he likes. He's also got a line on a roadster down south. He is a bit between a rock and a hard place though, he'd like to keep the present rod and drive it while he's building the new one. Wifey would like him to sell the present rod before the building starts. A dilemma for sure, but one that I think will be amicably solved and solved to everybody's satisfaction. It is nice to have one to drive while building another. I'm not sure which is the most fun for me.

'Course, while building the '32, and hitting the car shows etc. with CK, along with the little fact that CK bought his Morris way after I got all the '32 parts and had it running a year before me, kinda inspired me to get to the driving stage. It is a fun car for sure and is the most fun car to drive that I ever owned. Mainly due to what I like to call "linear acceleration". A lot of cars, and especially sweetie's little 5.0 liter Mustang pull hard in high gear, but there's
a point where depressing the throttle much past halfway at about half rpms doesn't gain much more in the acceleration department. The roadster though, with it's built for torque 462 inch engine and 2400lb weight is a different story. Push the throttle, the car pushes back. Push it some more, it pushes even harder, which means that half throttle usually has it pulling away from a stop pretty hard. You do have to change some of your driving habits though. First time I passed a set of doubles (tractor, two trailers on a two lane highway) I got a bit of a surprise. Normally, you just nail the throttle when it's safe and let off when past, right? Well, I started at 50 mph full throttle with the, at that time dual quads and big cam, and when I saw the truck in the right rear side mirror, I took a look at the speedo; 90 mph. No wonder I went by the guy so fast.

The roadster is not the fastest car in the world or the fastest car I've driven, but it is different. Probably is the fastest street car I've driven though.

Little brother has let me drive the HJ off and on at times, and with the car running low 10s and 126 mph at the time, also my personal best in it, that thing is a whole other ball game. When he went to alcohol, I never got a good opportunity to drive it again. And I can only imagine what it's like now as the HJ has run a best of 8.13 and 166 mph.

After the swap meet, CK and I hit the car show. Lots of neat cars. A couple of my favorites were a highboy roadster with Pontiac engine and a '31 on '32 rails roadster running a lightly modified A engine. We got to see some of the Shifters car club cars. They were parked on the south end of the stands next to the fence and the cars were straight out of the '50s. For us, it was double Deja Vu all over again.

Since we'd found a note from a friend (Don) in the roadster earlier, we went looking for him. We found his neat little small block Chevy powered Model A coupe parked behind the stands at the 1000 foot mark. We walked around to the front and climbed to the top of the stands right behind the coupe. After about 20 minutes of watching the races and Don's, coupe he showed up at his car, found our note and heard us yelling at him. We got to spend a couple of hours with Don watching the races and also met his little brother. A strong looking kid which leads me to believe that maybe us older brothers shouldn't pick on little brothers so much when they're little. They do grow up and usually bigger than you. Last time I pushed my little brother around, I ended up getting tossed into the kitchen and getting my wrist broken. 'Nuff said there.

Don picked a great time to leave the stands. Right after he left, one of the bracket racers, I think it was a Vega, got a little loose at about the 500 foot mark, let off, got straight and got back on the gas. It looked like it was all under control, but at about the 1000 foot mark, right in front of us he started getting loose again. He let off, and it looked like all was well until he started sliding around a bit, then totally lost it and went sliding into the left lane in front of the other car, a yellow one. He, aside from the dial-in, looked like he had lost the race to the sliding Vega. The Vega crossed the track and hit the left lane rail just past the lights and rolled once, bounced up in the air still spinning and by that time we lost view of it in the smoke and dust. He tossed off quite a few parts, looked like body and trim pieces for the most part and from what we could see and hear, it appears he rolled about four times. The driver of the yellow car was pretty heads up and when things started getting wild, he got into the right lane and somehow got past the rolling Vega without contact as far as I know. The emergency crew got on-scene pretty fast and had things well in hand when a few spectators at the top end tried to climb over the four foot cyclone fence and get on the track. They were run off pretty quickly by track personnel. Reports were that the driver was not hurt.

Interesting thing about all this was, first the clunking and thudding which you could hear quite well. The other part was the lights showed the times at, if I remember right, 11.58 seconds et and 128 mph.

Don came back after a short while and then CK and I headed for the pits as it was about time for little brother to be in line for the second run of the day. Then of course, a little later the fueler made a five second run and we missed that. Kinda sorry there. I would really have liked to see a nostalgia fueler run in the fives.

The A/gas second run was supposed to be at 3pm, but with the rollover and other delays, it didn't happen until about 5 pm. Kinda typical of drag racing, no big deal, just part of the game. There's plenty to do and look at anyway, so the delay didn't bother us too much.

We got back to the pit and found the HJ and tow car gone, so we dragged the roadster out and drove to the top end and watched the finals of fuel qualification while parked next to the fence just up from the last turnout. Ended up standing on the tires and leaning on the fence. Sometimes no fenders can be downright handy.

If you've never seen the drags from here, it's interesting. You get a good impression of the very high speeds these cars are capable of and get a good idea of how short the shut down area is when running at the higher speeds.

They ran maybe half a dozen races and then started running A/Gas cars. After a short wait, we saw the HJ coming down and got some good photos of the chute coming out and watching it slow down. Little brother ought to enjoy these as I don't think he has any pictures that were shot in the shut down area.

We waited for the gang near the timing shack and returned to their pit area with them. Interesting little parade with a black Suburban tow car, the black HJ and my black roadster bringing up the rear. Makes for an interesting group in the pits too. Looks like one of us is going to have to break down and paint some for-real color on one of our project cars, probably me. Little brother likes the black car bit and has a '74 Ford 1/2 ton at home, black of course, he purchased it new and it's a nice little truck. It runs an FE 428 among other things.

Times turned by the HJ this time were a little quicker than the earlier run – 8.40 et and 162 mph. We talked racing and roadsters for a while and watched the cars start filing out of the show area. It was still a good show. A few old friends came by that we hadn't seen for a while and we ended up staying a little longer than planned. No big deal, rather be late for home than miss seeing a friend. Since the racing we were interested in was over, and most of the visiting friends had drifted off, we ended up leaving about a half hour before dark. Plans were to hang a right out of the strip entrance/exit onto the Famoso Road, go two miles to Highway 65, turn north and head for home. At the exit the traffic guy tells us the road is one-way and we had to turn left. We did, and traveled about 10 miles to a darned good traffic jam that must have extended the remaining 2-3 miles to the 99 freeway. Well, heck, we're Valley boys, so to speak and no, we don't need no stinking directions. First north road we came to after hitting the traffic jam, we hung a right and took off. Plans were to parallel the freeway north and get on it further up the road.

Not to be, after a few miles the road took a hard right and later a 45 degree left and we found ourselves on one of the few diagonal roads that run a long ways in this farming valley. It was a most cool trip, as CK and I had both just about lost our voices, mainly from trying to talk over the wind in the roadster and also talking to everybody at the races. By now it was just about dark. we were running along, lights on in the soft twilight and heading northwest. We could see the tops of the snow covered Sierra in the distance, so we knew we'd intercept Highway 65, one of the major north/south routes in the area.

With a wind that was not cold, just a touch cool blowing through the roadster, it had settled out at a smooth and comfortable speed and we were clicking off the miles. There were several sharp "S" turns where I just let off the throttle, coasted up to the comer, leaned into the throttle a touch and at the apex just started pressing a little harder. Exiting the corners with no strain, no pain and no effort from the big motor. With virtually no traffic, it was one of the more pleasant driving experiences I've had for a while. Nothing fast and not dangerous to ourselves or others, it's just a pleasure to push the throttle smoothly down and find yourself whisked back up to the desired speed in no time.

No heater was required for the trip home, as it was still warm from the 75-80° F. temps of the day. I was doing okay with a T-shirt/sweatshirt combo and CK had his T-shirt and unzipped jacket. Not much talking either, we were just grooving on sliding down a black ribbon of road. the Sierra snowpack in the distance, some clouds still visible in the sky and watching the farm country scenery slide by.

All too soon, our little trip through the black void was over, and we found ourselves dumped out on a parallel road next to Highway 65. We promptly saw a black 'Vette being awarded an official Highway Patrol citation for speed on that stretch of highway. A little ways up the road, we got next to some of the citrus orchards and the temperature took a radical drop. I stopped the roadster and grabbed my jacket out of the trunk. It's surprising how much the temperatures in an area differ, simply due to what's planted where, how much shade it's in and when it was watered last, not to mention those little pools of cold or hot air, depending on the season, that you find yourself in. Street bike riders know where all these are at. And the roadster guys find out pretty fast too.

You can even navigate by smell, and it wasn't too long before we could smell the Mickey D's up the highway. We kept on truckin though. We knew the girls had hot, home-made burritos and cold beer waiting at home. These two girls have our number and have had it for some time. Heck, we're easy. 'Course, by the time we got there, and things got squared away, dinner was about 9 pm. A little late for all of us, but that just made it all the better. Goin' to the races, makin a roadster run, or going shopping at great stores are all things to be relived and rehashed after dinner, often far into the night. Many old stories and many new ones. A pleasant time for all.

The thing with a roadster, and a hot rod coupe is probably not far behind, is that sailing down the blacktop, on a soft and dark evening, whether by yourself, with a friend, or best of all, with sweetie is one of life's little treasures ....

I started out to write a little treatise about roadster rides, but fear I have failed. It is something everyone should experience at least once for themselves. It's such a different and strong experience, that once you're strapped in and the car is rolling, it's all pretty much like watching a movie or even a dream in your mind. Sometimes I wonder, was that really us?

The HJ report for Sunday: Finally got hold of little brother, seems like we ended up playing phone tag for a couple of weeks. The little HJ got eliminated first round on Sunday. A Camaro running in the high sevens got him. Since the HJ runs in A/Gas, which nowadays is a very tough class with an index of 7.50, it's tough to get very far up the ranks. The HJ fits into B/Gas much better and the competition is more even, but B/Gas is not run at all the nostalgia races, as was true this time. It was A/Gas or nothing. Little brother is a darned good driver, but overcoming the half second et advantage the other cars have is tough. Makes no difference, I think little brother is a touch like me, winning is nice, but it's not everything, and just taking part is many times enough. I think just running the fast little HJ is enough for little brother. Every time he steps out of the car he has a big grin on his face. As I did when I ran it in the 10's. Running in the eights I can only imagine.

'Course, now and then the little HJ breaks and usually something expensive. The grins don't last too long then!

"...The hats, his and mine, had a somewhat tall and fully rounded top and the brim hung down all the way around, not to mention that it came down to just above the ears. Any lower and the ears would have been the support point for the hats. Anyway, I decided it was kinda cool, the other guys thought I was nuts..."

CHAPTER TWENTY-FOUR
THE BLACK HAT
SET ABOUT 1958 - 1963.

Sometimes it's interesting how people remember you. Maybe it's just a small case of fame and only fame in a small circle for the most part. Bein' really famous looks like a total drag to me. Better to be well known as a bit of a character with family and friends than to end up owned by the world.

In this case, what was remembered, was not so much a guy in a black hat, but simply the black hat itself. Kinda surprising to say the least. I'd have thought that what was remembered was my Olds powered '50 Ford coupe. Seems with the car guys and gals especially, and with most other folks for the most part, the vehicle and owner get tied together pretty strongly. Witness how a friend, family member or even an acquaintance won't get recognized if they drive up in a different car. Not for a while anyway.

This is just a simple story about a simple black hat, a '50 Ford coupe, the drag racing venue and a touch about my sister, Shari. Sis always was a bit of a tomboy and did most anything and everything the boys did, many times, even better. She is a fast runner and a good athlete. Kinda tough sometimes too. Sometimes I think the only way that I made it to this stage in my life, taking into account my penchant for terrorizing, playing tricks on, and just generally giving her hell, was that I was two years older. That meant, when we were both smaller, where the girls are bigger than the same aged boys, which meant that sis was almost my size, she could more than hold her own. It wasn't always sister that went crying to mom.

Kinda funny too, the folks tell me that she was most eagerly anticipated by me before her birth and well loved afterward. Mom and dad have an interesting photo of the two of us sitting on the fender of dad's chopped '36 Ford five window. Her, an infant, about two months old, me just entering the terrible twos at about 26 months old. You could tell by just looking at the photo that I was thrilled to death to have my very own sister, although to paraphrase a bit, it was like the old song sung by B.B. King and Lucille. It was only a short while until "The Thrill Was Gone".

As life would have it, the love story didn't last long and the competition was underway. Competition about what, I didn't have a clue then and pretty much still don't know. Probably just the old sibling rivalry thing. We went through the usual growing pains that anyone can attest to that's been in a sibling relationship, although our grandson and older granddaughter, brother and sister, have always been able to get along well. Probably something to do with new genes being introduced into the family gene pool – and having a pretty good set of parents.

Anyway, as mentioned, sis was an excellent athlete and was the first to learn to skate on the neighborhood sidewalks. I wasn't too far behind as far as learning to skate went, although I never really caught up to sis. Even being two years older didn't help here, she was and still is, the more gifted athlete of the two of us. In fact she qualified for the Nationals in skating competitions a couple of times by placing well in the Pacific-Western regionals. Kind of a big deal in the skating world as it encompassed seven western states. Both times, she qualified in the freestyle events, but could not attend because it was so darned expensive. Not so much the entry fees and all that, it was simply that the travel and living costs were beyond the budgets of many families at the time.

The above is an unsubtle way of introducing my favorite sister, at least that's what I always call her when I introduce her to people. That leads to a wondering look on the face of many of them, at least until she tells them she's the only sister. It's a great little joke and one I've used for years. 'Course, once sis forgot to explain that she was the only sister and the lady I introduced sister to, thought for a long while that I was a bit of a cad for choosing one sister over the other. Something that happens I'm sure in many families, but not openly admitted.

Sister grew up, a strong young woman, a gifted athlete in one of the world's most graceful athletic endeavors, and as destiny decreed, became a most beautiful woman. She had a good personality too, one thing I didn't realize until I was about 16 and she was 14. That was about the time the boys started showing up at the house, sometimes alone, sometimes in twos and threes and fours. Sister's friends, recognizing a good thing when they saw all the boys, ended up hanging out at the house too. To boot, we had our cousin Judy live with the family for a few years, she was in between sis and I in the age department and had her own group of friends which meant that even more boys were coming over as well as Judy's friends. Plenty of boys for all the girls. Plenty of girls for all the boys.

Put all that together with the guys I ran around with, toss in the occasional girlfriend we brought over, and we had a house full of kids most times. Truthfully, I don't know how my folks put up with it. Patience is a virtue I guess, they sure were patient with us. Somewhere in here, sister and I had our last fight. No winners declared as in any conventional battle. Sister, having a bit of a temper, young and strong, along with being about 5'4" and 105lb. picked up what had to be about a 50lb. chair and threw it at me. It missed, but I was quick to note that it hit the wall half way up. Since I was reasonably smart, and her temper was at full throttle, I did the sensible thing any reasonably smart guy would do. Simply put, I ran for it. I bailed out of the door, into the coupe and left the premises. In a bit of a hurry I might add.

I've had big dogs after me and once got caught in a pasture with a big and mean bull. Neither time was I hurt, but neither time scared me as bad as sister throwing the chair. To this day, I don't remember what the fight was about, and I suspect neither does she, but I do remember the chair hitting the wall half way up. It made an impression on me much deeper than the dent in the wall.

When sis got to about 17 or so, she had a steady boyfriend named Karrol. He was a skater too and lived in Long Beach which was about an hour's drive down the coast from Ventura where we lived. He spent all his time either working, driving or skating with sister and kind of burning the candle at both ends. He owned, at the time, a slick little blue MGA. I thought it was a nice car, but not much in the hot rod department. 'Course we figured that anything that didn't accelerate strongly was beneath us. We never gave a thought that the little MG would and could eat us up on a twisty road.

Karrol was a more than nice guy though, and we enjoyed his company. When I found he worked for McCullough Corporation, I got real interested as McCullough was the forerunner of the Paxton Supercharger Company. For a while there, I thought we had an "in" to some serious horsepower. At the time, GMC blowers on the street were a bit rare, although you'd see the occasional '50 or so Olds running a 4.71 with a small four barrel poking through a hole in the hood.

The McCulloughs were what was generally seen on American cars. Usually they were owned by older guys who had more discretionary income than we did, although we figured any income we stumbled across was totally discretionary. The McCullough equipped car I saw around the most would drop into the Texaco gas station I worked at. Owned by a young doctor, it was a very clean and at the ripe old age of four, it should have been, '54 Buick Century. It looked totally stock, no problem with me, the '54 Centurys had always been a good looking car as far as I was concerned, but from what we heard he'd cleaned the clock of more than a few "wannabee" hot rods. Even stock, the Centurys were no slouch, clicking off zero to 60 mph times in the 10 second range. Good performance at the time and with a blower, a lot more than simply good performance.

It worked well living at home, working and attending school. Once school was out, after graduation day anyway, real life raised it's sometimes less than beautiful head. Real life in the form of rent. Looking back, a good learning experience, although at the time, it put a serious dent in the hot rod and run-around budget. Maybe it helped the folks a little too. I hope so, in my case it wasn't a whole lot, but it was a steady expense and I got used to it.

The McCullough connection was not to be though. Turned out that Karrol worked in the two stroke engine division. Cool if you were a go-kart racer, but not much help to us serious hot rod guys. At least we thought we were serious. Oh well – we tried and I did end up with a McCullough

Supercharger a couple of years later, one that was pulled off one of the very rare factory supercharged '57 Fords, brackets and all. I didn't have it long as it made good trading material. Today, it would be darned near worth its weight in gold.

Karrol as mentioned, was a more than nice guy. To top if off, he was a sharp dresser too. He was always well turned out with ironed button down shirt and well pressed slacks. A bit of a contrast with our usual uniform of T-shirts and Levis. We weren't the tough appearing group that rolled their cigs up into their shirt sleeves, and in fact only WB smoked at the time. It was just an accepted mode of dress for the times and the activities. Some of us actually owned dress slacks and a few owned suits, most times, hidden in the dark recesses of the closet and dragged out only when necessary. Church, weddings and the like. Not our weddings, other peoples weddings. It was the older guys that were getting married. We figured that was a long way off for us. Looking back, I can see it really wasn't too long, maybe 3-4 years for most of us.

With Karrol being the sharp dresser that he was, and having a "real" job, meaning a good paying, full time job, that is what most of us wanted, not the part time work at the gas station and similar places. More money equalled more car parts as far as we were concerned. For Karrol, it meant that he had more spending money than we did and of course, he was smarter in the financial department than we were and usually had a little more cash. That led to the Black Hat.

Somewhere along the line he saw somebody with a black Stetson – the Stetson being the Premier American Cowboy hat. As far as the cowboys were concerned, there were no other brands to consider. I think it's the same way now. Karrol bought himself a most cool black Stetson. 'Course he still wore the button down shirts, but to go along with the Stetson he started wearing Levis. Sister thought he was a fine figure of a man dressed as he was. We thought he looked cool too, but the price of the Stetson, for us at least, was not so much out of reach as it was out of the question. Heck, a guy could buy some serious speed equipment for that kind of money. Used speed equipment for sure, we didn't end up with a lot of new stuff, but the used stuff worked well, for the most part.

Karrol's career as a drugstore cowboy came to an end a few weeks after he got the hat. Too bad in a way, as we had become used to his "cowboy" look and figured it fit him well. The end was simple and one that more than a few cowboys had suffered as well. He set the hat down on the right rear decklid of my coupe and got busy helping us with something under the hood. The hat was forgotten and once the moderately built little flathead engine was fired, the hat vibrated right off the back of the car landing on the driveway. The next step was to back the coupe out as it had only the front end stuck in the garage, close up the garage and take it for a test run. The hat, forgotten for the moment, was run over and smashed by the right rear tire and probably the right front tire as well. Since it was black we didn't find it right away. It was camouflaged lying on the asphalt driveway.

Karrol spotted it, picked it up, and signs of disgust were soon etched on his face, not to mention he was totally PO'd. Not at us, but at himself for leaving a prized possession in a potentially dangerous place. I figured it could be straightened out, but the sweat band was torn loose and it was quite flat to boot. Karrol, being disgusted, gave me the hat with the admonition that "it's yours". I accepted, gladly. I figured it wasn't that bad off, and a free Stetson was not something sneezed at.

In fact, the whole week turned out not to be Karrol's week. As mentioned, he spent a lot of time driving back and forth between Long Beach and Ventura as well as working and skating. Skating could consume a lot of energy by itself, but it was the late hours and the long return home that got to him. I noticed one night that he looked tired and asked him once when he slept. His comment was that he slept on the drive home. A short quip and a funny one at the time and as it turned out, a bit prophetic too.

That night, on his return home, he fell asleep at the wheel. The little blue MG drifted off the Pacific Coast Highway and tore out 200 feet of the Zuma Beach cyclone fencing. The car ending up in the beach parking lot pretty well wrapped up in the cyclone fence. Karrol, aside from a few bumps and scrapes was unhurt, but the little MG was totalled. A bad week for sure, he lost his favorite hat and his beloved little MG.

In a small way, the Black Hat really was badly damaged, not to mention that it was slightly too small for me. Not a problem, I just pulled the sweatband completely off and it fit fine. 'Course, it had lost its fine looking cowboy bends and creases and was a bit sad looking. Being tossed in the closet for a few years and smashed under things now and then didn't do it a whole lot of good either. Along with me getting married and moving out of town to a new job, the Black Hat suffered many indignities, not the least, getting shuffled around between and sometimes beneath boxes.

I was fortunate in that CK, who figures prominently in most of the stories in this little book, introduced me to a personable, outgoing and most beautiful young woman. To say I was smitten would be putting it mildly. We married, much to my delight and I think much to her surprise. As far as I was concerned, life was starting out on the right foot and I was supremely happy. Her too, I think, hope so anyway.

To top it off, CK and I are still the best of friends and even though we live 160 miles apart, we still do all the hot rod stuff together that we can. A couple of years after getting married, I had the second version of the '50 Ford coupe, with built up Olds engine, Caddy trans and Spicer station wagon 4.27 rear end running. About this time, 1963, we started hitting the drag strip pretty often. At the time safety rules were pretty lenient. Perhaps lax is a better description. The basics were, at least in the gas classes, no hubcaps, all the lugnuts in place, battery held down with factory or metal straps, no clear plastic hose in the fuel lines, the car generally in good mechanical condition and seat belts. All the windows had to be installed and rolled up. No safety helmet required.

The big boys, meaning the dragster drivers, had much more stringent requirements. For them, the basics as above, where they would apply, plus shoulder harness along with the seat belts, an on-board fire extinguisher, fuel shut off controllable from the cockpit, face mask, leather jacket, safety helmet, goggles and gloves. In the gas classes, as well as the stock classes, we were left pretty much to our own devices. Which meant the typical Sunny California outfit of T-shirt and levis. It was the uniform of choice for many years, dating back to the early days of the dry lakes and is still the preferred mode of dress today, at least amongst the "hot rod" gang and drag race troops.

The San Fernando dragstrip almost always had fair and sunny weather, no matter the time of year, and in summer could get so darned hot in the asphalted pits that people would simply faint from heat exhaustion, men and women alike. This was a point in history when men, for the most part, did not wear hats. Pretty much true for the girls too. In fact, I darned near passed out after we flat-towed the coupe down behind the '57 Buick Roadmaster. We'd arrived there a little later than normal and on a heat wave day to boot. The coupe always traveled the highways with street tires and we swapped to slicks at the races. Usually I'd do the tire swap and little brother or the other guys would pull the tow bar and park the Buick. I must have skipped breakfast and been working too hard trying to make the time trial cut-off time. After I got the tires changed I was more than dizzy. I ended up laying in the back seat of the Buick while little brother ran the coupe. He did just fine, but it was just one of those days in which the really fast cars came out making C/Gas a tough class to be in for us. We didn't win, but little brother had a good time. He grinned all the way home.

I decided that wearing a hat at the races would be the sensible thing to do. The black and well crushed Stetson was remembered and a little searching through the closet soon brought it to light. It was in sad shape though. Along with being smashed by the coupe, it had lain under some stuff for several years and bore absolutely no resemblance to the fine hat it had once been. The crease in the crown was gone and the brim was completely flat. It just kinda sat there, limp and lifeless. The crown would stand up okay after a few days of being out from under the weight, but the brim would not take a roll and simply sagged down all the way around. One of the guys, and it may have been little brother, made the comment that "you look just like Grampa McCoy" in that hat. Well, true enough. Not so much in the age department, but the hat sure did look like his.

By way of explanation, Grampa McCoy was played by Walter Brennan in the TV series "The Real McCoys", a popular show at the time, it was a comedy series set on a farm. The hats, his and mine, had a somewhat tall and fully rounded top and the brim hung down all the way around, not to mention that it came down to just above the ears. Any lower and the ears would have been the support point for the hats. Anyway, I decided it was kinda cool, the other guys thought I was nuts, wasn't the first time they'd thought that, so I wasn't really bothered by the carping. After awhile they got used to it.

It became the official go to the races hat. Since we didn't run safety helmets at that time, I ended up wearing the hat when I drove as well as in the pits. It was different for sure.

One interesting thing that San Fernando did when they ran the stock class, gas class and any other street driven class was to have the timing ticket guy tell you where to go after the race. Interesting in that the timing ticket stand was down near the main grandstands and near the pit entrance that led off the drag strip itself. You'd get your timing ticket and it would have an "L" for loser or a "W" for winner written on it, sometimes right across the whole thing. Once I got the big "L" written in red. Kinda reminded me of the "Scarlet Letter" book. Felt about the same way too.

Anyway, the timing ticket guy would hand you the timing ticket and point out which way to go. Losers turned left into the pits, banished forever, or at least for the day. Winners went straight and parked in front of the grandstands near the start line. Once there, we were allowed to get out of the cars and mill around talking to each other and talking to crewmembers across the four foot cyclone fence.

San Fernando had a good, well organized and quick program. Starting at noon, an hour and a half of time trials. At 1:30 pm, an hour and a half of eliminations. Before and after those times open headers were not allowed. Made for a good race for the spectators and I only saw a few top fuel eliminations that went a minute or two past the curfew time. They were able to get the racing all done by 3 pm. After that, muffled cars and fun runs for a while. Hanging out in front of the grandstands with the other elimination winners was kinda cool. We were right down there in the middle of all the action and had an excellent view of what was going on.

Fuel rails would come down the fire-up road from the "hot pits", located at about the 1000 foot mark, light the engine off and make the initial part of the turnaround right next to us. After a bit of wrestling the car backwards due to no reversers and having a crewman pick up the laid over front wheel – laid over due to the extreme amount of caster these cars had dialed in – the driver could not return a fully turned wheel to the straight ahead position by himself and getting teary eyed from the alcohol/nitro fumes we had a front row seat to all the action.

Being parked right there, and kind of handy, the staging guy would have us lined up and quickly run out. There were no opportunities for repairs in the pits, once in a while a guy would make it and come back, but not often. If your car broke, overheated, or otherwise was not ready to make one run pretty much after the other, that was it for you. One reason our oriented to the street car did so well. The engine was milder than the top dogs and ran cool, so we never really broke anything and the car never overheated.

And for the Black Hat? For some reason I was remembered for it. Maybe for being in front of the grandstand crowd when I got lucky, but probably from just wearing it in the coupe and being the only guy with such a hat. The hat remembered more than the neat little '50 coupe that we ran. I've met guys that attended the San Fernando drag races at the same times we did. Not many ever remembered the coupe, or me, but many of them remembered the black hat.

We eventually went to wearing a safety helmet on our own, before the rules required it. Even with the car running a flat 100 mph, losing it on the top end could be a bit of a disaster. One that we did see on occasion and the results were always spectacular.

The Black Hat disappeared into the mists of time like so many things do, although I'll bet that little brother has it stashed away somewhere. Seems I saw him wearing it at the Palmdale drag strip, known today as LA County Raceway, a few years later. It wouldn't be a surprise. Little brother is good about saving things. Especially things I left behind when I moved out of the folks' house, like my BB gun, hydraulic floor jack, which he still has, and that's okay, a pair of fuzzy dice knitted by one of my girlfriends and Lord knows what else. I sure don't.

The Black Hat – would I want another one? Naw, I got one for Christmas a few years back and it's so nice that I hardly ever wear it. My favorite, specially in the rainy season is a beat up 20 year old or so Australian Bush hat. Not the one the Australian soldiers wear, but the one the outback guys use.

Another Olds powered '50 Ford coupe? You bet. In a New York minute. Always one of my very favorite cars. If I had a chance to get another one at least as good as the one I had, it could be worth your life to stand in the doorway.

There'd probably be three more guys right behind me. I'd bet the old "coupe gang" would like to revisit the past one more time. I know I would.......

"...Somebody said teacher was coming into the shop from the adjacent classroom. We of course, got very busy, and when teacher walked in, what he saw was the class working very hard on our engines, and WB silently whistling through space on the end of a chain. Teacher just turned and went back into the classroom. I think he'd long ago given up on us..."

CHAPTER TWENTY-FIVE
AUTO SHOP DAZE
HIGH SCHOOL AUTO SHOP WAS A MOST INTERESTING PLACE. HERE'S A FEW LITTLE STORIES.

One kid getting shut in the little tiny bathroom while two more held the door shut. A third kid just about emptied a CO_2 extinguisher into the bathroom. When the victim came out, he looked like something out of a National Geographic Antarctica expedition. He had ice in his hair, his eyebrows and clothes were just about completely white. Didn't seem to hurt him, although the purveyors of the deed did pay for their sins.

Some guys liked to crush stuff in the hydraulic press. For me, one of the scariest tools in the shop. After a few of these little stunts, one of the pieces being crushed came flying out of the press, hitting one kid's hand so hard, that stitches were required and he bled all over the place. You'd have thought the teacher would have placed the press off limits. Not so, after that one, most left it alone.

A most spectacular event was "The Earthquake". One of the things that most out of state folks think of when they think of California and disaster at the same time. I do note that the south and the east have their very own major faults. An extremely large one is centered in the Memphis, Tennessee area. With the Mississippi river nearby, and geologically speaking I can sure see a big lake forming here if the right kind of quake happens. Lake Memphis kind of has a nice ring to it. Along with tornadoes and such, inland areas get to worry about earthquakes as well.

Another fault is in the state of New York and I believe reasonably close to the Big Apple. Looks like a couple of things could happen here. We'll get a brand new stretch of East Coast and the Isle of

Manhattan will be relegated to the mists of time. A bonanza for archeologists of the future.

California does have other fun stuff, just as any other place does. The Santana winds are one, and they've been clocked in excess of 100 mph in some places. In fact, one year, a train of boxcars in the Dez were blown over while just sitting on the tracks. I've personally seen the Santanas at 70+ mph on an accurate wind gauge at the power station where I worked. We were an official LA County weather station and were supplied with a nice little bank of quality weather instruments.

Brushfires are another. These usually get set off, most times by arsonists, sometimes by accident and combined with the Santanas can get big and dangerous in virtually no time. But it's the earthquakes that get the most press and probably for good reason. We have a lot of small ones, quite a few medium ones and once in a while a big one. The one that happened in auto shop was a bit over the medium range and didn't do much damage. Nonetheless, the town was talking about it for a while.

I was in the auto shop, when the earthquake hit. Right behind me was a very nice, black, dropped in front, nice wheel covers, tuck and roll interior and pinstriped '51 or so DeSoto up on the hoist. When the quake hit, the DeSoto owner got out from under real quick and I got away from it just about as quick.

It was obvious the DeSoto was coming down. The auto shop building, built of masonry wall construction with metal roofing, was well braced internally and rode the quake out quite well. For what it's worth, the building was still in use a couple of years ago when I cruised by the school in the roadster.

A whole lot of noise went on during the quake as the quake makes quite a bit of noise by itself, and the building with its metal roll up doors and other metal stuff falling over made quite a bit of racket. We did okay in the auto shop and no one was hurt. After picking up a few things that did fall over it was back to work. At least that was the order given by teacher. We did wander outside for a bit to see what the rest of the school looked like as the main building was an old one and not earthquake rated.

Today the main building is gone which is a shame. It was a nice piece of California style public school architecture, now replaced with a slab sided piece of ugly. No pride there.

After shop class was over, we went to the next class in the main building
and heard a few interesting stories that had taken place in the classrooms. A few kids from out of state that had never experienced a quake ran for the door. The teachers, almost all of them California natives quickly stopped them and had the class take the earthquake posture of under the desk and cover your head. 'Course, by the time most got under there, the quake was pretty much over.

The most interesting story was the out of state teacher that had only lived in California a short while. He bolted out the door and ran out of the building. The class, composed totally of California kids simply remained seated with a few getting under the desks. For the teacher, it must have been a long walk back to the classroom. From what I heard, no one in the class ever said a thing about it to the school administration.

The thing about the quakes is that the first one is the scariest. After that they become interesting, until they get too big. Then they get scary again no matter where you're from. As for the DeSoto? It simply slipped off the hoist pads and remained hung up on the hoist and never did fall down. It did require a bit of a struggle with a floor jack and about six guys pushing to get it loose, but it suffered no damage.

The shops had roll up doors that were driven by an electric motor. One clown was forever grabbing on and riding to the top of the about 10 feet high door. That came to an end when we simply left him up there. Don't know how he got down, when the bell rang, we cleaned up and left for lunch.

The roof had a bank of large chain operated skylights, with the chains hanging down over the engine cages. All the engines which were on rolling stands had their own lockable cage as each engine was assigned to two guys. A bit of sabotage was always done if you left your engine unattended too long. Of course with the chains hanging down, and many in the shop class being clowns of the first magnitude, with my friend WB being one of the worst, guys would climb up on the engine cages, grab the chain and go swinging from side to side of the shop. Not the coolest stunt in the world as there were a lot of bad things to fall on. As fate would have it, WB got hold of a chain and started swinging and WB wasn't the biggest guy in the shop. A couple of the big guys got hold of him and started swinging him in a giant circle. Now the shop roof must have been 20 feet off the ground so the chain was long enough to give him quite a ride around just about the entire shop. No way he could jump off, with all the stuff in the shop, he would have killed himself. Somebody said teacher was coming into the shop from the adjacent classroom. We of course, got very busy, and when teacher walked in, what he saw was the class working very hard on our engines, and WB silently whistling through space on the end of a chain. Teacher just turned and went back into the classroom. I think he'd long ago given up on us.

What of WB? We climbed up on the cages, got him stopped and he let go the chain. He said it was a great ride, but we noticed he never went near the chains again.

Sometimes the simple stunts were the best. One kid had an absolutely beautiful, and very straight, black '49 Ford coupe. He'd worked hard and saved his money for this car, but the engine was a bit worn. He talked to teacher and decided to do an engine rebuild as his class project. Got to give him credit, for most of us it was venturing into unknown territory. It took a couple of months to get it done. An hour of shop class and all the stolen lunch hours he could, along with help from a friend, helped shorten a long project to a reasonable time. Once assembled it fired right up, the teacher oversaw the engine timing and decided all was okay. It didn't leak a drop of oil or burn any. So far, we hadn't fooled with his car or engine, as we did respect what he was doing and no one wanted to see his hard earned money wasted. The car ran great, but the kid was a bit of a worrywart. He was always checking the oil and looking for leaks.

That was enough for us, we started carrying coke bottles about half full of oil and every time we saw his car we'd pour some under the pan. It drove him nuts, he couldn't find

CERS

LADY LUCK

"...A few guys shot primer and a few even painted the complete car with a vacuum cleaner. Some vacuum cleaners came through with a wide range of accessories and with a cheap spray gun plugged into the outlet end you were in business. Sort of. Most of these jobs were pretty sad looking..".

CHAPTER TWENTY-SIX
PRIME TIME
SEEMS LIKE THERE IS A STRONG INTEREST IN THE '50s. PART OF THE NOSTALGIA DEAL I SUPPOSE.

Some of the people doing the most and putting forth the ideas on how it really was, weren't there at all! The only folks that really know, were there, and took part. 'Course the flaw here is, an event, even a long running one such as the fifties, is colored by the narrator's viewpoint. Something to keep in mind whether reading about the '50s or about history in general. As the saying goes, the victors get to write the history and for sure they are going to put their own favorable slant on things. So here's my view on how the fifties went, and like the victors, it has my own little slant on things. I guess just living through them makes you a victor of sorts. As did living through the admittedly more dangerous in some cases, more complex in others, and for sure downright weird in some places, the '60s. An era for some, colored by considerably more than rose colored glasses. As said, this is just a short bit on the '50s and maybe a touch on how it segued into the early '60s. As far as the car thing goes, the early '60s were pretty much an extension of the '50s. At least until the muscle cars started showing up in large numbers.

For me, the muscle car era started about '60. Which pretty much put an end to a lot of the '50s ways of doing things. A friend bought a '60 Ford Starliner Coupe, the hardtop model. First ride in this car pretty much showed the handwriting on the wall. A nice car to be sure, new, pretty, it had the 'FE390' engine, did have a stick shift and it hauled down the highway pretty well. No slouch in the acceleration department either. I realize that earlier Fords and Chevies had a pretty strong engine package and you could argue the muscle car era started there. Maybe so, seems like most accept the early to mid '60s as where it started. In the end, it made no difference and hot rodding was forever changed. With the introduction of the muscle cars a guy or gal didn't have to go to a lot of backbreaking work and struggle to build a good looking and strong running rod. And for those that never really cared to learn much about building a strong running engine, here was the answer to keeping up with the faster cars. Heck, all a guy needed was a payment book and he was driving a very nice, brand new and in some cases very fast car.

The average street driven hot rod was hard pressed to keep up in a lot of cases, and once some of the more mechanically astute got their hands on one of the factory hot rods, it got really tough. Generally speaking, this is what I saw and what I experienced in my area, a small coastal California town that was fairly close to the great hot rod centers of LA, Long Beach and the San Fernando Valley. Locals, and there are a lot of em, call these towns, along with a lot of other ones, with the all-inclusive term 'The Greater LA Area', or just plain LA. A lot of fads that started somewhere in the backwaters of the LA area soon spread to the outlying areas. LA for sure, was where these fads and styles started, got exported and stayed around a while.

I saw a few neat things done to some local cars by some talented and thinking owners, but strangely enough the local fads never seemed to go back to LA. As far as LA was concerned, they were the Kingdom of Hot Rod and no interlopers wanted or needed. No one ever made a comment to this effect, it was just one of those unwritten little rules understood by all. And truthfully, we needed LA, they didn't need us. We were the perfect customer. We brought money in, took products out, had no say in the matter and for the most part we were happy with our place in the scheme of things. I've heard and read the comment that there really weren't many hot rods or customs in any one particular area in the '50s. Not true. At least not for the place I grew up in. I'm guessing this is just a sour grapes quote from some of those that show up at today's rod runs and shows, don't have a rod, couldn't build a rod, wouldn't build a rod and wouldn't own one anyway. I don't know why some of these people keep showing up at the rod runs and similar. I guess they just need to look down on something.

A few people today, say that the coupes and roadsters of the '50s were few and far between, and that the American Graffiti movie was romanticized to a great degree and overly full of rods and customs. My comment is baloney. Actually my comment isn't, but since I'm such a polite and even tempered guy, baloney will suffice. It really was pretty much like the movie. The only place where the movie doesn't quite ring true are all the rods in the traffic scenes. Then again, if you hit the right traffic and the right times, the streets were loaded with hot rodded cars.

In my home town, with the economy based on the oil industry and the many large farms, there was only one football stadium, shared by the High School and the Junior College. The high school games were on Friday nights and Saturday was reserved for the Junior College games. If you liked football and hot rods, when the season was on, this was your kind of town. Like the old joke, about the only time you could walk down the street with a girl on one arm, a blanket on the other, and no one thought a thing about it. Toss a good running, well done rod into the mix and you had all the things required for a fun time.

Generally Saturday nights were the night for the car thing. We did take in the Friday night football games and cruise main afterward, but the night that counted for the most with the car gang was Saturday. Not a whole lot of the high school, out of high school and non-Junior College people took in the Junior College games. Along with the usual rods from the High School, rods and customs the older guys drove in, and rods and customs from out of town, the usual younger generation hangouts would be loaded with some really nice cars. Some primed, partially and completely and a few painted. At least half the kids that drove had rod type cars and when I say rods, I'm including the customs too. I say type because most were fairly close to stock, usually had nice paint, fancy hubcaps or the very latest, chrome wheels. To the owner's mind they were on the way to having a genuine rod. Looking the part was the first step as far as many were concerned.

The home town was fairly small as far as population went. Memory probably fails me here, but my graduating class had about 250 students in it. And a few years later it was still not over the 350 mark. The town was also the county seat and the county included quite a few really small towns. For the rod owners that lived in these small outlying towns, it was common to come into town on Saturday nights. Sometimes in a small caravan of 2-3 cars and most times a single car with just the driver and a friend. A few of the 'out of towners' became Saturday night regulars and were a part of the local scene.

Things were pretty friendly in those days, rod driving strangers were usually accepted at face value and usually ended up being part of the group. Sometimes they got challenged to a street race right away, sometimes not. If they raced, they ended up somewhere on the ladder or pecking order depending on who they'd beat to get there. Nothing official and no records, everybody just knew where each car stood in the speed department. Sometimes no race was required. Show up in the right car and you didn't have to race anybody. Then, like it is today, it's pretty obvious which cars were good ones to stay away from as far as street racing went.

Street racing was a fact of life then, it doesn't make it okay and it doesn't mean it was a good idea. Even though we used some of the really deserted country roads to race on.

Just as a small illustration, here's a rather incomplete list of hometown cars that showed up at the local hangouts on Saturday nights. Not listed are all the nice coupes and sedans that were virtually stock. These cars did their part too in adding to the background and overall feel for the era. Roadsters then, as now, were somewhat rare. Coupes were the number one choice for many, with the two door sedans running a close second.

'41 Ford coupe, 3/8 x 3/8 flathead, hard runner, done by a very knowledgeable flathead owner. He gave the late models fits for a while. DeSoto powered five window '32. The fabled Deuce, the fastest car in school and in town for quite a while. '39 Chevy coupe with Nailhead. '56 Chevy pickup with tri-power, Corvette cam, stacks. He tore the stock three speed out with distressing regularity. He had the habit too, of winding the snot out of it and eventually tossed a rod out the side. '56 Ford pickup, totally stock, holder of the 1/4 mile record in its class. His folks purchased it new. First time out, he bettered the record for his class. I don't know why, but this little truck ran very hard. Racing prep consisted of opening the cutouts and that was it. Several '49-'50 Ford coupes, some had slightly built flatheads, one had Olds power. '50 Ford coupe, one of the famous 'Fordillacs', purchased as a virtually new car that an LA company had stuck a Cadillac crate engine in. '49 Ford four door, complete with shaved rear door handles and Nailhead power. Olds powered '40 Ford coupe. 348 Chevy powered '38 Buick coupe, five 'carbed' straight eight powered Buick Century coupe, '29 Model A-V8 highboy roadster, with a reputed to be stock '48 Merc engine that just about cleaned everybody's clock due to it's light weight. '48 Merc coupe, quite a few custom touches, still a rod with a mild flathead. '50 Olds coupe, well done car, Cad-LaSalle 'floorbox', mildly built Olds engine, tuck and roll, nosed and decked, frenched headlights, '56 Olds Fiesta wheel covers. Another '50 Olds, a fastback, pretty much the same as above except for the '55 Olds Fiesta wheel covers. These two were friends from their grade school days. '51 Olds sedan, built Olds engine, triple carbs, Cad LaSalle 'sideshift' with home-brewed floor shift made from a '48 Ford column shift. Chrysler Hemi powered '40 Ford coupe, probably a 354. '29 Model A roadster, full fendered with a 241 inch Dodge Red Ram Hemi. '34 Ford Vicky, mild flathead. The owner rolled this one into a ditch, I bought it for parts, he soon bought a Buick Century coupe, bent up the front suspension on that, sold it, bought another '34 Vicky, got into street bikes, never saw him again. '53 'Vette', six carbed 283, four speed etc. '48 Ford coupe, custom, candy apple red, Buick Nailhead power, tuck and roll. '27 Ford Model T roadster pickup, pretty much done when purchased and it was a well built full fendered car with cloth top, very low in front, ran a mild flathead and later got a small block Chevy swapped in. '57 Corvette. '58 Corvette. Not much more to say with these two, both had all the factory go-fast options. '56 Chevy with factory powerpack and a four speed replacing the factory supplied Powerglide. Funny thing with this car was that it was a strong runner just as it came from the factory. It would cut 102-103 mph times when similar Chevies were doing well to run 100. Lusting after an even faster car, he went the total build up the engine route and when done the car ran about 100-101 mph. They never did get it sorted out and it was obvious to most that he should have left it as is. 20-20 hindsight, as always, is highly accurate. Got to give him credit for doing it. He would have been a hero if it ran faster after the buildup. The car was painted a nice candy blue and shortly thereafter was stolen and found pretty much stripped. '57 Chevy hardtop run by a very sharp local who's still in the hot rod biz and today still running very fast. In short order this was the fastest street driven car in a two county area. As for the primered cars? Like anything else it depended on your area and what you saw. Completely primered cars were common in my area. When I was 14 and walking to Jr High school I saw the very first one I ever noticed as being a complete primer job. A '40 Ford coupe primered black. Not too long afterward the primer was rubbed down with 30 wt. I'm not sure why, I think it may have had to do with the porosity of primers and rust starting shortly afterward. Bad part about this was, in a day or two it would be completely dust covered and tough to clean. This car ran in primer for a couple of years before getting painted a finish color. I would bet the painter had many disparaging remarks about the owners ancestors once he found the primer had been oiled down.

My friends and I did the black primer bit. Most of the paint jobs on our '49-'50 Ford coupes were faded factory colors with a few primer spots from nosing, decking and getting the dents out. It was easy and cheap to apply at home. Mine ended up more than interesting first time around as not knowing any better I shot it with black lacquer primer and used the 100 psi straight from the compressor to the spray gun. Who knew about regulators, let alone moisture traps? The paint was probably half dry when it hit the body surface and it ended up looking like a giant sheet of 80 grit wet/dry had been glued on. Felt just about as smooth too. A weekend of sanding for four of us and shooting it again with the proper spray equipment left it a nice suede finish. Since we had good paint underneath, the primer porosity was not a problem for us. The tough part about painting at home was simply getting access to an air compressor. With dad working in the oil patch, he could usually bring home a compressor for the day. Said compressor belonging to one of the oil field supply outfits. If not, there were rental outfits. With the group 'spraygun' that actually belonged to one of the dads, we were in business. At least we thought so.

A few guys shot primer and a few even painted the complete car with a vacuum cleaner. Some vacuum cleaners came through with a wide range of accessories and with a cheap spray gun plugged into the outlet end you were in business. Sort of. Most of these jobs were pretty sad looking. Part due to the poor spraying qualities, part due to lack of painting experience and part due to a poor choice in paints. The best and cleverest of all were the guys that primed some of the bodywork, usually smaller bits from dent removal, nosing and decking and the like with a fly sprayer. The fly sprayers were simple gadgets and not seen at all nowadays. They looked a bit like a tire pump laid on its side with a large screw-on metal can attached. The plan was to fill the can with the purchased fly spray, shoot it at the potential fly victims by pumping the handle and hoping for the best. Most times all that was accomplished was to create a bad smelling room and add a poison cloud to the indoor air. These things were cheap enough to buy one new, shoot primer as required and heave it out. In most cases they didn't clean up well enough to re-use. Probably our fault, you'd think anything would clean up if you used enough lacquer thinner. Some guys got pretty good with these things, and at times, it was difficult to tell what kind of paint spray device was used.

Rattle cans were fairly new at the time and not the greatest paint in the world, although one friend painted his '50 Merc coupe a metallic green with rattle cans. It sounded like a good idea at the time, but like many of what we thought were good ideas, it didn't work out too well in practice. Seems like he started with about 12 cans and ended up buying eight more. The really big drag was getting all the cans well shaken up. The paint ended up thin and uneven and the car didn't really look all that great. In the end, he paid more for the rattle cans than he would have for 'real' paint. To boot, he worked for the power company and had all the requisite equipment on hand to do a nice job in the company garage. The car ended up in light grey primer in a short while.

An interesting short story on this car was when the owner got married a year later. It was running the fake snap-on Moon discs and he had pulled the wheel bearing dust caps for clearance. His little brothers tied on all the requisite cans and streamers like you see on a lot of 'Just Married' cars. Being clever guys they also put rocks in the hubcaps, an old trick and one that would drive a guy nuts. The owner lived at the beach, as did his folks, which meant that when the little brothers put rocks in the hubcaps a bunch of beach sand got in there too. He and his new bride got about 100 miles from home when one of the wheel bearings failed. His occupation was mechanic for the power company and I heard his bride was most impressed with this one. Life goes on.

Black generally was the favored color for a completely primered car with a few of them being completely primed in red oxide and a very few in light grey. One '41 Chevy coupe was done in all white primer. Somewhere along the line some of the 'lowrider' contingent discovered that white primer mixed with a bit of toner made a neat finish. For a while, there were quite a few pink and purple 'lowriders' running around and even a couple of these were yellow. A suede rainbow for sure. For the few that pretty much didn't care what color the car was, there was always the 'mistake' paint. This was simply a gallon of most times enamel or sometimes lacquer that the paint mix guy had screwed up on. These were usually refused by the paint shop, and for good reason. What often happened was, somewhere along the line one of the toner colors was left out, or too much of one color added. Sometimes it was painfully obvious when comparing the mixed paint with the color chip. These cans of paint, usually a gallon were stored under the paint mix bench and had a dollop of the color on the lid for identification. The stores usually sold these out for two bits on the dollar. Quite a bargain when you figure a gallon of red enamel cost a little over $10.00 list price at the time.

'Course if you were the paint mix guy you could mix up some interesting colors. I knocked out a quart of metallic orange once and never did duplicate it. Kinda similar to the pearl orange that was popular a couple of years back. Worst screw-up I did in the paint department was to leave the dryer out of the enamel. Dryer was a molasses colored liquid added to the enamel at the end of mixing, seems like it was about 5% by weight. In fact, all the toner colors were added by weight, the empty can was set on a balance scale, the scale set, toner was then poured in until balanced and the scales reset for the next color. The painter shot a complete car on Thursday morning with the no-dryer paint and was pretty steamed when he came in Friday afternoon, with the comment that the paint had not dried after the requisite overnight stay in the paint booth. He left it in there all weekend and when he got it out Monday morning, the paint had leveled and flowed out nicely and he commented that it was one of the best enamel jobs he'd ever done. No runs, the paint just looked great. Although I'd bet it was a bit soft all the time it was on the car.

As far as the paint vs the totally primered cars goes, a lot depended on where you lived. In my town, a lot of cars were in total primer and ran that way for quite a while. In almost all cases, primer was viewed as a step toward a finished paint job. Problem for most of us was the simple lack of money. We usually spent our money on engines, 'drivelines' and tires. The guys that didn't do the hot engine bit spent their car money on paint and wheels. My town was considered in a small way, to be a somewhat poor town, loaded with blue collar workers, oil patch workers, farm workers and all the related industries, one reason I feel why a lot of the cars ran in primer. The perceived to be richer, old money, touristy, historic town to the north almost always had cars that had a real paint job. I don't remember seeing any rods from that area that ran in solid primer. I did spend a lot of time up there as I worked there, they had great beaches and I was involved in a Chevy oriented car club, with a flathead Ford coupe to boot! I was sort of an honorary member and it was expected that I would swap in a small block Chevy first chance and that would make it official.

I would imagine that most of the younger rodding set that lived there had the same problems as us as far as getting to the finish paint job. That was true for the group I hung out with, just that more of them seemed to do it. Simply put, there were a lot of primered and a lot of totally primered cars in the '50s, but in every case I knew about it was simply a step on the way to a finished paint job.

Maybe this is one of those topics in which everybody is right. If you lived through the '50s and there were no totally primered cars, then that's the way it was. If you lived through the '50s and there were a lot of totally primered cars, then that's the way it was too. No one's right and no one's wrong. It really came down to where you lived and what the local trends were. The thing to keep in mind though, and contrary to those that think they are re-living the '50s is that virtually no-one considered primer to be the finished paint job. That's just the way it was, but only for a while ....

"...One in particular I remember was a black '68 GT fastback with 4.5 miles on it. A nice stick shift car, it was purchased locally, during a rainstorm. When the new owner, driving his new pride and joy, exited the dealership, he stuck his foot in the throttle a bit much and promptly slid into a power pole..."

CHAPTER TWENTY-SEVEN
TERMINAL ISLAND TO INYOKERN
I GOT OUT OF DRAG RACING FOR WHAT I THOUGHT WOULD BE A SHORT WHILE.

I didn't know I was getting out, but as life goes, stuff happens. The short while turned out to be a long while. A very long while in fact. I was still involved as a spectator, sometimes on a pit crew and most times just following it in the hot rod and drag racing oriented magazines. Even so, there's nothing like being right in the middle of it as an active participant.

The Olds powered '50 Ford coupe was now in about its seventh version. That being the one, the last one as it turned out, geared toward street use. With the need for a second car we decided to return the coupe to street duty and the easiest way out looked to be finding another coupe and embarking on yet another engine swap. I was fortunate in finding a very good one at a paint shop. The car described earlier in the book.

The coupe we found, a very nice, totally stock one, ended up with the running gear that was pulled out of the, for the most part, drag racing coupe. The drag race coupe had ended up with the bumpers removed, a gasser style bumper on the rear, the back seat removed, grille removed, side window glass removed and replaced with amber Lexan and the rear wheel wells radiused for the hard slicks we ran, along with a set of aluminum wheels. All in an attempt to get the weight down and remain competitive, at least locally, with the somewhat mild engine, if you can call an engine with 290 degree advertised duration, .500" lift cam, a lot of duration and lift at the time, and running either six two barrel carbs or three two barrel carbs, dual coil ignition and all the rest, mild.

The little coupe was up and running and equipped with all the stuff that had been on the engine in its drag racing mode, except for the six two barrels. It now ran the three two barrel setup. It was a touch radical for a street driven car, but it turned out to be very dependable and a good runner in its street duty guise. It still ran the 4.27 rear end. Admittedly this was a bit low for the street, but the highway driving on the way to work had a speed limit of 55 mph, so it wasn't spun up too much most times. Now and then though, the dependable old engine got spun up to the 6200 rpm redline just for the heck of it. It still had the great sounds and it still ran hard.

The end for the engine came during a move to another city 120 miles away. That came about as the result of a small promotion and the move to another Edison switching center near Rialto in 1966. Sweetie and I had found a house to rent and she was at home in Piru getting ready for the move. The nice part was that Edison paid a moving company when a promotion was involved, but like always, there was lots to do. I'd spent my first week at the new job living at a motel. When Friday came, I hit the freeway to head for the old house and to help finish the small stuff for the movers. Somewhere near Sunland the engine started a mild rod knock. Since Sweetie didn't know the area very well near there, I decided to try to make it to the Mission in San Fernando, an easily found landmark and Sweetie had been there before. The saving grace would be, at least I thought so, WB got a good discount at the parts house and could pick up a turned crank pretty cheap so I figured it was worth the risk.

I almost made it, the rod was knocking a little louder by the time I hit the Mission Boulevard off-ramp. Once I took my foot off the gas, that was it, the engine locked up solid as a rock. Sweetie tossed the towbar into the trunk and drove our '57 Buick Roadmaster hardtop out for the rescue.

Brilliant me, I'd never given a thought to the little fact that maybe an engine that had seen quite a bit of drag racing as well as several years of street duty ought to have the bearings checked now and then. I figured it would be easy to fix, but as life does many times, there were other things to fix as well as other things to take care of. The main one being sweetie's little four door '53 Ford six cylinder. It had a knocking rod too, but it had been shut down before things got very far out of hand. The crank was turned, block bored and I completely rebuilt the engine. The pleasant surprise was the "in effect" 25% discount as only six of most items had to be purchased. The bill from the machine shop and parts house was considerably lower than expected.

The new neighborhood we moved into was cram packed with dirt bike riders. I decided that there was no beating this group, besides I liked dirt bikes anyway and had owned a BSA 500cc Alloy Clipper for a number of years. I'd sold it to Sweetie's brother a couple of years back. Nothing to do here but adhere to the old maxim of "If you can't beat 'em, join 'em". I did and it turned out to be a fun three years. I bought a 1967 Montesa 250cc Scorpion Enduro and rode it for about a year and a half. It only lasted the year and a half due to the poor parts supply on the part of the importer. The bike was made in Spain and was a nice little motorcycle, but in looking back, I should have bought one of Spain's premier motorcycles for dirt, the Bultaco.

Deciding that the BSA had been a great bike, and aside from the usual oil leaks, which were kept in check for the most part just by tinkering with the bike and taking care of things before they got too far out of hand, I decided that a new BSA 441cc Victor would be the perfect replacement. And so I headed for the BSA dealer in San Bernardino, not so far away as Rialto where we lived was simply a suburb of San Bernardino. They started out as a separate towns, but as both towns grew toward each other it wasn't long before they were all the same town for the most part.

Turns out the BSA dealer was also a Ducati dealer and felt the Ducati was the better bike, to the extent that he rode the Ducati in competition. The crowning achievement for both the Ducati, himself and one of the riders in our group, one of the very fast riders for sure, won the Baja 500 one year on a desmodromic head 350cc enduro model. The desmo head being pulled off the new Ducati 450 engine and stuck on the old 350cc race bike.

The Ducati turned out to be a fun and dependable bike, but even so, there were times I wished I had bought the BSA. 20/20 hindsight is a marvelous tool. As it turned out, with me doing the dirt riding and racing bit, the little coupe languished in the garage for about six years. It was always in

the back of my mind to get it running again, but having two major hobbies was just too expensive an undertaking for a family guy. Having two daughters, I was finding, was the most expensive hobby of all. That's alright though, with time comes reward and I feel I've been rewarded quite well by these two young women, not in the monetary sense of things, but I'm sure you understand, no further explanation is required.

In the summer of 1971 we moved to Saugus, to a company house, coupe in tow behind our second '59 Ranchero. We'd been through several cars since our move to Rialto. The '57 Buick had the trans start slipping and it was parked for a while until I discovered Sweetie's brother Tom was

Brother-in-law Phil Bledsoe in his very best James Dean-like pose leans against his stick shift '57 Chevy hardtop. The dress and pose is evocative of the times.

interested in buying it. We worked out a swap with our Buick and some cash going for a stick shift, 292 engined '59 Ranchero. The Ranchero was a nice addition to our rolling stock, as hauling the dirt bike up to now had been done either in the neighbor's '57 Ranchero when going riding with him, or on a simple bumper rack I made for the rear of the '53 Ford.

Somewhere in here, my other brother in-law, Phil, who I like to call bother in-law, although the simple truth is that I'm more of a bother to him than he is to me, had bought a '59 Ranchero the year before. Since his '59 Ranchero was in nicer shape than mine was, plus it had the bigger 352 engine, new paint and upholstery as well as an automatic, I put in the old request of; "If you decide to sell it, let me know first". Sure enough, before too much time passed, he developed "new car lust" and was ready to part with the Ranchero. With two darned near identical '59 Rancheros, the '50 coupe and the '53 4 door, we were pretty squared away in the rolling stock department.

After the move to Saugus in 1968, we sold the first Ranchero, the 292 powered one, to a good friend who painted and upholstered it right away and had it looking very good. It still ran good, the only fly in the ointment with this car was still the automatic trans diff. I don't know the ratio, suffice to say, it was quite high for a stick shift car. It was livable though, it made such a good highway flyer out of the Ranchero that I left it as it was.

In a small case of ignorance, although like all ignorant stunts, it didn't look that way at the time, I swapped the good running and very cherry, equipped with white and blue tuck and roll interior, '53 Ford four door to brother in-law Tom for Sweetie's mom's ex-'61 Ford four door hardtop. Tom had just bought it from his mom. It was a nice car, black in color, ran a 352 and had air conditioning along with a perennial overheating problem. Somewhere along the line the trans let go and it was parked, permanently as it turned out.

Shortly thereafter a co-worker had developed new car lust and his very cherry '62 Ford four door station wagon came up for sale. One test drive and I bought it. Equipped with a six cylinder engine and three speed, I figured that it was such a nice car that I could live with it. Besides, a guy could always stick a bigger engine in it. Turns out the bright red station wagon was a very good and very dependable car. We drove it as it was for quite a while. After all, I had the 352 powered '59 Ranchero, now equipped with eight inch wide wheels and equally wide tires. Lowered a bit at all four corners it went around corners like gangbusters. With a set of duals, it sounded good too.

The '50 Ford coupe was stored in a garage and it was always in the back of my mind to rebuild the engine, but with the dirt bikes, the almost a hot rod Ranchero, working lots of hours and doing the family guy/dad bit, I never quite got back to it. About 1969, my friend who lived next door, and had a couple of brother in-laws running a body shop in Rialto, which figured, as we'd just moved from there the year before, told me the brothers had started rebuilding the wildly popular Mustangs and selling them. The process was simple, they would bid on totaled cars, buy the necessary parts from the dealer and bring it up to snuff. They turned out some nice cars for sure. One in particular I remember was a black '68 GT fastback with 4.5 miles on it. A nice stick shift car, it was purchased locally, during a rainstorm. When the new owner, driving his new pride and joy, exited the dealership, he stuck his foot in the throttle a bit much and promptly slid into a power pole. The left front fender and front suspension, along with the hood and door were pretty damaged and the insurance company wrote off the car, surprising to me to say the least. Even with my limited skills in body work I figured I could have fixed it. The brothers did such a nice job that you couldn't tell it had ever been in a wreck.

Along with their purchases of rebuildable Mustangs, they also bid on and got Mustangs that were too far gone to rebuild and were purchased solely for the parts content. When they picked up a wrecked in the rear '67 Shelby fastback for parts, they had the Shelby 390 engine, an FE series model as well as the Ford Toploader four speed for sale. I went down and took a look at it and ended up telling them I would be back next Saturday with the cash. It was a good deal, not to mention the engine/trans had very low mileage.

Saturday came and since I had four days off, Saturday through Tuesday, I called 'em and said I'd be down on Monday instead. Not a problem for them, but as it turned out, a problem for me. Sunday, their shop was burglarized and the four speed Toploader was stolen, along with several nodular carrier equipped rear ends. The brothers knew what was valuable to the local hot rodders and kept the most desirable pieces from the totalled, not to be rebuilt cars, for later sale.

Monday, when I got there and found the trans gone, I was tempted to let the whole thing go, but they came up with an all-synchro three speed trans that bolted right up to the Shelby 390 engine. I figured that would work ok until they could locate a four speed, which as it turned out was never. Not too big a problem though, the three speed, equipped with a Hurst "Mystery" shifter worked very well in the Ranchero. Only problem was that I felt I was missing the fun of rowing a four speed around town.

The easy part was swapping the Shelby 390 into the Ranchero. The '59 motor mounts bolted right on to both engine and frame, a clutch pedal was easily obtained and after building a simple adapter plate for the transmission to mount on, we were in business, all except for an exhaust system. Even that wasn't too big a problem as I figured one of the Hedman Hedders for the 390 engine in the Mustang would be a total bolt in. A quick trip to Long Beach to get a set and it looked like there would be no problems in the header department. The right side bolted right on, the left side required the alteration of one pipe. Not too big a deal for most oxy-acetylene torch owners as I was, and count myself fortunate in owning one. It was the first "big" tool ever purchased and I have it to this day.

With the Shelby 390 engine, the wide tires and wheels, the lowering job and a nice set of quality gas shocks, the Ranchero made a great hot rod. It cornered well, accelerated well, in fact to the tune of 90 mph flat at the drag strip, which is pretty adequate street performance considering the era, but considering even more the weight of the Ranchero. The big flaw was brakes being prone to fade. This was easily cured by installing a set of the Velvetouch brake shoes along with a total hydraulic rebuild.

Not too much later and the center section of the dash had four of the 2-1/8 inch Stewart Warner gauges installed. Seems like I've always had the S-W gauges in my cars. The more the better as far as I'm concerned. In fact, the '32 roadster I drive today has nine of them installed, seven on the dash and two on a panel left of the steering column. They can make life easier for sure, as potential problems can be spotted right away and under-way trouble shooting can be accomplished.

While living at Saugus I was given little brother's '54 Ford two door, the one purchased new by our grandfather, then by dad and later by little brother. Little brother got drafted into the Army and eventually went to Vietnam as did many young men. He sold the good looking, good running overbored Y-block powered car to a friend who promptly destroyed the engine as noted earlier.

We ended up moving to Fillmore in 1971 as the company was doing away with company housing and the sad fact was, that with only a two car garage, two running cars as well as the still got a damaged crank '50 coupe, there was no room to store the '54. A few parts were stripped for '54 owning friends and it went to the junkyard, another one of those cars I should have kept.

April of 1972 we took the Ranchero to Mexico for a vacation. Three couples, four children, one 4 x 4 International Harvester Travelall, one ski boat and one Honda 305cc dirt bike, the bike, now at 331cc and modified for desert racing. We took the vehicles south, about 10 miles down the beach from San Felipe and camped out. We had a pretty good time for the most part.

Spring of '72 we built a cabover camper for the Ranchero, stuck on some air shocks and headed out for Arkansas for a two week vacation. The camper turned out to work well and it was a bit of a novelty as well. We had many requests as to where one could be purchased. I think one of the reasons it looked professionally done, was good wood-working advice from dad as well as windows salvaged from a wrecked house trailer. The biggest thing though, and one not seen much on the few home built campers I'd seen, was the typical camper style, embossed white enameled sheet metal we used. We'd simply gone to a camper builder in the San Fernando Valley and bought enough to cover our home built camper as well as the rain gutter trim strips and a whole bunch of hex headed screws.

We kept the camper for about a year and when we decided to sell it, it went fast. There aren't too many, if any campers available for the Ranchero sized vehicles.

The Ranchero had travelled quite a few miles on the Baja beach flats during low tide the year before. With the 22 foot tidal range in the Northern part of the Gulf of California creating a large expanse of sand, and sometimes mud covered flats at low tide, the Ranchero had traveled through quite a bit of salt water in the rush to get north and back before the tide came in. I rinsed it well after we got home, but once the rust started, it rapidly took its toll, to the extent that a year later it was starting to show. I decided to mine it for the good parts and build another one.

Of course, since I now needed one, finding a rebuildable Ranchero was proving difficult. It wasn't long until the faithful old six cylinder '62 Ford station wagon caught my eye. It too had been equipped with the eight inch wide wheels and equally wide tires. Running little hubcaps and sitting quite low on a stock and unaltered suspension, it looked like a do-able deal, which it was. The swap was just as easy as the Ranchero swap had been, once again the '59 V8 motor mounts worked well, just a bolt-on, a slightly different adapter plate was made up for the trans mount and a second set of headers was modified for the wagon. This little deal of selecting a set of headers for the smallest car that your engine was in was working out okay. Again, just one pipe modified on the left side and again, the right side just bolted on. An extra leaf was added on top of the rear spring pack for traction control purposes. Leaving the column shifter in place gave us a good looking, good running, easily maintained sleeper. It seems the performance was even better than the Ranchero, probably due to the stock 3.89 carrier in the factory installed nine inch rear axle. A set of Velvetouch brake shoes went on this car too.

The Ranchero was sold to a guy in a nearby town, but not before being stripped of all the good parts. I think he envisioned it as a good parts car. I never did see it running on the street again. Wouldn't be surprised though, California license plate #88078A.

Departing from the hot rod bit for a while, we fell in love with sailing and bought a Columbia 23. A very nice and very trailerable little sloop that slept four, had a head, which the ladies always appreciated, as well as cooking facilities. We spent a lot of time on the sailboat at California's always interesting Channel Islands as well as the big desert lakes, namely, Lake Mead and our favorite, Lake Powell. It was a most interesting time to say the least. Aside from living an adventure or two, and once not sure we'd live through one of them, we had a good time on the sailboat.

It was interesting in retracing Cabrillo's steps. Cabrillo, in 1542 discovered the western United States, wandering up and down the California coast, but for the most part was ignored as Columbus got all the press 50 years earlier. It was especially interesting seeing, visiting and viewing many of the historical areas of the west when visiting Lakes Mead or Powell. The most interesting being the areas of the Colorado river where the pioneers crossed and camped out. Many tales to relate here, the pioneers, not mine, but suffice to say, there's a small bit of wonder and a lot of reverence for those who came before.

In 1974 little brother got new truck lust. He bought a black Ford short bed half ton and sold me his very nice '63 Chevy short bed, big window, half ton pickup. He was the third owner and had just finished installing a fresh 327 engine, new clutch, tires and brakes, as well as new upholstery. I drove this little truck for about 10 years and did very little to it except for the required maintenance and of course, some hot rod stuff. The best, at least I thought so, was to replace the weak kneed three speed with a Corvette four speed with Hurst shifter, as well as going to a set of 4.11 gears to complement the very large back tires.

The Vette trans was a smooth shifting rig, as it turned out, an easy swap too. Aside from just bolting it in, all that was required was to bend the emergency brake guide down a touch, cut the driveshaft and cut a hole in the floor for the shifter. The 2.36 low gear in the trans was better than the 2.20 close ratio low gear that came in many of these cars, but the 2.64 low gear would have been perfect for the truck. The 2.36 low gear worked well for the most part. The only time it was a problem was when starting up from a dead stop on a grade when towing a trailer or boat. It just took a little planning ahead, and for the most part it never gave us a problem.

Other hot rod stuff consisted of a set of American five slot mags, rebuilding the dash for the always in favor, at least with me, S-W instruments and moving the radio closer to the driver. A coat of the popular Porsche India Red and it was a sweet little truck indeed.

We about lost the little Chevy pickup and did lose the '62 Ford station wagon when our home was flooded in the 1978 Fillmore flood. We had four feet of water and about two feet of mud in the house as well as having the back wall of the living room blown out and most of the brick walls around the property go down. Biggest regret, besides the year and more it took to rebuild, was the losing of many family photographs. It was a good learning experience. Good because it's surprising what people will do when a disaster strikes a community. People showed up with shovels, unasked, and just started the digging out process. Many of them were unknown to me. About 25 Edison guys showed up for a working weekend digging us out and did in a short time what would have taken me and a couple of friends and family quite a while to dig out.

As things went while the flood was in progress, we had time to take out one vehicle and the Chevy pickup was my choice. When I went back to get the station wagon, the water in the street was too deep to drive it out. A sad end to a neat little car. Neat to me and sweetie at least. Our older daughter Cheri called it the "Pink Pig" as a play on the name sweetie had given it. To sweetie, it was her "Red Rocket" and it was a rocket of sorts, with the Shelby engine and the 3.89 diff, she left more than a few of the newer cars in the dust.

The '68 Buick 430 engine and Turbo 400 trans came from my mom-in-law's poor old Buick when it burned a valve several years back.

Around 1984 I sold the nice little Chevy pickup and bought bother in-law Phil's very nice '77 3/4 ton 4x4 Ford pickup. Cool part with this truck was that bother in-law had already done quite a bit of hot rod work to it and I got to enjoy the fruits of his labors. Hot rod stuff to the tune of a Norris cam, recurved distributor, headers, Edelbrock Streetmaster intake manifold and a Carter 625 carb. The big tires and chrome wheels were a decided plus too, although the chrome wheels were swapped out for a set of five slot mags before too much time went by.

We did quite a bit of sailing up and down the California coast as mentioned and did a lot of the dirt bike thing in the mountains and deserts of California. The dirt bike stuff came to an end about 1987 when I sold my last dirt bike. The old gang had kinda just fallen apart after CK quit riding due to the fact that his back wouldn't take it any more. The sailing had come to an end the year before after one last trip to the Channel Islands with a couple of good friends. Four days of sailing, exploring, skin diving, fishing and just having a good time.

California's coastline was changing a bit too. Navigation wasn't quite as critical as it used to be as you could just sail from one oil platform to the next. Not that the channel was littered with oil platforms, just that you can see them from a long ways away.

In 1985 I'd come to the realization that I could swing the cost of the major components of a reproduction '32 roadster. I had a few components already on hand too. The main one being the '68 Buick 430 engine and T-400 trans I'd pulled out of mom in-laws poor old Buick when it burned a valve several years back. She decided to junk it rather than have me do a valve job. I think she had her eye on a new Dodge anyway and the burnt valve Buick was a good reason to step up. I'd stored the Buick engine away in the garage as I figured somebody could use it and the T-400 would be a good spare for little brother's 455 Olds powered Henry J drag race car.

While I was searching for parts and ordering the frame and body, I'd pretty much decided that a 351 Cleveland would make a great engine for a street roadster. I really liked the Cleveland 400-M in my '77 Ford pickup. A decided plus was that it would be different as far as roadsters went. Different, within the bounds of good taste, has always been one of my theme songs as far as the hot rods went. Even when running the popular early Olds in the '50 Ford coupes, we'd always done them a bit different than most other guys.

About that time, Hot Rod magazine came out with a series of articles titled "Dare to be Different". They had some good points, but one of the very best was listing the very light weight of the big block Buick engines. With the 400-430-455 Buicks weighing about 15lbs. more than the ever popular small block Chevy once the heavy cast iron intake manifold was replaced with an aluminum one, the Buick sitting in the garage was viewed in a new light. Other advantages were, rear sump pan, simple motor mounts, easy to find automatic transmissions as the Buicks used the common B-O-P as well as Cadillac bellhousing pattern. The biggest plus was the front mounted distributor. The distributor was off to the left side and out of the way, leaving the top of the engine free for whatever mad scheme may cross your mind.

I started building the '32 in late 1985 and got it to the roller stage in about a year. Time was the difficult item for me, seemed I was working a whole lot of hours. It helped in purchasing the necessary items, but it seems time was always limited. I let the roadster sit for about a year because I'd purchased a metal lathe and was learning how to run it. A metal lathe, as I was finding, is a lot of fun to operate and a whole other hobby itself.

Along with some buying and selling other lathes, refurbishing them and making tools for the lathe, the '32 pretty much languished under its cover. Wasn't long before boxes started getting stacked up on it. You can tell your project has come to a halt once it starts getting covered up with other things. Little brother, being a bit disappointed at the lack of progress on the '32 and always able to get things accomplished on his car came up with the best advice of all. He told me to just work on it 20 minutes a day. That was excellent advice and as things turned out, I ended up working on it several hours instead. I think he knew that just getting started is the hardest part.

In the end, the buying and selling of lathes allowed me to end up with two of the last USA made ones that Craftsman sold, a 12 x 36 inch and a 6 x 18 inch as well as a nice drill-mill. Having a 12 x 36 inch lathe left over so to speak, that one went to little brother as an early Christmas present one year. He's always been good about sharing with me, and what the heck, I've been buying him toys since he was a little guy, so one more didn't hurt a bit.

In 1988, Southern California housing prices were still at an all time high, so I bid a job in Central California. Having lots of seniority by then meant no problem in getting it. Sweetie and I, now equity refugees as the saying goes, moved to Visalia in Central California and so far it's turned out to be the most fun place to live that we have ever been. I used to drive down this big, flat agricultural valley, roughly 100 miles by 400 miles, and wonder what folks did for fun. It wasn't long before we had an answer. Visalia is close to two of the country's best national parks, Sequoia about 30 miles away and Yosemite about 120 miles away. We visit Sequoia in the roadster every year. Always something new.

Lots of other recreation available too, golf courses, lakes for fishing, good hiking, but best of all is Famoso drag strip at 60 miles away and El Mirage Dry Lake about 200 miles away. The very best part is the friendly people and many, many hot rodders in this valley. I thought when I moved up here that I'd find hot rodding in short supply and speed shops few and far between. Not so, there are hot rods everywhere and one of the very best speed shops in the valley is about six miles from

my house, namely, Speed Frame Engineering in Farmersville. They've got a little bit of everything there as well as good advice. It's always a pleasure to stop by and talk to Al as well as his ex-partner Chris. Chris went on to another equally interesting endeavour, but I still run into him at the speed shop now and then. Funny part about the shop is, they knew little brother before I moved up here. This is the shop he got his Alston frame kit from, as well as the recent funny car roll bar kit he stuck in the HJ.

The Henry J started out as two cars. The best body and the drag racing chassis were combined and the remainder went to the swap meet at Pomona. Beow is the Henry J as it appears today with chopped top and DRCE engine.

Little brother still had a strong interest in drag racing. Since the only potential racer we had between us was his bike, it was elected to do the job. We built the 'Sportster' into a strong runner. He drag raced the bike a lot at Long Beach and won several trophies with it. Not all the strips would allow bikes to drag race, Long Beach was one of the few. I raced dirt bikes at the time and ran his 'Sportster' at the drags once in a while. Dirt bike 'wheelies' were lotsa fun, but pulling a third gear 'wheelie' on this thing was downright scary. It was kinda spooky racing the cars, especially the faster ones. We could get them out of the hole, but you could hear them coming up on you. We always hoped they would stay in their lane, as some of them got a little loose about halfway up the track. The bike ran in the twelves at around 105-108 mph. and was still ridden on the street regularly, with a few long trips thrown in. (We hadn't gone totally crazy with the engine, it was still pretty tractable on the street. In fact it's still got all the speed equipment on it today that we installed back then and it still starts easy for a kick-start 'Sportster').

Little brother decided to get into drag racing with a car. He kinda got tired of 'beatin' up on the bike. 'Course by this time, between the two of us, dad, and the machinist/welder at an oil field machine shop had beefed up and reinforced most of the weak links that had broken on the Harley. ('Irwindale' had been the last serious drag race for me, although I got to drive his cars at several different strips. He's been very generous about that. (I ran 125 mph at 10.26 at 'Inyokern' in the Henry J with the new tube frame and a pretty mellow motor, a fun ride for me, a bit worrisome for him as 'Inyokern' strip is worn fairly smooth and the car skated around a bit, especially in high gear. I guess it didn't worry him too much, I got to do it twice!)

He had a good friend that ran a strong running '37 Chevy coupe with a Pontiac 389 engine and B&M Hydro. It was a really nice, well done car. The friend is a thinker, likes to build and tune and does drive now and then. Generally the wife did the driving. (And at 90lb., 'unobtainium' was not required to make a light car/driver combo.) She is a very good driver and handled the car quite well. Today they run a six second alcohol dragster and run a small business making parts for fuel cars. She's the driver for this one too. (Bob and Heather Sanders of Titan Engineering.)

Little brother, Louie, put the chassis for the Henry J together from an Alston chassis kit. he tacked the chassis together and then had it heli-arc welded by a certified welder friend.

Little brother, admiring his friend's car, bought a '37 Olds coupe and 455 Olds motor. (The Olds theme sorta stuck to him) We did get the engine swapped into the '37 and had it about ready to run. During all this, I was trying to talk him into running a lightweight roadster and getting a really fast ride with a pretty moderate engine. Went over to his house one day and there sat a Henry J, the '37 Olds had been sold and went on to be a street rod. He pulled the body and started building up the stock frame and a roll cage. Went over to his house another day and here was another Henry J. An ex-drag race car with a cherry body and well done 'radiused' wheel wells. We tossed this body on his completed frame and got it running with the Olds engine. He started drag racing with this and did fairly well, winning a few trophies in the process. Surprisingly it handled fairly well.

Talking to ex-Henry J owners who had drag raced them, we found that many of them were evil handling little cars. He did have an interesting ride once when the left axle broke and came out of the housing far enough that there were no rear brakes. He got it off the track okay. Summers Bros. axles were installed shortly thereafter. The surprising thing about this first incarnation of the Henry J was the modestly built Olds 455. Among other things he ran a hydraulic cam, single 850 Holley and stock, stress risers ground off, shot peened rods. He consistently shifted this thing at 7200 rpm and occasionally at 8000 rpm. I used to just cringe, to hear that big motor spin like that. Other guys would be watching and ask me where he was shifting at. I would tell 'em and then watch their eyes get really big. Then I would tell 'em the engine had stock rods and their eyes got even bigger. Some went away shaking their heads.

I don't think he ever did break this engine. It was kind of a 'change the oil and we'll go racing' thing. It generally ran in the high 10s. He had a lot of fun with this car and won now and then. On one of the first outings we took the Henry J to Terminal Island Drag Strip, at the Los Angeles Harbor. (This was the original configuration – 468 inch Olds, Turbo 400, 850 Holley, hydraulic cam, about 10.5 or 11.0 to 1 compression ratio, 4.57 gears, stock frame, straight axle etc. which had been

running about 122 mph at 10.60 or so.) He was very concerned with weight and would not run a fuel filter. (I offered to buy him one but he still didn't want it.) We got to the end of the staging lanes and got called to the burnout box. We were running against a really nice Chevelle. The motor would hardly run after start-up. We had the tilt front end open to access the engine, it was running way too rich. The totally brilliant pit crew, (me) had failed to bring tool one. Once called from the staging lanes, there's virtually no time to do much of anything. The Chevelle at this time has the race

The above photo shows the Henry J in action at Bakersfield while below it is shown in much earlier times at Palmdale. In those days the Henry J was powered by a 455 Olds with Turbo 400 trans and nine inch rear end. It ran low 11s.

effectively won but does a tremendous burnout across the start line (which was verboten), promptly eliminating himself. As neither car had properly staged, the staging lane guy told us if we could get to the end of the track we would have a win. We shut the tilt front end, fired up, staged and launched. The car promptly died about 100 feet out, (brother forgot to turn on the electric fuel pumps after the shut-down) got started again, coughed and stumbled the rest of the way to a 33 second et. At the end of the track I pulled the Holley primary needle valve. (I'm sure you see this one coming). Sure enough there was a small piece of sand/rock stuck in there holding it open. Rinsed it out with the water hose at the cool-down area and went on to win eliminations. Little brother is pretty religious about running fuel filters now.

Eventually he moved to the country and ended up with a total of three Henry Js and two fiberglass front ends. That was the drag racing end of it. He also found an already built, quite nice

Henry J, with small block Chevy and four speed. Since he had always been an automatic fan, he promptly yanked the four speed and stuck in a Turbo 350. (He could drive a stick just fine, listening to him shift my car at the drag strip made it sound like it had an automatic in it. He's probably surpassed me in the driving department by now, although a few years back he let me drive the drag race Henry J at Bakersfield. My ET was better than he had been running, his friends gave him a bad time for weeks after that one. I was simply lucky and had hooked up good, 'course I never mentioned that to anyone.)

Towing back along the return road at Palmdale. Compare the profile of the Henry J as shown in this early photo with its current chopped and tube chassis equipped configuration.

He had the street Henry J about 4-5 years when the original owner called up, made a good offer and bought it back. Not bad, drive a car for 4-5 years, do very little work on it because it ran so well and sell it at a profit. Somewhere in this time period he built the tube frame for the drag racing Henry J, which was probably the very best thing he ever did for the car. I helped him a bit here, mainly building the headers and doing some glass work on the front end. Just as in the past when I was the group carburetion expert, mainly by default, I was now the group fiberglass expert since I owned a sailboat. My main fiberglass expertise with the boat was; drilling holes in it for different things. And repairing a chunk taken out of the bow. Anyway the glass work turned out okay since I usually follow the directions pretty well. (If you can make mud pies, you can probably do fiberglass work). Just after the tube frame conversion was completed a second Olds engine was built. This engine was fitted with a fuel injection system he got from a friend that also ran Olds engines. In fact only one of his drag racing group of friends ran a Chevy. It was generally Fords and Oldsmobiles. After running this engine for a while it was converted to alcohol. This engine had about 11.5 to 1 pistons and had a solid lifter cam. Several different cams were tried, eventually returning to the original one. With this engine, the car ran 134 mph and 9.90 'ets'. Of course, to any right thinking hot rodder the question was: How can we go faster? Another engine was built, this one with 15 to 1 pistons, aluminum rods, roller cam, and Batten heads. A magneto was also installed. The fuel injection system remained. Alcohol was still the fuel of choice. We had learned that an alcohol engine can be tough to start on a cool, damp morning. At times, starter fluid would have to be used to assist starting. There were many 'pullings' of the plugs, drying them out and trying again. Our vocabularies improved considerably. Finally, we got smart and started putting a couple of gallons of the best racing gas we could get in the tank. The engine started up easily on this, but it really rattled the pistons. 15/1 cr was a bit much even for the racing gas. After the heads got some heat in them, the gas was drained from the tank and alcohol put in. The car would start great for the rest of the day, (or night). This engine pulled the car to 143 mph and 9.1 second 'ets'.

About this time he installed a parachute. I had been trying to talk him into running one, but since they weren't required until 150 mph was exceeded he didn't want one. I think his mind got changed due to two things. He went to Fremont for the day as did several of his drag racing friends. There must have been 3-4 home-town cars there. About this time he was running mid 130s. He raced a tube framed Opel. The Opel was in the right lane, little brother in the left. The Opel was running 142 mph with commensurate et's, and was faster than the Henry J. He had won the race and was in front of little brother when this escapade started. It appears the Opel went into reverse instead of neutral at the finish line. The Opel skated around a bit, got totally out of control, slid into the left lane in front of little brother and started rolling. All the time remaining in the left lane. Little brother, being no dummy, promptly got into the right lane and had a great view of all the action. The Opel must have rolled three or four times. This all happened about dusk.

The home town group, watching the race thought little brother had rolled the Henry J. They didn't see the high speed lane changes. They went driving and running down the return road to see what happened. When they got there, little brother was out of the car, obviously okay. The Opel was on its roof and the emergency crew was helping the driver get out. The Opel was constructed from an Alston kit, as was little brother's car. It held up really well, considering the multiple roll-overs. It appeared the Opel could simply be re-skinned and it would be ready to race again. The driver suffered only a bruised leg. Little brother decided that maybe a chute would be a good idea after all.

The other parachute escapade was a simple one. While at the Bakersfield drag strip, we were a little past the finish line in the return road (which at Bakersfield is used for tow cars to go to the top end and retrieve the race car) when we watched a 140 mph Mazda get really loose in the shut-off area. The rear end was swinging from side to side and getting worse each time. It didn't look like he would get it back. The Mazda driver popped the chute, the car oscillated about three times and straightened right out. It looked to me like little brother was ready to buy a chute. Little brother had two friends that were running a tube framed '57 Chevy and a tube framed '57 Ford. The Chevy ran about high 150s in the high eights. The Ford ran 163 mph at 8.63. Of course, little brother decided that running at these speeds and ets would be a most fine thing.

After a bit of searching and perusing the ads, he found a GM 'DRCE' engine at about 1/3 of the new cost. This engine was a couple of generations older than what the big time racers were running. It had dynoed at 1040 hp. He got the whole ball of wax, enough parts to rebuild it once, and other than the little things like crank trigger ignition, carbon fibre clutch, Lenco four speed, a couple of Dominators, and a new set of really big tube headers he was about ready to go. The only thing that stood in his way was $$. The general plan was; keep racing the alcohol injected motor while gathering the requisite parts for the 'DRCE' motor over a period of time. Sort of a 'Have your cake and eat it too' kinda thing.

Little brother got the HJ running and the new tube frame sorted out, although not much in the sorting out department was needed due to the engine/trans was a proven combination and the Alston tube frame went straight to start with, the sorting out done at Palmdale Dragstrip if I remember right. After that we took the car to Terminal Island Dragstrip and little brother made a few runs with it during time trials. I believe it was still running the first 455 Olds engine at the time, hydraulic cammed, Holley 850, T-400 etc. Little brother, ever generous, asked me if I'd like to make a run with it. The simple answer, yes I would. No problem here. I was always ready to drive at the dragstrip. I made one run with it, seems like it was in the high 10s and around 120 mph. Little brother at the time had been running mid 10s and about 122 mph or so. Once the car was cooled down, I got to make another run, with results similar to the first. It was definitely a fun car to drive.

The new frame, along with the narrowed rear axle showed its worth, it launched well, went straight, handled well and was easy to get stopped. Even though the original stock frame with full roll cage went pretty straight, the car tended to wander a bit, probably due to the wider rear end with the slicks sticking out a bit. With the change in steering input required when shutting down, it was apparent the stock frame, even with the cage was under a bit of a twist due to the torque applied by the big Olds.

The steering changes required when running the tube frame required less input and things generally went much smoother. I did learn though, at a later race at Famoso dragstrip that I really should follow little brother's driving instructions to the letter. I made a run in the low 10s at about 125 mph and instead of clicking the trans into neutral in the traps as instructed, I decided to leave it in gear and just roll off the gas. Once the acceleration torque load was off and the deceleration torque load was on, I found myself with the steering wheel cranked way over to the opposite side while trying to keep the car straight. Nothing dangerous, but I can see where it could have got away from me. I decided that next time I'd listen to the voice of experience, even if the voice of experience was younger than me.

After the initial runs, initial at least for me, we trekked out to Inyokern dragstrip. Inyokern being located a ways out in the desert, near Highway 395 a main route between the southern and northern part of the state and located on the east side of the Sierra Mountain Range. Inyokern was one of the first dragstrips in the country and I believe it's still operating. That makes it the record holder for longest continuos operation of a dragstrip in the US.

Inyokern is an interesting, kinda low key, calmly run strip. Quite a few locals show up as well as racers we'd seen at the Palmdale dragstrip. One of the interesting points about the Inyokern strip is that it's part of the Inyokern airport, a history common to many dragstrips in the nation. What better use for an old airport than drag racing. At least from the eyes of a drag racer. I'm sure the airplane pilots would have other opinions.

Inyokern, like San Fernando and Santa Ana dragstrips, both of the latter being located on airport property ran the race cars as well as had airplanes flying in and out on the adjacent airstrip. A novelty, at least for us, Inyokern did quite a bit of sailplane flying out of there, which meant something to see for everybody. If the racing was a little slow, or for that matter, stopped, it was interesting seeing the sailplanes getting towed to altitude, releasing, and the eventual landing. With a sailplane, you gotta get the first landing right. None of this "go-around" stuff like you would with a power plane if you didn't like the approach or the looks of the landing. As it turned out, Inyokern's strip surface was one of the slipperiest strips we'd ever been on, for several reasons. We'd been told that the dragstrip had been the takeoff site of many jet powered drone airplanes. The F86 being the primary one used, at least when they still had lots of them to use. The story being that a private company with no access to military airports used Inyokern instead.

With that in mind, and realizing that the heat and velocity of the jet blast would be tough on any surface as well as the constant baking in the desert sun, had the oils in the asphalt evaporate away at a fairly high rate. This left the small rocks and pebbles used in the asphalt mix about half exposed on the surface. With the exposed rocks getting polished by landing airplanes as well as the drag race cars it's lucky we had the traction we did. Seems like the HJ ran about 2-3 tenths of a second slower than it did at the other strips. Which is the long way round to explaining a couple of the rides I took in the HJ. Nothing dangerous or scary, just interesting.

Little brother had made a couple of runs and offered me a chance to drive. Never being one to say no to a spin in a fast car it wasn't long before I was suited up and belted in. First run was against a dragster, one built for the brackets and running a mild engine. His times were about the same as we had been turning. We lined up and launched. I was fortunate in getting a good bite in low and got about a half length on the dragster right away. A shift to second at the right time and the little HJ started pulling strongly. And then the rear end started coming around. I'd been here to a small extent on the dirt bikes and what always worked here was to click it up to the next gear. Worked every time on the bikes. 'Course the little fact that the rider tosses in a bit of "Body English" was forgotten. I stayed on the throttle and clicked the trans into third and the HJ straightened out just fine. Body English not required in this instance, although as little brother told me, apparently the dragster driver had been there before and had shut off when the HJ started its drift. The HJ never left its lane or really got out of hand, but the dragster driver was probably wise in doing what he did, even though it cost him a race. It was a time trial race at that, but for most drag race drivers, a time trial race is just about as important as the real thing. A race is a race! Getting to the finish first is the important thing.

Just like Terminal Island, I got the chance to make another run, although this time it was a single. I think too, like most of us, little brother liked to see his car run and what it looked like going down the track. The viewpoint from outside the windshield being just about as good as the one from inside the windshield. Not half as exciting though! Since the run was a single, I elected to place the T-400 in drive and see how it would work out. The car was equipped with a rev-limiter so not too much danger there in case it didn't shift properly. As it turned out, it worked great. The car launched good, ran through the gears as it should and the only thing different from the other runs by little brother or myself was the very large arc described as the car went from the left side of the left lane to the right, toward the dividing line, about mid-track and back to the left side through the traps, all inside the left lane as it should be. It was kind of a strange ride, but as the car seemed to be handling well I just stayed on the throttle all the way. Little brother tells me that it was pretty interesting to watch.

Aside from one more run in the HJ at Famoso dragstrip that was about the last time I drove the car. When he converted to alcohol it never worked out that I had an opportunity to drive it again. With the DRCE engine/Lenco trans combo in the car now I'm not so sure I want to drive it, at least not until I get some experience under my belt running my own car. Even then, I'm not sure.

Of course, the alcohol motor, knowing what was going on, and seeing the 'DRCE' motor waiting in the wings, chose the next race to self-destruct. It let go in the traps at 143 mph. Little brother popped the Turbo 400 in neutral and had no problems shutting down. (Who says motors don't have a soul?) He sent me videos of the pieces hanging on the hoist. Never have I seen a more destroyed engine. The center webs were broken out of the block. The crankshaft was in three pieces. The camshaft was in many pieces. Not all the lifters were found Pushrods were missing. Not one of the aluminum rods was salvageable. The pan had several holes in it. The magneto drive/mount had

sheared off and the top of the magneto was hanging on to the engine only by the plug wires. I believe the only salvageable things removed from this engine were the Batten heads, roller rockers and the fuel injection system. Utter destruction! This put the drag racing on hold for about a year and a half.

The '31 on '32 rails project resides in my crowded garage. The cherry body with recessed firewall is a steel reproduction roadster from Brookville Roadster.

Little brother worked hard and got the 'DRCE' motor running with Lenco etc. First time out it ran about 152 mph at about 9.1. It broke several valve springs, one or two each run. He was finding out what running a big-time motor was all about. A lot of between rounds maintenance. Next time out he ran about 154 mph or so and broke several valve springs again. He was getting re-supplied by a friend who ran an alcohol dragster and had a couple of sets of 'no longer the hot set-up' springs. Gave 'em all to little brother. Say what you want about the drag racers, they are a generous group of guys and gals. He ran one other time after that and it seemed the valve spring thing was working out okay. I believe he was running about 157 mph at about 8.9 seconds. Next race was the 1996 Hot Rod reunion. I believe this was the first time out for the chopped top. His friends at the body shop that did this chop and the subsequent re-paint did an outstanding job. It made the car look considerably different. The top was not chopped to the max as drag racers tend to do, just chopped a reasonable amount. It blends in well with the body lines, and I feel this is the way the designers originally intended it to look.

Of course at the time this car was made (it's a '52, they were made '49-'53) men wore hats and a tall roof line was called for. One thing that made the chop easy was in planning ahead when the tube frame was built. It was built to fit under a chopped top, so all that was required was the bodywork. He had made several other changes in the car, and had a 'primo' set of 'officially really good' valve springs that were well matched to his engine combination. His first time trial there was after dark. After nearly taking out the lights at the start, he made a strong run and shut down about 200 feet in front of the finish line. CK and I were camped out with his 5th wheel on the east side. We figured he blew the motor. We fired up the roadster and went to the pits on the west side to check. The answer was very simple, the Henry J had a pair of wimpy sealed beam headlights that glowed yellow and only lit up the area in front of the car – and not too well at that. No wonder, with the crank trigger ignition, big MSD ignition module incorporating two rev-limiters and who knows what else, didn't leave much left over in voltage department. (He really needs an alternator, but being very weight conscious and somewhat of a conformist in the drag racing area he won't put one on). The other part of this is the lighting at Bakersfield – the main strip is fairly well lit, the shut off area is not, and is quite dark. Anyway he had made the run, the car pulling very hard. About 200 feet short of the traps, he had to shut off. He simply could not see where he was going. As he put it, it was like failing into a 'black hole', even shutting off in front of the traps. This was his best run yet. It ran 161 mph and 8.60 et. Lotta big smiles floating around the pits.

Next day he was in eliminations and ran 164 mph at 8.50. He ran in the combo class and made it to the semis. The next race we attended was the March Meet 1997. Once again my friend had brought his 5th wheel up, I drove the roadster down and we were really set up to watch the race, assist little brother in the pits, wander through the manufacturers midway, (where we actually bought some hot rod goodies and about six T-shirts each) visit the swap meet, check out the cars in the tech area and visit with old friends.

This photo, taken in 1985, shows me removing some of the engine components so that I could use the 430 Buick engine as a dummy block during construction of the '32 Ford roadster.

It was too cool. We were parked next to the fence on the east side about half way down the track. We parked the friend's pickup hood under the 5th wheel front, bed toward the track, had comfy chairs in the pickup bed, a portable radio to hear the announcer (sometimes the east side speakers fail) and copious quantities of refreshments. We ended up buying a 10 foot square collapsible shade Saturday morning and set that up over the truck bed. We were set up so good that it was almost sinful.

Parked next to us was a group of nice guys from a couple of small towns near Bakersfield and we ended up visiting with them, sharing the barbecue fires, bench racing and telling lies far into the night. Depending on the class running at the time, we would spectate or drive the roadster over to the pits on the west side, helping little brother in the pits. (Although that's a moot point as his younger son is getting to be a pretty good tuner in his own right – generally we assist when we can, get tools, chase parts and stay out of the way.) Usually after deciding they had things pretty much under control, we would leave the roadster parked in his pit area. We would return from another T-shirt buying spree, fire up the roadster and wander around. This year we only put 18 miles on the roadster inside the track area. Anyway, (kinda forgot about the Henry J remembering what a good time we had) little brother got squared away for eliminations and the class was called to the staging lanes. He won the first round at about 166 mph at 8.4. The car ran straight and true. He won the second round too, although he had to drop out of the running due to engine problems. That was the end of the day's racing for him.

Turned out, this engine (cast iron block – aluminum ones are available) had cracked a lifter boss. Whoever heard of such a thing. I guess the side loading on the roller lifters, with the killer valve springs and high lifts these engines run, really stress the bosses. I understand this is a somewhat common problem with these engines when a cast iron block is used. The engine was pulled, stripped and dragged into the machine shop little brother goes to. These machine shop guys have been around a lot of racing engines and really know their stuff. They brazed the cracked boss, bored out all the lifter bosses and installed bronze bosses. Hopefully this will cure the problem. If not, it's Sayonara for the block. The option after that is simply to get one of the newer aluminum blocks, which I understand do not have the cracking lifter boss problem. A little less weight won't hurt either. (Although, aluminum blocks are - shall we say – expensive)? I believe it will save about

The guy under the cowboy hat is none other than CK himself, complete with patriotic red, white and blue apron. CK puts on a BBQ each 4th of July after the local car show.

40-60lb. The car ought to pick up a bit as 100lb. is worth about a 10th in the ET department. As of today, the Henry J is back in running form and ready for the next race.

Little brother is still drag racing the Henry J, not as often as he would perhaps like to, but often enough. He usually makes the March Meet, Pomona Goodguys, California Hot Rod Reunion and the Hangover Nationals at Palmdale. The hangovers, aptly named, are on New Years day every year. He attends a few car shows with the HJ every year. Most times, his wife Marcie takes her restored '56 Porsche along and enters it too. Both the race car and the Porsche win a trophy now and then.

Little brother still has his black '74 Ford half ton pickup that he bought new, a good looking truck, equipped with a set of five slot mags since virtually new and now running a 428 FE engine along with a white Stockland camper shell. Said shell has the windows covered with participant stickers from many, many drag races over the years. It was the original tow vehicle for the HJ. The little black truck is still very nice and is darned near a collector's item itself. Last thing he did to it was lower it a bit. I'm guessing it won't be long before it starts getting entered into the car shows, although, with his penchant for detail and tinkering being even stronger than mine and the HJ not needing much in that department right now, I wouldn't be surprised to see him get started on a roadster, more than likely 455 Olds powered. He was a bit disappointed that I didn't stick an Olds in my roadster, but he has to admit the Buick is working out well.

Little brother never ceases to amaze me. He comes up with some clever and simple fixes to difficult problems and not much really slows him down. I can't wait to see what he comes up with next. As for the rest of us? Like in – where are we at now?

Skip, the wild man of our little coupe gang and probably one of the most interesting guys I ever knew, is not doing much of anything in the hot rod world. He's retired, turned into a bit of a computer guru and aside from a little shooting and reloading he's just cruising along enjoying life and still living in the old home town. I heard he went "calm" on us, but knowing Skip for many years, I'm not so sure. There are probably some interesting things he's been thinking about and has simply not got around to doing them yet. Time will tell here.

WB, long famed for his red '49 Ford coupe is retired too. He put in many years at the same power company I worked for, namely Southern California Edison Co., although today they call themselves Edison International. He was a bit of an electronics guy in his early twenties, but a gifted mechanic and ended up as shop foreman for one of the Edison garages. He doesn't do the hot rod thing anymore. He always liked fishing and his main interest is now shark fishing. Plenty of those in the channel offshore from the old home town.

Bud, CK's little brother is retired too. After his stint in the Army, Bud did the dirt bike thing for a while, but since he always liked hunting and still is an avid fisherman, the outdoor thing is his main interest, salt water fishing in particular. Last time I was at his house I noticed one garage wall had 15-20 salt water fishing rods and reels hanging on it. Understandable for sure. Living right next to the Pacific Ocean all his life, with some of the very best fishing available he spent all the time on the water that he could.

CK; you pretty much know about CK. He figures prominently in many stories in this book. We're still friends and he's still doing the hot rod bit. He still owns his bright yellow 1938 Morris 12 and got started on a full fendered '29 Model A roadster a couple of months ago. CK being ever the hard worker, has the A up on wheels and in the roller stage and it doesn't look like too long before it's on the road. Looks too, like it will turn out to be every bit as nice as the Morris. Once again, CK got a project car way after I did and will get it running way before my latest project. Kind of the story of our lives so to speak.

As for me? I retired about three years ago and am still doing the hot rod bit. I've still got and probably always will have the Buick powered '32 roadster that I've written about and a '50 Plymouth coupe that runs so well stock that I'm not sure if I will ever get around to street rodding it, although adding a large slug of horsepower would be nice. Horsepower isn't everything as some say. Maybe, but for me, it's way ahead of whatever is in second place. My latest project is a '31 Model A roadster on '32 frame rails, slated to be a dry lakes roadster in the street roadster class – A/Street Roadster class to be exact, and plans call for it to have a full complement of street gear. So far, it's turning out pretty good. Very traditional in appearance except for the roll bar and aluminum seat.

This project got started when a participant, Skip, but a different Skip from the wild man in our little coupe gang, on the Rodders Round Table, a hot rod oriented web site with participants from all over the world, made an interesting observation to a bit of carping I was doing about drag racing and how it's run today. He commented that since El Mirage Dry Lake was close to my house, actually 200 miles, but close enough, I should try some Dry Lakes and Bonneville racing. I thought about it for a while and when down at CK's shop a while back, engaged in some serious bench racing, CK really got the ball rolling by donating a disc brake caliper adapter kit, along with a later donation of a complete Ford nine inch rear end. After digging out some usable parts that I had stored in the garage, the whole thing looked like a do-able deal. Like the '32, it will also be powered by a bored out 455 Buick.

The new roadster is a fun project and is keeping me busy, as are the other cars. It's good though, a guy, and the gals too, need hobbies and interests to make life interesting, especially true after retirement. I determined a long time ago that I would not be one of those bitter old guys that sat on the porch and watched the world go by.

Life's easy. Family. Friends. Interests, some old, some new. Doesn't get much easier than that.......

A FORTUNATE LIFE
AFTERWORD
MEMORIES.... MAKE SOME GOOD ONES

There you have it, a short trip down the sometimes slippery road called memory lane. Some aspects, perhaps remembered differently by those who were there. Like all things remembered, a differing viewpoint by each.

The thing to remember is, my friends, my family, and myself, were and are, just "little guys" in the California Hot Rodding picture. We learned a lot, had a lot of fun and for many of us, we're still doing the hot rod thing and still learning. Some say life is a great circle always meeting at the end. Maybe, my opinion is that life is simply a grand love story painted on a broad canvas. Love for family, friends and interests, in about that order.

Writing this book has been a bit of a trip in a time machine too. When you get right down to it, a good running hot rod is a time machine in its own right. Sometimes, it's hard to remember how old you are when you're in a roadster cutting through the dark of night, the wind singing softly around the car and the engine singing a Zen-like song of smoothness and tranquility. Returning to younger days is easily accomplished by a simple press on the loud pedal. Once the engine hits its stride, bringing forth all the good mechanical sounds, and you're shoved back hard in the seat, the wind noises rapidly increasing, and the tach winding its way toward the redline, it's hard to tell where you are in time. In the end, time is all we have. Spend it wisely, you only get one trip through life. In my opinion the only thing you get to take out of life is memories. Better make some good ones........

Jay Carnine

GRAFFITI Publications

The Essential Holden V8 Engine Manual
by Larry O'Toole.
The Essential Holden V8 Engine Manual tells you everything you want to know about the Holden V8, from how to identify parts through to completely rebuilding an entire engine and stroker versions. An introduction tells you the story behind the design and development of the engine. Full specifications are included and you will also find extensive coverage of aftermarket involvement.

Engineering Street Rods *by Larry O'Toole.*
How to go about building your own street rod using examples from existing rods. Based on engineering methods and principles known to be sound. It's one thing to build a street rod but it can be quite another to have it comply with current regulations and engineering requirements. How to minimise the hassles by using 100's of photos and diagrams to explain what is required. For the first time rodder or experienced builder there is plenty reference material to incorporate into your next project.

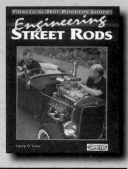

Nostalgia Street Rods
by Larry O'Toole.
Our latest full colour production featuring the best in nostalgia street rods from all around the world . 112 pages in landscape format so you get to see the cars at their best with concise, accurate information and no through the spine photos.

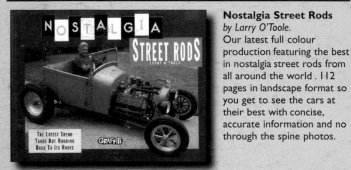

Street Flathead
By Mike Davidson.
This is the ideal book for nostalgia hot rodder who power his or her street a sweet running sidevalve Everything you will ever want to know about buil high performance street is contained in this book A follow-up his best selli Flathead Fever book wit great title for flathead Fo

The Colourful World
by Larry O'Toole.
A landscape format publication to show rods at their best in full living colour. No "through the spine photos" or close ups of hubcaps, just large format, glorious colour photos of your favourite street rods with short captions giving you all the basic information about each car.

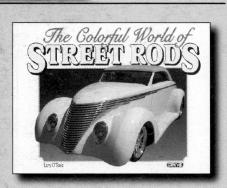

Flathead Fever
By Mike Davidson.
Detail the methods and tricks Mike has used to build two versions of the Ford Flathead engine. One is mildly modified for increased performance in a street driven hot rod, with occasional outings to the drag strip, while the second is an all out race engine for the salt flats, where Mike's knowledge and ability with this engine has been proven with speeds in excess of 160 m.p.h.

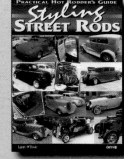

Small Block Chevrolet Tuned Port Fuel Injection
By Frank 'Choco' Munday
'Choco' Munday's experience really shows through with simple and logical, yet comprehensive detail. An extensive content list makes it very easy for the reader to quickly find the section dealing with any particular aspect of the TPI system. Combine this with extensive lists of diagrams, tables and photos and you have a very complete package that will impress even the most knowledgable Tuned Port Injection mechanic.

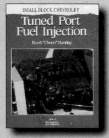

Custom Auto Electronics
By Frank 'Choco' Munday
Here's a book that tackles the electronic world in language that we can all understand and from a viewpoint of the hands-on enthusiast who wants to work with it on his own hot rod project. The book covers conventional wiring including the fitting of an entire loom into a hot rod type vehicle. Custom Auto Electronics and Auto Electrical Reference Manual is extensively cross-referenced to make your research easy.

Styling Rods
by Larry
Here's guide t your st using o rodder vehicle Ten cha over 3 give an to how rodder
designed all aspects of their street ro front and rear end treatment, engine and vision, interiors, running boards a and even accessories.

GRAFFITI PUBLICATIONS PTY LTD
PO BOX 232 CASTLEMAINE 3450 VICTORIA AUSTRALIA
TELEPHONE: 613 5472 3653 FACSIMILE: 613 5472 3805
www.graffitipub.com.au   graffiti@netcon.net.au